TRANSACTIONS OF THE

AMERICAN PHILOSOPHICAL SOCIETY

HELD AT PHILADELPHIA

FOR PROMOTING USEFUL KNOWLEDGE

VOLUME 72, PART 4, 1982

# Pavia and Rome: The Lombard Monarchy and the Papacy in the Eighth Century

JAN T. HALLENBECK

Professor of History, Ohio Wesleyan University

THE AMERICAN PHILOSOPHICAL SOCIETY

INDEPENDENCE SQUARE: PHILADELPHIA

1982

Library of Congress Catalog
Card Number 81-68190
International Standard Book Number 0-87169-724-6
US ISSN 0065-9746

# CONTENTS

## ACKNOWLEDGMENTS

In writing this book I have enjoyed generous and valuable assistance from numerous sources. Staff members of the New York Public Library and the libraries of The Ohio State University and The Pontifical Institute of Mediaeval Studies went out of their way to locate materials, especially periodicals. Ohio Wesleyan provided me with several grants for travel and manuscript preparation and Christopher Finlay, an Ohio Wesleyan senior, drew the maps. Professors Katherine Fischer Drew, James M. Powell, and Richard E. Sullivan were kind enough to read and evaluate the manuscript. Their criticisms, particularly those of Professor Sullivan, have been essential in strengthening the work and saving me from a number of important errors. Those which remain are of course entirely my own. Finally, I am indebted to the members of my family, especially to my wife, for their constant support, interest, and patience.

December, 1981
Delaware, Ohio

# LIST OF ABBREVIATIONS

| | |
|---|---|
| *AHP* | = *Archivum Historiae Pontificiae* |
| *Ann. Ein.* | = *Annales Qui Dicuntur Einhardi* |
| *Ann. Laures.* | = *Annales Laureshamenses* |
| *ARF* | = *Annales Regni Francorum* |
| *Ben. Chron.* | = *Benedicti Sanctae Andrae Monachi Chronicon* |
| *CC* | = *Codex Carolinus* |
| *CHR* | = *Catholic Historical Review* |
| *Chron. Moissiac.* | = *Chronicon Moissiacense* |
| *Chron. Sal.* | = *Chronicon Salernitanum* |
| *CMH* | = *Cambridge Medieval History* |
| *Cod. Dip. Long.* | = *Codice Diplomatico Longobardo* |
| *Ep. Lang. Col.* | = *Epistolae Langobardicae Collectae* |
| *Fred. Chron.* | = *Fredegarii Chronicon* |
| *Hist. Lang.* | = *Pauli Historia Langobardorum* |
| *LP* | = *Liber Pontificalis* |
| *HZ* | = *Historische Zeitschrift* |
| *MGH* | = *Monumenta Germaniae Historica* |
| *Pauli Cont. Cas.* | = *Pauli Historia Continuatio Casinensis* |
| *Pauli Cont. Lom.* | = *Pauli Historia Continuatio Lombarda* |
| *Pauli Cont. Rom.* | = *Pauli Historia Langobardorum Continuatio Romana* |
| *Pauli Cont. Tert.* | = *Pauli Historia Continuatio Tertia* |
| *QFIAB* | = *Quellen und Forschungen aus Italiensichen Archiven und Bibliotheken* |
| *RH* | = *Revue Historique* |
| *RSCI* | = *Rivista di Storia della Chiesa in Italia* |
| *SMC* | = *Studies in Medieval Culture* |
| *VG II* | = *Vita Gregorii II* |
| *VG III* | = *Vita Gregorii III* |
| *VH* | = *Vita Hadriani I* |
| *VS II* | = *Vita Stephani II* |
| *VS III* | = *Vita Stephani III* |
| *VZ* | = *Vita Zachariae* |

## LIST OF MAPS

# INTRODUCTION

The years from 712-774 saw the Lombard Kingdom of Italy emerge under royal auspices, develop, and then be seized by Charlemagne, who substituted Frankish rule for Lombard authority at Pavia, the monarchy's capital. This period also provides much material from which to analyze, primarily from a royal point of view, relations between the Lombard monarchy and the papacy. "Relations" between the monarchy and papacy will mean political dealings—diplomatic exchanges, agreements and treaties, hostilities and disputes of various kinds, and policies toward one another. Although there are great risks in calling either the monarchy or the papacy in the eighth century a state in the modern sense, hence seeing their relationship as a matter of international relations, a greater risk would be to define the subject otherwise. The events, developments, and issues to be treated were all political in character and involved the aspirations and fortunes of two political entities. Most emphatically, we are not embarking upon a study of church-state relations. Contemporaries in both the Lombard kingdom and Rome did not see things that way, nor should we. Ecclesiastical matters will be treated to an appropriate extent whenever they have clear bearing upon the political and international fields under consideration.

The need for a study of the eighth-century relationship between the Lombard monarchy and the papacy appears to be considerable. Most importantly, the relationship itself has yet to receive sufficiently thorough attention. The older standard works dealing with the eighth century lack a clear and persistent focus upon the dealings between the monarchy and the papacy. Such is the case in the sixth and seventh volumes of Thomas Hodgkin's *Italy and Her Invaders*, Hartmann's *Geschichte Italiens im Mittelalter*, and Bertolini's *Ròma di fronte a Bisanzio e ai Longobardi*. There is little change in such recent surveys as Peter Llewellyn's *Rome in the Dark Ages*. The relationship has fared better in the flood of periodical literature pertinent to eighth-century Italy as it is made the central concern of several articles, most notably David Harry Miller's "Papal-Lombard Relations During the Pontificate of Pope Paul I: the Attainment of an Equilibrium of Power in Italy, 756-767," David Sefton's "Pope Hadrian I and the Fall of the Kingdom of the Lombards," and, perhaps, my "Rome Under Attack: An Estimation of King Aistulf's Motives for the Lombard Siege of 756." While these studies point in the right direction in their specific examination of the royal-papal relationship, their restricted scope leaves the relationship as a whole still in need of treatment such as that attempted here.

An imbalance in the historiography of the relationship compounds the problem of insufficient attention to it. Attention has centered upon papal, Frankish, or papal-Frankish perspectives: the standard Hodgkin, Hartmann, and Bertolini works are so oriented, as are other older treatments such as Mann's *Lives of the Popes in the Middle Ages*, Duchesne's *Beginnings of the Temporal Sovereignty of the Popes*, Erich Caspar's *Das Papsttum unter Frankischer Heerschaft*, Karl Rodenberg's *Pippin, Karlmann und Papst Stephan II*, and Arthur Kleinclausz's *Charlemagne*. There is similar commitment in more recent works such as Llewellyn's survey and the steady yield of German scholarship, especially Wolfgang Fritze's *Papst und Frankenkönig: Studien zu den päpstlich-frankischen Rechtsbeziehungen* and Robert Holtzmann's *Die Italien politik der Merowinger und des König Pippins*. The royal side of the relationship does occasionally receive limited discussion in the periodical literature, but it is generally handled from papal, Frankish, and papal-Frankish points of view. Examples of such studies are Miller's "Papal-Lombard Relations During the Pontificate of Pope Paul I," Percy E. Schramm's "Das Versprechen Pippins und Karls des Grossen für die römische Kirche," Leon Levillain's "L'avènement de la dynastie carolingienne et les origines de l'état pontifical," and H. Hubert's "Étude sur la formation des états de l'église. Les papes Grégoire II, Grégoire III, Zacharie et Étienne II et leurs relations avec les empereurs iconoclastes (726–757)." Study of the relationship between Pavia and Rome from the royal point of view has come some distance, but it remains a largely unexplored territory.

Since the standard judgments about the relationship have arisen from scholarship which has seldom had it as the principal focus and has largely ignored royal points of view, one may fairly ask whether those judgments are accurate and complete. At minimum, they need to be tested by measuring them against conclusions reached through specific study of the relationship which takes full account of the crown's perspectives. Reappraisals and revisions of standard understandings may thus be in order, particularly concerning motivations for royal Lombard hostility toward the papacy and the degree to which the kings were actually inclined toward peace with the papacy and independence for Rome.

A few additional observations are in order concerning the book's content. The methodology employed is relatively simple, if at times cumbersome: chronological narrative accompanied at appropriate points by analysis and interpretation. Readers will look in vain for detailed discussions of such celebrated and intricate matters as the papacy's eighth-century separation from the Byzantine empire, the formation of the papal-Frankish alliance, the foundation of the papal state, and the papal ideology associated with all three. These and other matters will naturally be dealt with, but only to the extent necessary to accommodate the needs of reporting and interpreting the royal-papal relationship from the royal perspective. Finally, efforts have been made throughout to write a book that is at once sufficiently credible in professional respects as to assure service to the cause of scholarship, yet also intelligible to the general reader and student, whether the latter be undergraduate or graduate.

Anyone who has not been exposed to early medieval history is warned at once that firm judgments about the subject at hand are virtually impossible to reach. The most important limitation is the nature of early medieval source material in general and eighth-century materials in particular. The latter are few in number, woefully thin in information, and usually devoid of cause and effect commentary. Dating is often highly problematical and deliberate bias in source composition is not uncommon. Above all, meaning is generally obscure owing to all of these difficulties and others such as problems of authenticity, lack of surrounding reference frame, and ambiguous Latin. In sum, the sources raise as many problems as they solve, which explains why scholars have had to hypothesize more than to reach exact conclusions, and why this book is so replete with conditional and guarded assessments. Completely certain judgments are not normal in the study of the history of any period; they are most unusual in studying the relations between the Lombard monarchy and the papacy in the eighth century.

# I. THE BACKGROUND

The early history of the Lombards is still largely hidden in myth and legend despite significant clarification being achieved through archaeology. Evidently originating in Scandinavia, the Germanic Lombards seem to have moved southward over a long period through Germany and Bohemia until they reached the Danube by the late fifth century. There they were an element in the constantly shifting barbarian world on the fringe of the troubled late Roman empire.[1] Tradition places the Lombard movement across the Danube into the Roman province of Pannonia in the 540s under the leadership of Audoin (546–565), regarded as the ninth of the Lombard kings. In Pannonia the Lombards become imperial allies, receiving Byzantine subsidies[2] and fighting the Gepids and other barbarians for Justinian as he sought to keep the inhabitants of the Balkan region divided among themselves. A further aim was to keep the Pannonian powers so occupied that they could not give significant aid to the Ostrogoths in Italy, whom Justinian was attempting to conquer in order to restore the empire in the West. Justinian went so far as to import some Lombards for use against the Ostrogoths, but they were quickly returned to Pannonia when they proved to be unruly allies.[3] The Ostrogoths were finally annihilated.

## THE ESTABLISHMENT OF THE LOMBARD KINGDOM OF ITALY

Soon thereafter, in 568, after the Lombards and the Avars, Asiatic relatives of the Huns, had teamed to destroy the Gepids, Audoin's successor Alboin took the entire Lombard people from Pannonia through the Alps to Venetia, the northeast corner of Italy.[4] Alboin's motives are not clear. Perhaps the Lombards found the Avars too threatening, or it may be that the previous Lombard experience in Italy coupled with the recent withdrawal of imperial

---

[1] Principal secondary sources on the Lombards from this point until the eighth century are Thomas Hodgkin, *Italy and Her Invaders*, Vol. 5, *The Lombard Invasion, 553–600* and Vol. 6, *The Lombard Kingdom, 600–744*; Ludo M. Hartmann, *Geschichte Italiens im Mittelalter*, 2.1 and 2.2; idem, "Italy Under the Lombards," 194–212; Lucien Musset, *The Germanic Invasions. The Making of Europe, A.D. 400–600*, pp. 86–95; Katherine Fischer Drew, tr., *The Lombard Laws*, especially Drew's Introduction and notes and the Foreword by Edward Peters; and Paul the Deacon, *History of the Lombards*; and H. Pabst, "Geschichte des langobardischen Herzogtums," pp. 405–518.

[2] Hartmann, *Geschichte Italiens*, 2.1 12.

[3] Paul, *History of the Lombards*, p. 53, n. 3.

[4] A variety of other people moved with the Lombards. Paul the Deacon specifies (*History of the Lombards*, 2.6.61, 2.26.80) Saxons, Suevi, Gepids, Bulgars, Noricans, Pannonians, and Sarmatians.

troops from Italy for service against the Sassanid Persians made Italy an irresistible target. Further, suspension of imperial subsidies may have provoked the Lombards to action.[5] Finally, a number of sources, especially the *Historia Langobardorum*, the great national chronicle by the eighth century Lombard historian Paul the Deacon, insist that Alboin responded to treason by Justinian's distinguished commander in Italy, Narses. The latter, embittered by his loss of command at the order of the new emperor, Justin II, urged Alboin to seize Italy and its wealth.[6] The assertion may have some basis in fact, but it is by no means certain. Whatever the reasons, the Lombards in 568 moved into the Venetian plain as enemies of the empire, beginning a new and vital phase of their history.

Meeting little resistance, Alboin spent the next four years taking most of northern Italy east of the Apennines from imperial possession. The first conquest was Forum Julii (Cividale). The place became the center of the Lombard duchy of Friuli, was awarded by Alboin to Duke Gisulf,[7] and was understood as the barrier to incursion by enemies into Venetia.[8] The people and the bishop of the city of Aquileia, knowing that the Lombards lacked sea power, fled to the island of Grado, there identifying with Ravenna and its church as a surviving bastion of imperial resistance on the Adriatic. Vicenza, Verona, and Milan all fell, as did the towns of Liguria except for those along the coast. Ticinum or Pavia, the eventual Lombard royal capital, was taken after a siege of three years, and in 571 Alboin's forces crossed the Apennines and absorbed much of Tuscany.[9] It was Alboin's last great triumph, however, for the king was murdered in a conspiracy concocted by his wife and foster-brother.

The assassination led to the reign of the insignificant King Cleph, followed by a ten-year period (574–584) during which the Lombard throne was vacant and war bands led by independent Lombard dukes established the central and southern Italian duchies of Spoleto and Benevento. By 575 or 576 Duke Faroald had seized Nursia, Spoleto, and other towns in the Umbrian-Sabine region, making Spoleto the center of his duchy and sponsoring an Arian bishop there.[10] To the southeast, in Samnium, Duke Zotto overran the city of Benevento and a large surrounding area. Faroald was unable to take Ravenna on the Adriatic and Zotto found Naples impregnable on the Tyrhennian side of the peninsula,[11] but the formation of the great Lombard duchies of Spoleto and Benevento was well under way. Growing from autonomous Lombard war bands, and taking significant shape in the period which knew no king, neither duchy had an original or natural sense of dependence upon the Lombard monarchy in the north or even of membership within a Lombard kingdom.

[5] Donald Bullough, "Germanic Italy: The Ostrogothic and Lombard Kingdoms," p. 172.
[6] Paul, *History of the Lombards*, 2.5.59–60.
[7] Ibid., 2.9.65–66.
[8] Hodgkin, *Italy and Her Invaders*, 5.160.
[9] Ibid., 164.
[10] Hartmann, "Italy Under the Lombards," p. 198.
[11] Ibid.

While Faroald and Zotto carved out their principalities, other dukes from the Lombard north raided across the Alps into Gaul. In 574 and 575, for example, Lombards pillaged in the Rhone valley of the Burgundian kingdom. Feeling threatened, the Austrasian Franks seized the key passes into Italy and even mounted a raid into the Lombard duchy of Tridentum (Trent). The Byzantine emperor was quick to exploit the developing Lombard-Frankish tension, subsidizing King Childebert of Austrasia against the Lombards. A number of Lombard dukes were also bribed into the imperial cause, and when Childebert in 584 attacked Italy in force the leaderless Lombards found the crisis sufficient to warrant restoration of the monarchy. Elected king in 584 was Authari, the son of Cleph, to whom the dukes gave up half their land to form a royal demesne. Authari was able to damage the Frankish-imperial association by arranging a truce with the chief imperial officer in Italy, the exarch, and by marrying Theudelinda, the daughter of the duke of Bavaria, a rival of Childebert. In time, however, Exarch Romanus mounted a major campaign against Authari, restoring severed communications between Ravenna and Rome and regaining such important places as Mantua and Modena. He also persuaded some of the northern dukes to side with the empire. Three more times Childebert invaded Italy, the last in 590 in concert with the exarch. Two Frankish forces were involved, one approaching Milan and the other advancing upon Verona. But the Lombards defended themselves successfully through arms and diplomacy. The Franks retired, not to significantly reappear in Italy until Pepin's great campaigns of 755–756. Authari had restored the Lombard kingdom and guided it through a great crisis.

By the last decades of the sixth century the basic outlines of Italy's new political organization were clear. The northern districts from the coast of Liguria to Friuli and as far south as Tuscany belonged to Lombard dukes under the auspices of the king. The area was the kingdom of the Lombards. The surviving imperial presence in Italy was now represented by the exarch, the emperor's deputy for Italy who held civil and military authority.[12] Except for the exarch's personal jurisdiction around his capital of Ravenna, local Italian dukes in imperial service defended the remaining imperial places: the duchies of Venice and Istria, to the north and east of Ravenna; the duchy of the Pentapolis—composed of the towns of Rimini, Pesaro, Fano, Sinigaglia, and Ancona—directly adjacent to Ravenna;[13] the duchy of Perugia extending southward from the Pentapolis across the peninsula; and the duchies of Rome and Naples on the west coast.[14] The imperial

---

[12] See Charles Diehl, *Études sur l'administration byzantine dans l'exarchat de Ravenne (568–751)* and A. Guillou, *Régionalisme et indépendence dans l'Empire Byzantin au VIIᵉ Siècle. L'exemple de l'exarchat et de la Pentapole d'Italie*.

[13] The Pentapolis covered the area between or perhaps beyond the Apennines and the Adriatic extending from the Marecchia to the Misco just beyond Humana (Numera). For geographical details see Guillou, *Régionalisme et independence*, pp 43–76 and Diehl, *Études sur l'administration*, pp. 59–63.

[14] The most detailed geographic description of the duchy of Rome is Diehl, pp. 63–68. See also L. M. O. Duchesne, *The Beginnings of the Temporal Sovereignty of the Popes, A.D. 754–1073*, p. 15.

territories were collectively known as the exarchate, a term which by the eighth century bore the much narrower meaning of Ravenna and its environs.[15] Bordering the duchies of the Pentapolis, Perugia, and Rome were the emerging independent Lombard duchies of Spoleto and Benevento, placing the Pentapolis-Perugia-Rome strip between the Lombard kingdom to the north and the central and southern duchies to the south. The great road from Rome to Ravenna, the Via Flaminia, had been denied to the empire by Faroald's Spoletan compaigns which placed part of the road in Lombard possession, and Exarch Romanus had had to struggle to regain Perugia from the Lombards in order to keep the strip clear, both developments indicating the imperial focus upon maintenance of trans-Apennine communication between Rome and Ravenna. To replace the Via Flaminia, a new strategic and military route was built, the Via Amerina.[16] Well-protected by a series of forts at key points,[17] the Amerina became the communications core of imperial Italy and the chief support to the claim that imperial Italy was still extant. In any event, the Rome-to-Ravenna duchies and the Amerina, threatened as they were by Lombard encroachment, also served as a wedge between the two Lombard worlds, that of the crown in the north and that of the great dukes in the center and south. Among other things, the Byzantine geographic position accentuated the sense of separateness and autonomy which was already keenly felt in Spoleto and Benevento.

At the end of the sixth century and early in the seventh, the Lombards exerted severe pressure to erode or eliminate the imperial territories. In the south Duke Arichis of Benevento, the successor of Zotto, gained numerous places and threatened both Naples and Rome. Faroald's successor in Spoleto, Duke Ariulf, in 592 cut the Via Amerina and unleashed a major campaign against Rome, taking fortifications in the Tiber valley to the northeast of the city. Pope Gregory the Great, having appealed vainly to Exarch Romanus for aid, concluded his own peace with Ariulf, much to the displeasure of Romanus, who viewed the pope as an imperial officer and subordinate.[18] The angry exarch promptly turned on Ariulf and before the end of 592 regained the Roman fortifications, retook Perugia, and cleared the Amerina. But in 593 King Agilulf, the successor of Authari, took up Ariulf's cudgel by seizing what Romanus had just repossessed and marching down the Amerina toward Rome. Pope Gregory met the crisis by arranging a truce, this time with Agilulf. But the Lombards continued to apply pressure despite negotiations until an armistice was reached in 599, with the empire

---

[15] More specifically, the term *exarchatus Ravennantium* originally referred to all imperial territories in Italy. By the seventh century, however, the exarchate was regarded as a specific district, the city of Ravenna and the region bounded by the Po in the north, the Apennine crest on the west, and the Marecchia River in the south. Guillou, *Régionalisme et independence*, p. 43.

[16] Diehl, *Études sur l'administration*, pp. 68–69.

[17] Ibid., pp. 69–70.

[18] The details of Gregory's long and able defense are given in Hodgkin, *Italy and Her Invaders*, 5.349–373, 413–420.

ALPS

KINGDOM

FRANKISH KINGDOM

Trent

Friuli
Aquileia

ALBOIN, 568

PANNONIA

LOMBARD

Milan • Monza
• Pavia Cremona
River Po
• Bobbio

Vicenza
Verona
Mantua
Monselice

Grado
VENETIA

ISTRIA

EXARCHATE OF

LIGURIA

Modena
EMILIA
RAVENNA

Ravenna

Rimini
Pesaro
Fano
Sinigaglia
Ancona

DALMATIA

Luna

PENTAPOLIS

Perugia
DUCHY
• Nursia
Spoleto
OF
SPOLETO

Rome

ADRIATIC SEA

CORSICA

DUCHY

OF

• Benevento
• Naples

CALABRIA

SARDINIA

TYRRHENIAN SEA

NAPLES

BENEVENTO

BRUTTIUM

IONIAN SEA

MEDITERRANEAN SEA

SICILY

EXARCHATE OF AFRICA

MAP. 1 Italy in about A.D. 600

paying tribute to the crown. The peace of 599 was a major settlement, agreed to by Agilulf, Ariulf of Spoleto, the papacy, and the empire. Fighting resumed in 600, but the focus was now in the north where Agilulf captured Monselice, Cremona, and Mantua, suppressed the restless dukes of Friuli and Tridentum, and used Avar troops to ravage Istria. The net effect of the northern operations was to threaten seriously the empire's hold upon Ravenna, causing the emperor to reach a new armistice in 605, this time yielding 12,000 solidi in tribute.[19] The peace held for the rest of Agilulf's life, until 616, suggesting that the struggle between the Lombard crown

---

[19] Hartmann, "Italy Under the Lombards," p. 202.

and Byzantium for control of north and central Italy was reaching a stalemate, a condition of equilibrium.

Agilulf was succeeded by his minor son, Adaloald, who reigned until 626 when he was probably murdered, perhaps by a party which resented his acceptance of growing Roman and Catholic influence in the kingdom,[20] a matter to be discussed shortly. The new king was Arioald, duke of Turin, who held the throne for ten years. During this twenty-year period (616–636) there was further fighting with the empire, but nothing of a decisive nature. More serious was an Avar invasion from Pannonia into Friuli which resulted in the death of the duke and the devastation of the duchy. The crown did nothing, the Avars retiring to Pannonia on their own account. Once again the monarchy was in need of rejuvenation, and it was King Rothari who provided it.

Elected in 636, Rothari was devoted to the ideals of further conquest, royal strength throughout the Lombard territories, and protection of Lombard identity, which he saw threatened by Roman influences. As Hartmann observes, Rothari aimed "to raise the king's authority over the nobles, and to this purpose war against the imperials, which had rested during two decades, was taken up again in order to strengthen the king's royal domain by new conquests."[21] Northwest Italy from Luni to the Alps was conquered, the king appointing no dukes and keeping the land as royal possession. Other successful action by Rothari against the empire was in Venetia and around Ravenna. Most significant, however, was perhaps Rothari's promulgation of the Lombard laws, which in his sight made his kingdom's status equal to that of the empire.[22] The law as articulated by the crown was common to all Lombards. Hartmann puts it well: "The kingdom . . . showed its power by the fact of issuing legal regulations for the whole country, which, if not at once, were at all events after a short time accepted irrevocably from Benevento to Cividale."[23] By the death of Rothari in 652, a little less than a century after Alboin's entry, the Lombard monarchy had been revived and pushed well past earlier stages of strength and coherence.

Authari's effective successor was Aripert, who succeeded Rothari's son after the latter was killed following a short reign. As will be seen, Aripert was the first Catholic king of the Lombards. His death in 661 after a nine-year reign was followed by the ineffective tenure of his two sons, who were both forcefully overthrown by Duke Grimoald of Benevento, the son of the Friulian duke who was killed by the Avars. Grimoald married Aripert's daughter and further legitimized his coup by securing election as king. For the first time there was a Lombard Kingdom of Italy as hitherto independent Benevento was joined to the traditionally north Italian royal zone. Only the duchy of Spoleto lay beyond the grip of the crown. For the next nine years Grimoald struggled endlessly to hold the kingdom together.

---

[20] Ibid.
[21] Ibid., p. 203.
[22] Ibid., p. 204.
[23] Ibid.

In Benevento, where his son Romoald served as duke, there was a difficult contest in 663 with Emperor Constans II who in person brought a substantial imperial army to bear after landing in Tarentum in Apulia. The Lombards were victorious, however, with Romoald subsequently being able to advance deep into Apulia with the seizure of Tarentum and Brindisium.[24] In the north Grimoald had to suppress the duke of Friuli and probably others, causing him to bring in Avar forces, which attempted to annex what they had occupied. The king pursuaded them to leave, however, and then installed a new and loyal duke. At Grimoald's death in 671 the Lombard Kingdom of Italy was still intact, a tribute to the unrelenting efforts of the king.

Anarchy threatened for a moment as Grimoald's son Garibald was overthrown by Perctarit, one of the sons of Aripert whom Grimoald had thrust aside. But Perctarit was able to hold the throne, although he had to share power with his strong son Cunincpert, who joined him as co-king in 680. Perctarit also let the duchy of Benevento resume its autonomy by allowing Romoald, the son of Grimoald, to stay on as duke. The new independence of Benevento, it should be emphasized, robbed the kingdom of the Italian status which it had enjoyed under Grimoald. It was probably under the joint kingship that a major peace agreement was reached in about 680 between the Lombards and the empire. In effect, there was a formal acceptance of the territorial status quo as the empire recognized the Lombard state and the Lombards pledged no further conquest. Remarkably, the peace held: there was no further war between the monarchy and Byzantium until the offensive of Liutprand in 726–727. After Perctarit's death in about 688, Cunincpert successfully defended the crown against the serious challenge of Duke Alahis of Tridentum, whom Perctarit had never been able to control. The triumph over Alahis was a victory for Catholicism and the monarchy in that Cunincpert was a Catholic and Alahis a schismatic. Cunincpert, who was well-loved by his subjects, also kept peace with the empire and left the monarchy in firm control of the north.

But deep trouble ensued after Cunincpert's death in 700. His young son, Liutpert, who was under the protection of his tutor Ansprand, was quickly challenged and defeated by the duke of Turin. The duke died, but his son Aripert issued his own challenge, defeated Liutpert again, and took him prisoner. Now bearing the title Aripert II, the usurper had Liutpert killed, drove Ansprand into exile, and killed one of the latter's sons. Ansprand's other son, Liutprand, was not harmed, because, says Paul the Deacon, "Aripert regarded him as a person of no importance and as yet a mere youth. . . ."[25] Liutprand fled to his father Ansprand in Bavaria. In 712 Ansprand had his revenge as he attacked Aripert with a Bavarian army and drove him to flight. "And when weighted down with gold", Paul

[24] On his way home Constans spent twelve days in Rome.
[25] Paul, *History of the Lombards*, 6.22.265.
[26] Ibid., 6.35.278.

reports, "he [Aripert] attempted to swim across the river Ticinus, he sank there and, choked with the waters, expired."[26] Ansprand had the throne, but he died after a reign of only three months. His son Liutprand, earlier spared by Aripert, was elected to succeed him. Although few were likely to have expected it, Liutprand would surpass even Grimoald in bringing the Lombard world to order and coherence.

The growth of royal power and a Lombard kingdom was a major aspect of the Lombard experience in Italy. The invasion itself was a royal operation, King Alboin appointing dukes both to help lead the military action and to govern territories which he granted to them after the conquest.[27] After the restoration of the monarchy in 584 King Authari and his successors were able to impose their authority north of Spoleto and Benevento, and from Authari's reign onward there was a royal demesne, that is, the king's personal estates and the land in each duchy which was designated as belonging to the crown. Each duchy also had a *gastaldius*, the chief royal officer in the duchy who had competence over an administrative district called the *civitas*, which was not often coterminous with the duchy.[28] The gastald served as steward over the royal demesne in the duchy, functioned as chief judge and legal authority, and represented the king in military affairs. Also supporting the king was the royal *gassindium*, the king and his sworn body of warriors, his *fideles*,[29] from whom were drawn the king's principal palace officers such as the treasurer (*vesterarius*) and the chancellor (*referendarius*).[30] Pavia gradually emerged as the chief royal residential center and thus as the royal capital, the permanent seat of the principal organ of the royal government, the writing office. Pavia also became the mint for a royal coinage, and minting itself was claimed by Rothari as a royal prerogative: "He who mints gold or strikes money without the king's command", says Rothari in one of his laws, "shall have his hand cut off."[31] The restriction is thought to have been effective from the reign of Cunincpert. As noted, the development of the royal law code from the reign of Authari onward also contributed greatly to the growth of royal power and prestige, especially as the king came to be viewed as both formulator of the law and provider of justice and peace through the administration of the gastalds. Finally, although the dukes retained military capacity of their own, the king never lost his position as national war leader, and, as the laws make clear, the Lombard freeman was first and foremost an *exercitalis* or *arimanus*, an army man owing service to the Lombard nation.[32] In sum, by the eighth century there was a kingdom of the Lombards whose monarch presided over a national law, boasted a national center, and conducted a national administration in both Pavia and the duchies.

---

[27] A good example of the latter is Alboin's grant of Friuli to Gisulf, described at some length by Paul, *History of the Lombards*, 2.9.65–66.

[28] Drew, *The Lombard Laws*, p. 241, n. 17.

[29] Ibid., p. 248, n. 62 and p. 251, n. 2.

[30] Hartmann, "Italy Under the Lombards," p. 210.

[31] Drew, *Lombard Laws*, Rothari #242, p. 100.

[32] Ibid., p. 24.

However, both the Lombard monarchy and the Lombard kingdom obviously suffered from severe limitations. Most notable among them was the autonomy of Spoleto and Benevento, save for the unusual reign of Grimoald. Although the royal law may have been applied in these great duchies in some degree, they were otherwise independent. Gastalds there were not royal officers but appointees of the dukes, and the crown had no demesne rights. Benevento minted coins, and both duchies conducted their own foreign relations. Except in the days of Grimoald, their separation from the monarchy effectively prohibited the emergence of a Lombard Kingdom of Italy. But there were other limitations. The ten years without a king (574–584) left all Lombard territory in ducal hands and accustomed dukes everywhere to autonomous military, judicial, and administrative competence. After restoration of the monarchy in 584, King Authari and his successors were able to impose their authority north of Spoleto and Benevento, but in effect by the late sixth century the Lombard kingdom had a dual administration, as one scholar puts it, "that of the dukes on the one hand and that of the king represented by his royal officials on the other."[33] Although the king was clearly the stronger and the superior, the ducal element never ceased to be vital, and, as we have seen, often fostered revolt against the crown, as is especially evident in the cases of the dukes of Friuli and Tridentum. Ducal power was particularly significant in royal elections (the elective principle itself being a royal limitation), inviting factionalism and civil war, inhibiting dynastic continuity, and encouraging the freeman soldier to attach his loyalty to the duke rather than to the king. It may be instructive that the kings never attempted to do away with the ducal system in the north; they asserted the right of appointing the dukes, but they knew that the ducal dualism was too entrenched to remove and so left it untouched, content instead to develop and maintain a strong corollary position through the gastalds and the law. At best, the Lombard kingdom was a confederacy of north Italian Lombard dukes kept in check by successful royal legal and administrative efforts.

## The Lombard Conversion to Catholicism

Originally the Lombards adhered to Germanic paganism, to the cults, rituals, and idols known to the folk for time out of mind. But, during their residence across the Danube from Pannonia about 500, Lombard leaders and presumably the people as well adopted Arian Christianity, perhaps as the result of Rugian missionary activity among them.[34] The Lombards remained Arian through the Pannonian period and that of the entry into Italy. During the entry, according to Paul the Deacon, Catholic churches were pillaged, priests were killed,[35] and St. Benedict's monastery at Monte

---

[33] Ibid., p. 240, n. 11.

[34] Musset, *The Germanic Invasions*, p. 87. For a recent and important discussion of Lombard religious development, see Stephen C. Fanning, "Lombard Arianism Reconsidered." Fanning doubts that the Lombards were ever Arian and sees the Lombard conversion to Catholicism as movement to it from paganism, not Arianism.

[35] Paul, *History of the Lombards*, 2.32.93.

Cassino was sacked.[36] But the Lombards in Italy were surrounded and far outnumbered by the Catholic Romans, with whom the Arian kings seem disposed to co-existence,[37] making Lombard movement toward Catholicism inevitable. The first step was the late sixth century marriage of King Authari to Theudelinda, the Catholic princess from Bavaria who stayed in the Lombard kingdom after Authari's death and married his successor, the great Agilulf. Authari did not become a Catholic, but Agilulf did, at least if we are to believe Paul the Deacon.[38] In any event, there were remarkable gains in the time of Theudelinda. St. Columbanus, the zealous Irish missionary, founded the monastery of Bobbio in the Cottian Alps near Pavia with Agilulf's help and used it as a center for converting Lombards.[39] The impact of Bobbio in the Lombard movement toward the new faith may have been decisive.[40] Missionaries from Rome and the Catholic bishop of Pavia were also permitted to preach against Arianism and baptize Lombards as Catholics. Notable converts were Adaloald, the son of Agilulf and Theudelinda, and Gundiperga, their daughter. Theudelinda founded several churches, especially the church of St. John the Baptist in Monza, and corresponded with Pope Gregory the Great. The latter saw in the influence of the Catholic queen hope for permanent Lombard-imperial settlement after he and Agilulf had reached the armistice of 599: "we exhort you," wrote the pope to Theudelinda, "that you so proceed with your most excellent husband that he may not reject the alliance of our Christian republic [the empire]. . . . Do you, therefore, according to your custom, ever busy yourself with the things that relate to the welfare of the parties. . . ."[41] Conceivably, Agilulf's long peace with the empire after 599 may be attributed in large measure to Theudelinda's influence and connection with the papacy. Theudelinda's important career lodged the Catholic faith at the Lombard court for a long period, probably strengthened the Catholic bishop of Pavia and the episcopate in the kingdom generally, and put Arianism very much on the defensive.

There ensued a quarter-century of reaction, from 626 to about 652. Agilulf's Catholic son Adaloald was murdered in 626, perhaps by Lombards resenting Roman (in this case Catholic) influences.[42] The next king, the formidable Rothari, was also reactionary, remaining an Arian (although not persecuting Catholics) and promulgating the laws in part to buttress Lombard customs and traditions. Even so, the Arian bishop of Pavia became a Catholic in Rothari's reign,[43] suggesting continued Catholic advances despite unfavorable conditions. This judgment is confirmed by the fact that

---

[36] Ibid., 4.17.162.

[37] Hodgkin, *Italy and Her Invaders*, 6.145.

[38] Paul, *History of the Lombards*, 4.6.153–154.

[39] Hartmann, *Geschichte Italiens*, 2.2.25. Both Theudelinda and Columbanus supported the Three Chapters schism. Hodgkin, *Italy and Her Invaders*, 6.138–142.

[40] Ibid., 6.133–134.

[41] Paul, *History of the Lombards*, 4.9.157.

[42] Hodgkin, *Italy and Her Invaders*, 6.150.

[43] Paul, *History of the Lombards*, 4.42.195.

a Catholic, Aripert I, succeeded Rothari. Only a few things are known about Aripert's Catholic commitment. He was the son of a brother of Theudelinda,[44] which may account for his Catholicism. He established a major church in Pavia,[45] And, like Theudelinda, he had Roman inclinations in contrast to the Lombard orientation of Rothari.[46] The assertion of an eighth-century poem that Authari proscribed Arianism is to be doubted,[47] but with the crown clearly won for Catholicism it was only a question of time before the triumph was complete.

After Aripert I there were no more Arian kings, with Grimoald, Perctarit, Cunincpert, Liutprand, and Ratchis all hailed as outstanding Catholics. Perctarit, we read, was "a pious man, a Catholic in belief, tenacious of justice and a very bountiful supporter of the poor."[48] Under Perctarit and Cunincpert, Lombard bishops pledged to the pope that henceforth whenever Lombard bishops-elect were confirmed by the pope they would promise to uphold the peace of 680 between the Lombard kingdom and the empire. Papacy, Lombard church, and Lombard crown were being specifically linked, even integrated in this understanding. Late in Cunincpert's reign a synod, probably a meeting at Pavia, settled the long-standing Three Chapters schism which had divided Lombard Catholicism since the days of Theudelinda and Columbanus.[49] This action, coupled with Cunincpert's defeat of the schismatic Duke Alahis, appears to have removed the last significant obstacle to the triumph of Catholicism.[50] Liutprand (712–744), never doubted in his orthodoxy, was pictured by Paul the Deacon as "very religious . . . merciful to offenders, chaste, modest, prayerful in the night watches, and generous in charities. . . ."[51] Liutprand's successor Ratchis (744–749) abdicated and became a monk at the restored Monte Cassino. We know little of the degree and quality of Catholic belief among the Lombard people, but if the service and commitment of their kings is any indication the Lombards were as Catholic as any Germanic nation in Europe in the eighth century.

## THE PAPACY, THE LOMBARDS, AND BYZANTIUM

Like any other bishop, the pope was obligated to look after the spiritual needs of his diocese. But, based upon a developing ideology which involved the concepts of the primacy of St. Peter among the apostles and of Rome among the sees of the world, the papacy claimed spiritual headship of the Christian churches everywhere. The claim was acknowledged by churches in Italy, North Africa, and some other parts of the West, but the recognition

---

[44] Ibid., 4.48.202.
[45] Ibid., pp. 202–203.
[46] Hartmann, *Geschichte Italiens*, 2.1.244.
[47] Hartmann, "Italy Under the Lombards," p. 204.
[48] Paul, *History of the Lombards*, 5.33.237.
[49] See above, n. 39 and Paul, *History of the Lombards*, 4.14.260–261 and notes 2 and 3.
[50] Hartmann, "Italy Under the Lombards," p. 206.
[51] Paul, *History of the Lombards*, 6.58.306.

brought with it a host of thorny problems such as defining relationships between bishops and the pope, clarifying the role of the papacy in ecclesiastical reform and articulation of theology, and directing missions for the conversion of pagans, Arians, and other heretics. In the East, Rome's assertion of spiritual primacy was generally ignored or opposed by the great sees of Constantinople, Antioch, Alexandria, and Nicaea.

On more mundane levels, like the bishops of many other cities during the disintegration of the Roman empire, the papacy exercised civil administration powers in Rome in cooperation with and in place of the failing Roman government. It fed, clothed, and housed the poor, provided and managed the city's food and water supplies, and maintained its public works. After Justinian annihilated the Ostrogoths and restored Italy and Rome to the empire, the popes continued to perform these functions and added new ones such as the provisioning and paying of the Roman army. There was duality in this situation, for while the inhabitants of Rome may have seen these administrative services as activities independently conducted on behalf of the city by the papacy, the legal reality was that the pope and his officials were officers and subordinates assisting in the government of Rome in the name of the exarch and ultimately of the emperor. Rome was an imperial city in an imperial district, a duchy whose civil and military officials were all responsible to the exarch.[52] In brief, the papacy was an institutional component of the Byzantine constitution. This condition was implicit in imperial ideology, which pictured the emperor as the earthly regent of God who ruled Christendom and directed all its governing agencies for the common good, making the pope a subordinate of the emperor, the Christian executive. Although the papacy was developing its own Gelasian or "two swords" ideology which posited the pope as Christian sovereign and the emperor as the pope's secular assistant in Christian governance, the popes actually accepted the imperial worldview and with it their own membership in the imperial constitution: each new pope-elect requested the emperor to approve his election to the papal throne and refused consecration by Roman suffregan bishops until the approval was granted. Further complicating the papal position was the fact that the papacy was one of Italy's foremost landowners.[53] Governed by a substantial ecclesiastical bureaucracy, peopled by a large population of papal tenants, and yielding a steady and good income, papal property was scattered throughout Sicily and Italy but was found especially in the duchy of Rome and around the city of Ravenna. Known as the patrimony of St. Peter, the property gave the papacy both the ability to perform its episcopal and administrative services in Rome and a set of local and Italian interests and responsibilities which were wholly separate from the empire.[54] In brief,

---

[52] See especially Diehl, *Études sur l'administration*, pp. 168–184.

[53] David Harry Miller, "The Roman Revolution of the Eighth Century: A Study of the Ideological Background of the Papal Separation from Byzantium and Alliance With the Franks," pp. 79–133, 92–93. See Ibid., n. 32 for additional references on papal property and related matters.

[54] Ibid., p. 93.

apart from its spiritual and episcopal roles, the papacy was two things: imperial assistant and independent leader of the duchy of Rome, or at least of its many patrimonial dependents.

In both of the latter capacities the pope was bound to resist the Lombard advances in Italy. As Byzantine official he could only oppose any Lombard attempt to seize the duchy of Rome, which the Lombards saw as simply one more imperial place to be conquered, albeit a particularly significant one. And, as independent leader of the duchy of Rome the pope was obligated to protect its people and the patrimonial land. But what resources did the pope have at his disposal? Armed force from local and imperial sources was surely questionable at best, as Gregory the Great learned in the 593 crisis presented by Ariulf and Agilulf. Defense by pursuit of peace through diplomacy, money, and armistice was therefore a mandatory supplement to arms. Thus, when Ariulf and then Agilulf in 593 seized Perugia, cut the Via Amerina, and advanced upon Rome, Pope Gregory sought peace with the Lombards: only in a Lombard-papal peace could there be satisfaction of the pope's double imperial and local responsibility. The peace of 680 between the Lombard monarchy and the empire is also worth recalling in this regard. The pope fully supported the settlement by insisting that Lombard bishops-elect promise to uphold the peace. As before, the pope was attempting both to meet his imperial obligations and to respond to his local Roman requirements by cultivating peace with the Lombards. In brief, dictated by the dual imperial and Roman functions, the papal attitude toward the Lombards was both defensive and pacific in quality.

What of the Lombard attitude toward the papacy and the Roman duchy? There is no indication that the various efforts against the duchy conducted by Agilulf and Ariulf were part of an Arian crusade against Catholics. The fact is that Rome was an imperial territory and a Lombard war against it was an expected natural feature of the general Lombard effort to conquer Byzantine Italy. Nor can it be shown that Lombard leaders were significantly hostile toward the pope. The Lombards most inclined to such hostility, Ariulf and Agilulf, both eventually came to terms wth Pope Gregory, and Agilulf entered into a long *modus vivendi* with him and his successors. Indeed, the evidence suggests that from the reign of Aripert I until that of Liutprand there was not a single case of tension between the Lombard monarch and the pope. Relations between the latter and the Spoletan and Beneventan dukes were more difficult, for both attempted to seize border places from time to time. But as far as the royal-papal relationship was concerned, calm apparently prevailed. Finally, it is clear that once Agilulf and Ariulf ended their campaigns, the crown lost interest in taking the city of Rome or any of its territories. Instead, there appears to have been only the inclination to remain faithful to the settlement arranged by Agilulf and reinforced in 680 under Perctarit and Cunincpert. Thus, from the early seventh century onward, the Lombard monarchy's attitude toward Rome and the papacy was as pacific as that held by the papacy toward the Lombards.

This fundamental royal-papal harmony depended upon continuation of two conditions, royal acceptance of peace with the empire and papal membership in the Byzantine empire. The latter reality was in question by the seventh century, however. In the first place, no love was lost between non-Germanic inhabitants of Italy and the empire because of the grim legacy of Justinian's Ostrogothic war, subsequent heavy imperial taxation, and Byzantine-Italian religious differences and tensions. Partly because of its patronage of thousands of Italians by virtue of its extensive land ownership, the church—especially the papacy—was seen by Italians as their more natural and preferred leader. This situation contained potential for Italian revolt against the empire led by the church, even by the papacy, a potential which obviously contradicted the papacy's membership in the empire but was also congruent with the other reality of papal independence.

The Byzantines seemed anxious to do what they could to convert the potential into actuality. In the 630s, for example, the exarch Isaac had the Lateran arbitrarily looted to help protect himself against dissidents in Ravenna and to pay imperial expenses there. Much more importantly, after Pope Martin I in 649 condemned theological positions being advanced by the empire, Emperor Constans II, finding that various lesser expedients were of no use, ordered the exarch to bring Martin to heel by force.[55] The exarch Theodore Calliopas in 653 broke into Rome and tried to arrest him. At this point the Roman laity and clergy rallied to Martin, causing Calliopas to doubt his ability to maintain himself in Rome and leading him to sneak from Rome in haste with the pope in tow. Martin was taken to the East, and in Constantinople was convicted of various charges, among which was that of inciting rebellion against the empire. Thereafter Martin endured humiliating and painful punishments in Constantinople and the Crimea, where he died.

In Italy, Martin's sufferings at imperial hands were followed with interest and outrage.[56] There had been an Italian revolt, and the pope had led it, or so many Italians, especially those in Rome, must have believed. A period of calm followed the episode of Martin, but anti-imperial sentiments continued. The most serious instances of such hostility occurred in 687 when the exarch tried but failed to settle a disputed papal election in Rome and in the 690s when the militias of Ravenna, the Pentapolis, and Rome abandoned the exarch and rallied to Pope Sergius I after he defied the rulings of a synod called by Emperor Justinian II which ordered recognition of the see of Constantinople as supreme in the church.[57] The outraged militia troops nearly lynched an agent of the exarch when he attempted to arrest Sergius; he escaped only by hiding from his pursuers under the pope's bed in the Lateran. Although calm descended once more, Italians now understood that Byzantium ruled in its Italian places only by their sufferance and looked to the pope as the focal point of Italian leadership. The irony was

---

[55] For details see Hodgkin, *Italy and Her Invaders*, 6.256–269 and Peter Llewellyn, *Rome in the Dark Ages*, pp. 150–155.
[56] Llewellyn, *Rome in the Dark Ages*, p. 155.
[57] Ibid., p. 160.

complete: Byzantium's chief agent in the governance of the city of Rome and ally in defense of the city and duchy against the Lombards was by the late seventh century the leader of an expression of Italian nationalism which found its essence in Italian hostility toward the empire.

This was the general Italian environment in which the eighth-century relationship between the Lombard monarchy and the papacy began. The royal power was considerable in northern Italy, but even there the ducal power was sufficient to limit it significantly. In the duchies of Spoleto and Benevento independent Lombard dukes ignored the crown and governed without reference to Pavia. Byzantium continued to possess the exarchate and the duchies of the Pentapolis, Perugia, and Rome, lands which linked Ravenna and Rome by the Via Amerina and severed the northern kingdom from the central and southern duchies. Until those territories belonged to the crown, and until the dukes of Spoleto and Benevento were subordinated to Pavia, no Lombard Kingdom of Italy was possible.

Despite its considerable territorial possession, the empire's power in Italy was nearly gone, for its subjects were hostile to the point of active rebellion and looked not to Constantinople or Ravenna, but to the church, especially to the papacy, for leadership. Owner of much land and lord of many tenants in the Byzantine duchy of Rome, the papacy was in an awkward and contradictory position: as proprietor and patron it was an independent authority and an Italian leader, while as administrator in the city of Rome it was an imperial constituent, a role which it specifically accepted. In both capacities the pope had to oppose any Lombard effort to take possession of the duchy and the city of Rome. But a *modus vivendi*, formalized in the status quo Lombard-imperial peace of 680, had been achieved between the Lombard monarchy and the pope wherein the crown refrained from any hostile action, allowing the pope to enjoy peace with Pavia. It remained to be seen as the eighth century dawned whether the potential for papal withdrawal from the empire would be realized, and if so, whether that fundamental change would affect the friendly relations between the Lombard monarchy and Rome.

## II. THE SEARCH FOR PEACE BY COMPULSION

**V**ery little is known about relations between the Lombard monarchy and the papacy in the earliest years of the eighth century. It appears, however, that the relationship was cordial, for the sources make no mention of any kind of trouble and point out that Aripert II returned a great donation in the Cottian Alps to the papacy.[1] Aripert's successor, Liutprand, was no less friendly, confirming the Cottian donation[2] and readily acknowledging the pope as the sole head of the church.[3] He also helped to defend Pope Gregory II (715–731) from imperial maltreatment in the 720s. Further evidence is lacking, but it is clear enough that no tension marked the early years of the eighth-century relationship between Pavia and Rome.

### THE EIGHTH-CENTURY ITALIAN REVOLT AGAINST THE EMPIRE

The relations between the Byzantine emperor, Leo III, and his Italian subjects were strained. In 726 Leo ordered heavy increases in taxes on land in order to pay for reforms in the East.[4] The papacy, owning its extensive Italian tracts, stood to suffer greatly from the increase and responded with what amounted to renewed revolt: Gregory II refused compliance with the tax by having the many papal tenants withhold payment.[5] Leo III would not tolerate such treasonous behavior from an officer of the empire.[6] Indeed, Leo went so far as to order Gregory's death, or at least the exarch Paul sent an expedition to Rome to kill the pope. But militia units in Rome joined with Lombard forces furnished by King Liutprand and the dukes of Spoleto and Benevento to thwart Paul's effort. Paul himself was murdered in Ravenna during rioting between imperialists and supporters of the pope.[7] In the meantime, Italians in imperial territories other than Rome, probably inspired by Gregory's example, refused their own taxes to Leo.[8] A new Italian revolt against the empire, the most severe to date, was in progress. As in the earlier troubles, the pope was perceived by the rebels as the

---

[1] Paul the Deacon, *Historia Langobardorum*, 6.28.174; *Vita Johannis VIII*, LP, 1.385.

[2] Paul, *Hist. Lang.*, 6.43.179. *Vita Gregorii II* 4, LP 1.398.

[3] *Leges Langobardorum, Leges Liutprandi* 33.4: ". . . papa urbis Romae, qui in omni mundo caput ecclesiarum Dei et sacerdotum est. . . ."

[4] David Harry Miller, "The Roman Revolution of the Eighth Century," p. 101.

[5] Ibid., p. 102.

[6] For what follows see *VG II*, 16, 403–404 and Paul, *Hist. Lang.* 6.49.

[7] *VG II*, 18, 405.

[8] Miller, "The Roman Revolution," p. 102.

leader. The revolt reached its climax when Byzantium lost most of its Italian military power as the Italian militias ousted their dukes appointed by the exarch and elected new leaders.[9] Henceforth the emperor and the exarch, who was now Eutychius, were powerless and would have to base their activities upon diplomacy, enlisting non-imperial agencies to do most of their fighting for them. Only in the city of Ravenna itself and its surrounding country did the empire apparently retain military strength.[10] Elsewhere—in the Pentapolis, Perugia, and Rome—Italians formerly under imperial rule looked ahead to a new era of independence.

In the meantime, Emperor Leo announced a major religious reform, generally known as Iconoclasm: sacred images must be removed from all churches in the empire.[11] The iconoclast rationale was that Christians were made vulnerable to the heresy of idolatry by the presence of images, for few could make the necessary distinction between worshipping the image and venerating the holy thing which it represented. To Italians, who relied heavily upon images in worship, the imperial decree was detestable. Pope Gregory II, already in sharp conflict with Leo over the matter of taxes, and already seen by Italians as a national leader against foreign rule, did the only thing he could—and probably felt that he must do on theological grounds: he convened a Roman synod and condemned Leo's Iconoclast decree.[12] If Leo III expected any good to come in Italy from that decree he was sadly mistaken. It only exacerbated anti-Byzantine feeling there, strengthened local autonomist sentiments, and encouraged former imperial subjects to view the pope as Italy's leader.

## KING LIUTPRAND'S RECREATION OF THE KINGDOM OF ITALY AND FIRST TENSION WITH ROME

As the Italian revolt reached its climax King Liutprand of the Lombards sensed that an unusual moment had come to advance the monarchy's interests.[13] Quite clearly, the collapse of the exarch's military power invited

---

[9] Ibid., pp. 102–103.

[10] Ibid., p. 104.

[11] For Iconoclasm see Stephen Gero, *Byzantine Iconoclasm during the Reign of Leo III with Particular Attention to the Oriental Sources*; Paul J. Alexander, *The Patriarch Nicephorus of Constantinople. Ecclesiastical Policy and Image Worship in the Byzantine Empire*; L. Bréhier, *La querelle des images*; M. V. Anastos, "Iconoclasm and Imperial Rule, 717–842."

[12] *VG II*, 24.1.409. Gregory also sent two sharply worded letters to Leo III asserting papal as opposed to imperial authority in dogmatic matters and telling him that imperial rule in Italy was at an end. *Epistolae*, Epp. 12 and 13, PL 89.511–524. On the question of the authenticity of the letters, see Miller, "The Roman Revolution," pp. 107–108, especially n. 70.

[13] Principal references for the period of Liutprand's reign are: Ottorino Bertolini, *Roma di fronte a Bisanzio e ai Longobardi*, pp. 423–489; idem, "I papi e le relazioni politiche di Roma con i ducati longobardi di Spoleto e di Benevento," pp. 1–57, esp. pp. 33–57; idem, "Le relazioni politiche di Roma con i ducati di Spoleto e di Benevento nel periodo del dominio longobardo," pp. 681–692, esp. pp. 685–688; Hartmann, *Geschichte Italiens*, 2.2 pp. 86–156; idem, "Italy Under the Lombards," pp. 211–214; J. Haller, *Das Papsttum, Idee und Wirklichkeit*, 1 pp. 351–364; F. X. Seppelt, *Geschichte des Papsttums*, 2, pp. 88–94, 100–107; Erich Caspar, *Geschichte des Papsttums*, 2 [*Das Papsttum unter Byzantinischer Heerschaft*], pp. 726–738; R. Macaigne, *L'Église Merovingienne*

# THE SEARCH FOR PEACE

Liutprand to strike quickly into the exarchate and the empire's other territories. If they were conquered the monarchy would control all Italy except for Gaeta, Naples, Apulia, and Calabria and the Lombard duchies of Spoleto and Benevento. Indeed, the independence of the latter two territories would be threatened, for royal seizure of the exarchate and the duchy of the Pentapolis would give Pavia a direct route from the Lombard kingdom to the duchies, the route from Pavia into the duchy of Spoleto by the Via Aemilia, the Via Flaminia, and the Old Flaminian Way.

In 726 or 727 Liutprand began to exploit his opportunity by capturing Ravenna's port of Classis,[14] thereby cutting off the capital's communications with Constantinople. He also laid siege to Ravenna itself, but was unable to take it.[15] In the Emilia, the region in the exarchate northwest of Ravenna,[16] however, Liutprand enjoyed greater success. There he took most of the towns to the west of the Aemilian Way and gained control of the road itself.[17] One further royal conquest was achieved in the Pentapolis as Liutprand took Auximum (Osimo),[18] the southernmost place in the duchy lying close to the border with the duchy of Spoleto and astride the Old Flaminian Way leading directly from the Pentapolis into Spoleto. Liutprand perhaps wanted Auximum for defense against potential Spoletan expansion into the exarchate.[19] The dukes of Spoleto from time to time had driven into the exarchate and a new attempt might be expected in the turmoil of the Italian revolt, but, having Auximum, Liutprand could block any such Spoletan invasion. Liutprand also may have had offensive reasons for taking the area, however, for the Old Flaminian Way through Auximum could serve as his point of entry into Spoleto for the subordination of its duke.

As Liutprand seized Classis, much of the Emilia, and Auximum, he doubtless watched for papal reactions, for, rebellious or not, the pope was still technically an imperial officer. Gregory II had been effectively neutral up to the occupation of Auximum in 727, neither helping to halt Liutprand's drive on the Adriatic nor cooperating with the king against Byzantium. But Gregory's neutrality was entirely consistent with his leadership of the Italian revolt. In fact, it amounted to indirect aid to Liutprand, assistance

et l'État pontifical, pp. 193–213; L. Bréhier and R. Aigrain, Histoire de l'Église, 5 [Grégoire le grand, les états barbares et la conquête arabe (590–757)], pp. 412–421; H. Hubert, "Étude sur la formation des états de l'église. Les papes Grégoire II, Grégoire III, Zacharie et Étienne II et leurs relations avec les empereurs iconoclastes (726–757)," pp. 1–40; Thomas Hodgkin, Italy and Her Invaders, 6, pp. 437–508; Peter Llewellyn, Rome in the Dark Ages, pp. 199–206; and Miller, "The Roman Revolution," pp. 102–113 ff.

[14] Paul, Hist. Lang., 6.49.181; VG II, 13.403.

[15] Paul, Hist. Lang., 6.49; VG II, 13.403.

[16] Eighth-century understanding placed the Emilia entirely within the Exarchate. Diehl, Études sur l'administration, pp. 52–53, n. 2.

[17] The Emilian towns seized were Feronianum (Zenzano or Frignano), Montebellium (Monteveglio), Buxum (Bazzano), Persicetum (San Giovanni in Persiceto), and Bonnonia (Bologna). Paul. Hist. Lang., 6.49; VG II, 18. 405. The identifications follows A. Guillou, Régionalisme et independence, pp. 57–58.

[18] Paul, Hist. Lang., 6.49; VG II, 18.405.

[19] Bertolini, "I papi e le relazioni politiche di Roma con i ducati," p. 48.

which was seen in Constantinople as treason.[20] At this juncture Gregory II may have regarded Liutprand as an ally in the Italian revolt since Liutprand's conquests in the exarchate and the Pentapolis were evidently perceived as liberations from imperial oppression and Liutprand did what he could to cultivate the image of liberator.[21] If the pope had such an impression of the king, it could only have been enhanced by the latter's congenial treatment of the pope: Liutprand had protected Gregory against Exarch Paul. Later, Liutprand steadily refused bribes and gifts from the next exarch, Eutychius, which were designed to obtain royal cooperation in a new attempt to murder the pope.[22] There was no papal anxiety or disapproval of the royal seizures of imperial territory on the Adriatic and the royal maneuvers against Spoleto; instead, confirmation appeared to issue from the Lateran. At the very least, in the relations between Liutprand and Gregory there was considerable warmth and solidarity. As the *Vita Gregorii II* puts it, "The Romans and Lombards were united as brothers. . . ."[23]

But royal-papal tension arrived quickly. At some point in 727 Liutprand entered the duchy of Rome and seized the fortress of Sutri on the Via Cassia about thirty miles northeast of Rome near the duchy's border with Lombard Tuscany.[24] Gregory II responded to the fall of Sutri in alarm by deluging the king with money and gifts, and sending many letters begging the king to bestow Sutri upon St. Peter and St. Paul as a royal donation. For four months Liutprand took Gregory's money but would not yield. At last he complied, however. As the pope had requested, Sutri was transferred to the papacy as a donation.[25] Lombard troops thereupon withdrew from the Roman duchy, although Liutprand maintained possession of some of the Sutri district.[26] As fast as it had occurred, the royal-papal tension had evaporated.

Why Liutprand appropriated Sutri is unclear. Perhaps the fortress was to serve as a second base for potential royal operations against the duchy of Spoleto,[27] but this may be doubtful because Sutri was not on any road leading into it. More plausible is the possibility that the seizure was effected in cooperation with the pope against the empire as part of the Italian revolt.[28] The obvious royal-papal tension over Sutri's capture by Liutprand leaves this argument questionable, however. Another possibility is that

---

[20] Miller, "The Roman Revolution," p. 102.

[21] Roberto Cessi, "La crisi dell' esarcato ravennate agli inizi dell iconoclastia," pp. 1678–1679; A. Gasquet, "Le royaume lombard; ses relations avec l'empire grec et avec les Francs," p. 76.

[22] *VG II*, 19.406. Eutychius attempted to buy Lombard support because he could not succeed against the pope as long as the Lombards were in league with him. Bertolini, "I papi e le relazioni politiche di Roma con i ducati," p. 42.

[23] *VG II*, 19.406: ". . . una se quasi fratres fidei catena constrinxerunt Romani atque Longobardi. . . ." Particularly emphatic in recognizing Liutprand's harmony with the pope is Haller, *Das Papsttum*, 1, pp. 353–355.

[24] For the seizure and what follows see *VG II*, 21.407; Paul, *Hist. Lang.* 6.49.

[25] The papal source (*VG II*, 21.407) is explicit that the donation was to the papacy.

[26] *VG II*, 21.407; Duchesne, *Vita Zachariae*, LP 1.437, n. 15.

[27] Hartmann, "Italy Under the Lombards," p. 212.

[28] Cessi, "La crisi dell' esarcato." pp. 1679–1680.

MAP. 2. North and central Italy in the early eighth century.

Liutprand occupied Sutri simply as a means of extorting money from the pope to defray the costs of his military expansion elsewhere. That Liutprand yielded Sutri only when he had amassed a small fortune favors this view. Finally, it may be that since the duchy of Rome was understood to belong to the empire, Liutprand's attack upon Sutri was actually but another part of his general offensive against imperial territory in central Italy. None of these possibilities is mutually exclusive, but none is very certain either.

What is much clearer from the circumstances is that no permanent rupture between Pavia and Rome arose from the Sutri episode. Despite the tension the matter was settled to apparent mutual satisfaction. The trouble perhaps signified that Liutprand's support of the papacy against the empire had its limits,[29] but the fall of Sutri did not mark the beginning of a sys-

---

[29] Bertolini, "I papi e le relazioni politiche di Roma con i ducati," pp. 46–47.

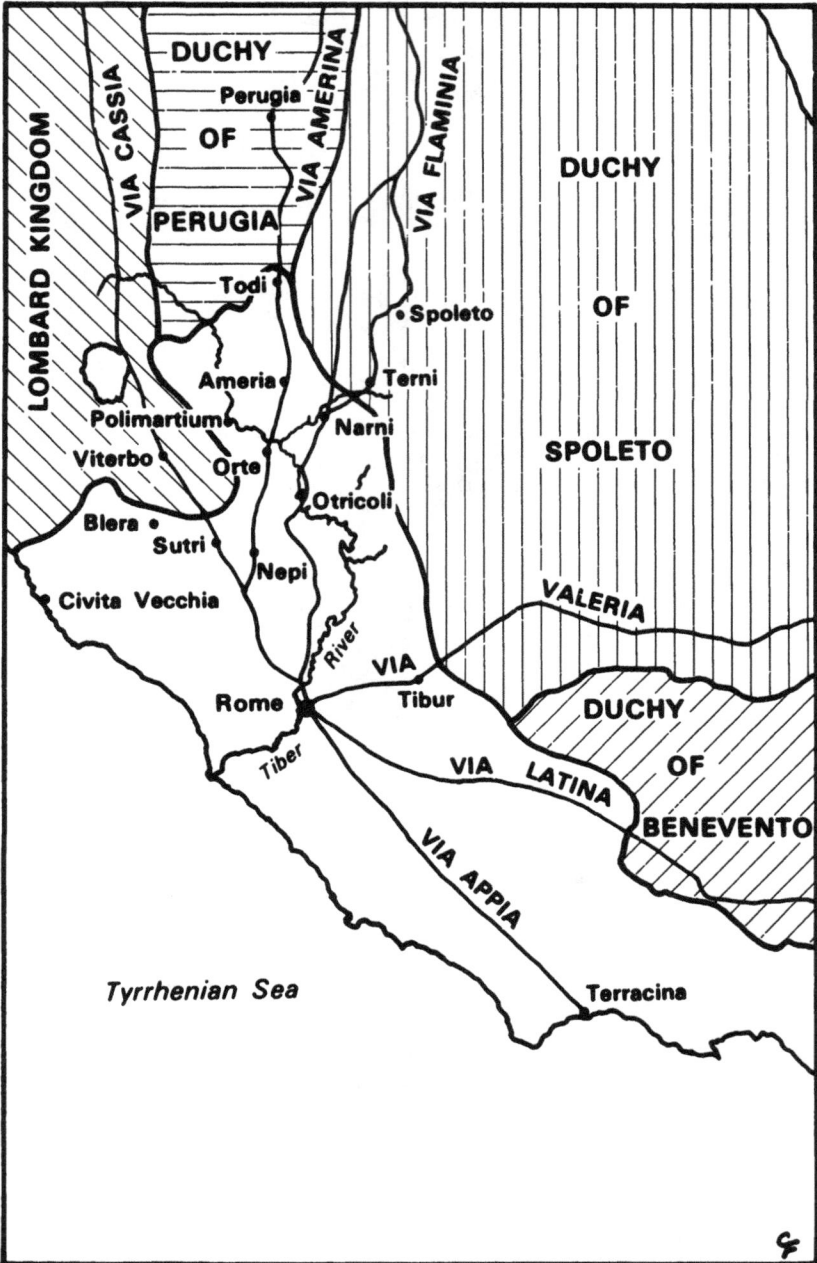

MAP. 3. Duchy of Rome in the reign of King Liutprand: Hodgkin, *Italy and Her Invaders*, 5 (1895): 353.

tematic royal campaign to conquer Rome's duchy. Thus while Gregory II was bound to have been uneasy after the Sutri settlement, nothing had happened to disturb the positive relationship between Pavia and Rome which had obtained earlier in the century.

A final observation about the Sutri affair needs to be made: the dealings were ultimately to the benefit of the papacy, not the empire, in that Sutri did not remain imperial property but became a papal possession. In Gregory II's demanding and receiving Sutri—an imperial place—as a donation *to the papacy* there is perhaps reflection of a changing papal perception of the duchy of Rome. We cannot be sure that such a perception was developing,[30] but at least some scholars think that it was at this point that the papacy began to view the duchy as papal rather than imperial in jurisdiction.[31] Such a view would, of course, explain why Gregory felt able to receive Byzantine territory as a possession of St Peter: to the pope, imperial authority in the duchy was at an end. Such thinking was perhaps a natural corollary of the extensive papal proprietary role in the duchy and the long public function in Rome; certainly it was to be expected as Gregory refused Leo's taxes, condemned his Iconoclasm, and let himself be seen as the leader of the Italian revolt. Thus, Sutri was perhaps a watershed in papal development. The pope was apparently emerging as the head of an independent Italian political entity—for the moment known only as the duchy of Rome.

Upon conclusion of the Sutri matter, in 728 Liutprand effected a surprising diplomatic revolution. The king became an ally of Exarch Eutychius of Ravenna, who had hitherto been his archenemy. We know little of the details except that Eutychius initiated the negotiations and that Liutprand received gifts and money for his cooperation. Something of the specific terms of the alliance is also known, terms which explain why the pope's biographer called it a "wicked" arrangement. The exarch pledged to help Liutprand subjugate Transamund of Spoleto and Romoald of Benevento, while the king promised to help Eutychius against Gregory II.[32]

Having formed the pact, Eutychius and Liutprand invaded Spoleto and easily brought Transamund to heel. No details are reported, but the campaign seems to have been very effective since the report of the invasion is followed immediately by the statement that Transamund took an oath of loyalty to the monarchy. Whatever the explanation, Transamund had clearly accepted dependence upon the crown in place of the traditional Spoletan autonomy. An oath similar to that of Transamund was taken by his powerful but threatened Beneventan neighbor, Romoald, although no royal troops appear to have entered his duchy.[33] The example of Spoleto was perhaps sufficient to achieve Romoald's submission.

An event of primary importance in Lombard history had occurred: Liutprand had recreated the Lombard Kingdom of Italy, or at least the essential framework for it despite the continuing independence of the surviving imperial territories. For the first time in more than half a century the

---

[30] To some, the Sutri donation was simply a return of patrimonies, not a transference of territory from imperial to papal jurisdiction. Bertolini, *Roma di fronte a Bisanzio*, p. 447; Hubert, "Étude," pp. 12–13.

[31] Hartmann, *Geschichte Italiens*, 2.2, p. 97; G. Pepe, *Il medio evo barbarico d'Italia*, pp. 163–164; Duchesne, *VG II*, 413, n. 36; Macaigne, *L'Église Merovingienne*, p. 198.

[32] *VG II*, 22.407. The 728 date rests on Duchesne, *VG II*, 413, n. 38.

[33] *VG II*, 22.407. Paul does not report these events.

monarchy had overcome the separatist powers of the Lombard world, and in this respect Liutprand was able to return the latter to the principles of national political order and coherence. Liutprand had every intention that the change would be lasting, for when he left the south in 728 he installed royal officers in both Spoleto and Benevento, gastalds who were responsible to the crown and entirely independent of the newly subdued dukes. The duchies, while permitted to retain their identity in the continuation of the ducal office within the framework of the Italian kingdom, were also to be integral parts of the kingdom, ruled by the king from Pavia. The Lombard world had been potentially transformed.

It is clear from the seizure of Spoleto and Benevento that restoration of the Lombard Kingdom of Italy was Liutprand's goal.[34] In this context, the Auximum occupation becomes explicable as a means of royal access to Spoleto and the meaning of the sudden royal alliance with the exarch is visible within it as well: Liutprand wanted Eutychius's military aid although limited, to subdue Transamund and Romoald.[35] Furthermore, as an ally Eutychius could neither make nor threaten trouble for the monarchy on the Adriatic while royal operations were in progress in the duchies. The exarch's objectives in the alliance with Pavia have been well established: cooperation with the crown would make a friend of the empire's principal Italian antagonist, thereby preserving what was left of the imperial territories and holding out hope for recovery of what had been lost. In particular, the royal siege of Ravenna would be ended. In addition, with Gregory II deprived of Liutprand's support and now opposed by his power, this intractable pontiff might be returned to imperial obedience or replaced by another who would be more congenial to the ideology of Roman and papal membership in the empire and more in conformity with the Iconoclasm of Constantinople.[36] None of the exarch's hopes ever came to fruition, however, suggesting that Liutprand simply used Eutychius and his aspirations to advantage as one means of giving life to his goal of recreating Pavia's Italian kingdom.

Once that kingdom was in being, its survival became Liutprand's paramount concern. The new realm was in jeopardy at every turn, always a potential victim of the instabilities of the time. The dukes of Spoleto and Benevento would naturally chafe against the yoke of dependence upon Pavia, so contrary was it to their long tradition of separatism. More omi-

---

[34] There is widespread agreement that Liutprand's goal was to create a Lombard Kingdom of Italy. See for example Hodgkin, *Italy and Her Invaders*, 6.457; Hartmann, *Geschichte Italiens*, 2.2., pp. 86–87, 126; G. Pepe, *Il medio evo*, p. 204; David Harry Miller, "Papal-Lombard Relations during the Pontificate of Pope Paul I: The Attainment of an Equilibrium of Power in Italy," p. 359, n. 1. One authority offers the dubious view that Liutprand's conquests had the effect of destroying papal chances for unifying Italy and even the entire West and assuring rule of Italy by foreigners. M. Roberti, "Liutprando re longobardo," pp. 91–102.

[35] Bertolini, "I papi e le relazioni politiche di Roma con i ducati," p. 55.

[36] Caspar, *Geschichte des Papsttums*, 2, p. 727; Llewellyn, *Rome in the Dark Ages*, p. 167; Anastos, "Leo III's Edict Against Images in the Year 726–727 and Italo-Byzantine Relations Between 726 and 730," pp. 5–41, esp. p. 33; Peter Partner, *The Lands of St. Peter*, p. 14. Brehier and Aigrain, *Histoire de l'Église*, 5, pp. 414–415; Miller, "The Roman Revolution," pp. 103–104.

nously, external developments could easily play into ducal hands. The old royal-imperial hostility might return at any time, leaving open the possibility of some form of cooperation between the exarch and the dukes against the crown. Nor could the papacy be overlooked. Having seen the creation of the Kingdom of Italy, Gregory II would naturally be anxious about Rome's relationship to it: the triumphant king might actually prove to be no menace at all, but he might just as well decide that Rome and the papacy had to be brought into the kingdom in some degree. Against such an eventuality, the pope might well seek protection—most logically from the dukes of Spoleto and Benevento, who could be expected to enter into a papal alliance against the king in order to retrieve their lost autonomy. This is not to say that Liutprand's new Italian kingdom was in a hopeless situation; rather, it is to suggest that it was new, fragile, and prey to the shifting politics of the time.

### THE ROYAL-PAPAL SETTLEMENT OF 728

With such considerations before him, after the subordination of Spoleto and Benevento Liutprand joined Eutychius in leading the combined Lombard-imperial army from Spoleto to the very walls of Rome. One must suppose that the exarch believed that Liutprand was about to render the promised aid against Gregory II. The latter sallied forth to meet with Liutprand outside the walls and plead for peace. The sole source which reports the meeting, Gregory's biography in the *Liber Pontificalis*, implies that the Lombard was overcome by the pope's presence and rhetoric. Liutprand is said to have prostrated himself before Gregory and submitted to him by placing various symbols of royal authority upon the *confessio* of St. Peter. Thereafter the king swore that he meant no harm, persuaded Gregory and the exarch to dwell in harmony with one another, and promised to "conspire" no further with Eutychius. Liutprand then departed while Eutychius went into Rome with pope, staying there for some time.[37] For the first time in recent memory all of Italy was at peace.

These events warrant more than the limited attention which they have received. In the first place, Liutprand made it plain that he wanted peace with Rome, its duchy, and the papacy. At a time when he could have delivered a powerful assault upon Rome, or at least subjected the duchy to frightful ravaging, no hostility occurred.[38] Instead, the king submitted to Gregory, swore not to injure Rome, and managed to bring the pope and the exarch to reconciliation. The papal source attributes the reconciliation to Gregory's influence,[39] but one may look beyond that influence and sug-

---

[37] *VG II*, 22.407–408.

[38] Hartmann ("Italy Under the Lombards," p. 212) seems close to the truth in saying that Liutprand "never wanted" to fight Gregory II in 728. One scholar asserts that Liutprand's appearance before Rome with the exarch was the time at which the Lombards could have taken the city. H. Pabst, "Geschichte des langobardischen," pp. 405–518, esp. 477.

[39] Agreeing with the source impression is Llewellyn, *Rome in the Dark Ages*, pp. 167, 199; see also Pabst, "Geschichte des langobardischen," p. 477 and Bertolini, *Roma*, p. 449.

gest that Liutprand was voluntarily revealing his genuine attitude toward St. Peter and Rome. In particular, Liutprand let it be known that the establishment of the Lombard Kingdom of Italy through the recent subordination of Transamund and Romoald augured no threat for Rome and its territory for neither the city nor duchy of Rome were made part of the kingdom. Thus, in his view, the new Lombard kingdom and the Roman political entity were to coexist in harmony as separate and independent states. But Liutprand evidently went further, trying to indicate that he still supported the papacy against Byzantium. That seems to have been the meaning of the king's successful effort to achieve some form of reconciliation of Exarch Eutychius and Gregory. Liutprand not only refrained from aiding Eutychius against the pope as he had promised but also sponsored the reconciliation, which obviously benefited Gregory in that it eased the deep papal-imperial division and, since it involved no papal submission to the empire, suggested a measure of imperial acquiescence in Rome's separation from Byzantium and emergent autonomy in Rome and the duchy.[40] In sum, far from threatening the papacy, Liutprand was clearly promoting conditions which offered positive benefits and peace with the new Lombard Kingdom of Italy.[41]

Liutprand's concern for peace with the papacy was undoubtedly motivated by his great concern for protection of the newly-founded kingdom through stabilization of the Italian scene at large. If peace reigned throughout Italy the kingdom would have an opportunity to develop without disruption, for its most dangerous enemies, the dukes of Spoleto and Benevento, would be without allies and therefore disinclined to strike against the crown. War in Italy would give them hope. For example, if Pavia and Rome came to blows, the pope would be apt to turn to them as natural allies against the king. In such a situation the new kingdom would be threatened with disintegration. Likewise, if the monarchy and the empire resumed their old struggle, the exarch might seek aid from the dukes, with the same harmful effects for the kingdom. But, in the event of a general Italian peace, no party would require allies, leaving Transamund and Romoald suspended in a void wherein their only choice was obedience to Liutprand. Thus, Liutprand cultivated peace with Gregory II to let him know that Rome and its duchy were to be safely independent of the crown. It was also thus that Liutprand caused the reconciliation between Gregory and Eutychius and, further, made no move to discontinue his own alliance with the exarch. The ultimate significance of the 728 Roman episode was thus the king's attempt to assure security for his new kingdom by putting hitherto unstable Italy to rest.[42]

---

[40] Miller ("The Roman Revolution," p. 104) calls the reconciliation "a truce between the exarch and the pope."

[41] An untenable variation is that in the 728 reconciliation Gregory was terminating his leadership of the Italian revolt in favor of cooperation with the exarch against Liutprand, who was now seen as a greater danger than the former. Cessi, "La crisi dell' esarcato," p. 1683.

[42] Compare with Miller's assessment ("The Roman Revolution," p. 106): Liutprand's aim was "not to bring genuine peace between the Romans and the exarch, but to gain time for

There was perhaps another side to the matter. Liutprand had consciously avoided violence, implying that if Rome pursued actions harmful to the monarchy, he would not hesitate to return to Rome with his army. He preferred peace throughout Italy, especially between the monarchy and Rome, and the signal to the pope that he would enforce the peace upon Rome proved both tactful and sufficient.

Before leaving the developments of 728 at Rome, it is worth noting that Pope Gregory did not abandon the new papal perception that the duchy of Rome was papal territory. He did not give Eutychius to understand that it was either dependent upon or returned to imperial authority, and that Gregory alone had responsibility for keeping both Liutprand and the exarch from damaging it and its capital suggests exercise of papal political juris-diction. Whether Liutprand appreciated this gradual emergence of an in-dependent papal territory at this juncture is not known.

FAILURE OF THE SETTLEMENT: POPE GREGORY III AND THE COLLAPSE OF THE
KINGDOM OF ITALY

Gregory II lived only three years after the conclusion of his Roman settlement with Liutprand and Eutychius. During that period there seems to have been no disruption of the peaceful Italian conditions established in 728. A *modus vivendi*, a new equilibrium was evidently emerging in a stable environment which replaced the conflict, disruption, and rapid change of the recent past. The new Lombard Kingdom of Italy remained in place, with its monarch maintaining sway over Spoleto and Benevento and holding to his peace with both Rome and the empire. Neither the pope nor the exarch disturbed the new conditions, and on one occasion Gregory and Eutychius even collaborated against an imperial pretender.[43] Two fac-tors may have been foremost in maintaining the status quo—King Liut-prand's policy of keeping the peace between Pavia and Rome, between Rome and Ravenna, and between Pavia and Ravenna; and Pope Gregory's willingness to co-exist with the new Lombard Kingdom of Italy. That king-dom may be viewed as the most substantive novelty of Italy's new political organization, and for its welfare Liutprand had bent every effort to achieve the status quo.

At some point prior to 735, however, hostilities resumed between King Liutprand and the empire. The sources are too confusing and restricted in information to make much sense of the trouble, but a bare outline is visible. The first conflict, which cannot be dated, was perhaps an attack by a certain Duke Agatho of Perugia upon Bologna, one of the places which Liutprand had taken from the exarch in his initial drive in the Emilia in 726. Agatho

---

himself to obtain control of the duchies, complete the conquest of Italy, and forestall papal efforts to hinder him."

[43] See *VG II*, 32.408–409. The pope and the exarch jointly took care of the problem. Hubert ("Étude," p. 14) regards this cooperation as evidence that there was still unity between the empire and the pope.

was promptly put to flight with great loss,[44] but a second conflict, also undatable, was more significant. In this case Lombard troops besieged Ravenna. They were led by Duke Hildeprand, a nephew of Liutprand, who, either before the siege or soon thereafter, was elected king of the Lombards while Liutprand was so ill that he was not expected to live. Hildeprand was kept on as co-ruler when Liutprand recovered. Hildeprand's siege was successful, with Exarch Eutychius fleeing to Venetia, one of the few remaining imperial districts on the Adriatic. There Eutychius pleaded for help to recover his lost capital.[45] Perhaps unexpectedly, Pope Gregory III (731–741), the able, ambitious, and energetic successor of Gregory II, also called for aid by urging Duke Ursus of Venetia and Patriarch Antoninus of Grado to assist Eutychius.[46] The appeals seem to have had the desired effect, for at some unknown time before 735 a Venetian naval force was able to drive the Lombards from Ravenna and to restore Eutychius.[47]

A number of observations concerning these events may be made. First, it is not clear who was to blame, but Liutprand's valued general Italian peace was obviously disrupted, for Pavia and the empire were again at war. To a degree, then, the security of the Lombard Kingdom of Italy was in jeopardy, for its safety lay in peaceful relations among all Italian powers. Next, the new pope was moving away from the decidedly harmonious relationship with the crown which had been pursued by Gregory II, as was evident in Gregory III's support of Eutychius as the latter sought to regain Ravenna. For the past several years peace had prevailed between Pavia and Rome. But in the Ravenna matter Gregory III was behaving as an enemy,[48] for he was clearly supporting the cause of a leader with whom Liutprand was at war. Did Gregory's new stance and support of the exarch signify a papal interest in helping Byzantium recover its lost territory apart from Ravenna? If so, the Kingdom of Italy was endangered by its own central portion which was composed entirely of former imperial land. Or, did Gregory's shift herald the beginning of a papal policy of general opposition to the crown through support of other royal enemies in addition to the exarch? If that was the case, pontifical efforts to dismember the kingdom through collaboration with the dukes of Spoleto and Benevento could be anticipated. Liutprand had no answers to these questions in about 735, for Gregory's shift was too recent to be assessed thoroughly. The only assurance is that the king must have worried about it since the other novelty of the

---

[44] Paul, *Hist. Lang.*, 54. 298.

[45] Iohannis Diaconi, *Chronicon Venetum*, p. 12, lines 8–11. For discussions on the date of the fall of Ravenna, see Diehl, *Études sur l'administration*, p. 377–378, n. 5 and Duchesne, *VG II*, 412, n. 11.

[46] *Epistolae Langobardicae Collectae*, p. 702, Epp. 11 and 12. The *Chronicon Venetum* (p. 12, lines 14–25) quotes the letters. For a discussion of the authenticity of the letters and the Venetian chronicle see Hodgkin, *Italy and Her Invaders*, 6.505–508. Miller ("The Roman Revolution", pp. 105–107) places the letters in the reign of Gregory II and regards them as spurious.

[47] *Chronicon Venetum*, 12, lines 11–14; Paul, 6.54, 183–184. Hildeprand was taken captive by the Venetians. That Ravenna was retaken before 735 is based on Duchesne, *VG II*, 412, n. 24.

[48] As perceived by Bertolini, *Roma*, p. 458.

period, the partial breakdown of the general Italian peace, was closely related to it and a troublesome thing in itself. At minimum, the *modus vivendi* operative in 728 and for several years thereafter was beginning to disintegrate.

The disintegration became complete in the late 730s in consequence of major new developments in central Italy. Perhaps looking to provoke a crisis which might liberate him from Liutprand's dominance, Duke Transamund of Spoleto in 737 or 738 attacked the Roman fortress of Gallese.[49] The latter was important to the Roman duchy—which in the papal sources was now being called the *sancta republica* or "holy republic."[50] Located about thirty miles north of Rome on the Via Amerina, Gallese helped to guard Rome's communications with the Adriatic, which would be severed if the fortress fell.[51] Perhaps fearing that Transamund's attack might lead to an effort against Rome itself, Gregory III repaired the city's walls.[52] But the crisis soon passed, for Gregory was able to save Gallese with bribes and negotiations,[53] and from the latter came an alliance between Rome and Transamund.[54] The duke rebelled against Liutprand,[55] thereby renouncing the submission which he had made in 728.

The king must have been thoroughly dismayed by these developments,[56] for the formation of the Roman-Spoletan alliance gave rise to the very conditions which he had worked to avoid: he was now confronted with enemies in central Italy in place of an ally and a subordinate, and the Lombard Kingdom of Italy had ceased to exist because of Transamund's defection in association with the pope.[57] Transamund had reverted to the traditional Spoletan separatism and as long as he remained out of control Liutprand ruled only the customary Lombard realm of the north and the newer royal districts of the exarchate and the Pentapolis.

What accounts for this disaster? The best explanation probably lies in Gregory III's willingness to take action on behalf of Roman interests which were harmful to the crown and in Transamund's determination to escape Pavia's dominance. It does not seem that Gregory's formation of the alliance with Transamund was a deliberate blow aimed specifically at Liutprand; naturally, the pope wanted to defend Rome and its republic from Spoletan encroachment by the most expedient means available, in this case that of

---

[49] *Vita Gregorii III, LP* I, 15.420.

[50] Ibid., 15.420–421: "potuit causam finire et in conpage *sanctae reipublicae* atque corpore Christo dilecti exercitus Romani annecti praecepit."

[51] Duchesne, *VG III*, 424, n. 32.

[52] *VG III*, 15.420. The chronology is unclear here. The repairs perhaps occurred before Transamund's seizure of Gallese, and may have concerned Byzantine and Saracen threats as well as Lombard. Duchesne, *VG III*, 424, n. 31. Bertolini (*Roma*, p. 458) asserts that Gregory repaired Rome's walls because he expected royal reprisals after the papal role in Liutprand's loss of Ravenna.

[53] *VG III*, 15.420–421.

[54] Duchesne, *VG III*, 424, n. 32; Hodgkin, *Italy and Her Invaders*, 6.474.

[55] Paul, *Hist. Lang.*, 6.55.184.

[56] Hodgkin, *Italy and Her Invaders*, 6.474.

[57] See Pabst, "Geschichte des langobardischens," pp. 474–476.

turning an enemy into an ally.[58] Nevertheless, Gregory knew that in align-
ing with Transamund he was making himself an enemy of Liutprand.
Simply put, the pope judged that security for Rome in the Gallese crisis
was more likely to be found in friendship with Transamund than in friendship with Liutprand, even if that decision invited severe tension with the
crown. As for Transamund, his game is very clear. The papal desire for
security opened to him the way to freedom from Pavia. He was presented
the ally which he needed for hope of successful resistance to Liutprand and
willingly took it.

Liutprand probably had his own perception. From his point of view,
Gregory III was to blame for the trouble. A while before the Gallese disaster,
Gregory had indicated an interest in opposing Pavia by helping to stir the
Venetians into assisting Eutychius to recover Ravenna from the Lombards.
Now Gregory was teaming with Transamund, striking at the heart of the
monarchy's interests, the maintenance of the Kingdom of Italy. For Liut-
prand, it appears, there was now an answer to an earlier question: Gregory
III had undertaken a policy of general opposition to the monarchy and was
Pavia's determined enemy.

Liutprand obviously had to apply military power in central Italy if his
kingdom was to be restored. But for the time being he could not act there
since he and most of his forces were in Septimania, fighting in alliance
with the Frankish mayor, Charles Martel, against Moslems who were a
threat to the Frankish and Lombard kingdoms alike.[59] In passing, it may
be suggested that Gregory III felt able to align with Transamund because
Liutprand was tied down in Septimania and thus unable to intervene easily
in central Italy. Whether this was the case or not, Liutprand finally returned
to Italy and in 739 swept into Spoleto, drove the fleeing Transamund into
Rome,[60] and replaced him upon the ducal throne with his own appointee,
Hilderic.[61] Victorious in Spoleto, Liutprand pursued Transamund to Rome,
knowing that the kingdom would not be safe as long as he was at large.
He promptly demanded that Gregory III surrender the fugitive, but the
pope, the Roman *patricius et dux* Stephen, and the Roman army all refused
to comply.[62] Liutprand therefore resorted to force, seizing four fortified
towns in the republic—Ameria (Amelia), Ortas (Orte), Polimartium (Bomarzo), and Blera (Bieda)—and looting papal property in the same area.[63] We
do not know why these places were singled out, but the intention may
have been either to prepare for a siege of Rome or to have Gregory believe
that one was forthcoming. Three of the towns—Amelia, Orte, and Bom-

---

[58] One scholar sees the alliance as a ducal alignment with the empire against Liutprand.
Diehl, *Études sur l'administration*, pp. 216–217. The view is predicated upon the untenable
premise that Gregory III was in service of Byzantium.

[59] Paul, *Hist. Lang*, 6.54.183.

[60] *Vita Zachariae, LP* I, 2.426.

[61] Paul, *Hist. Lang.*, 6.55.184.

[62] *VZ*, 2.426.

[63] Occupation of the towns is specified in *VZ* 3.426. See also *Pauli Historiae Continuatio Tertia*,
p. 207. Looting of papal property is referred to in *Codex Carolinus*, p. 477, #2.

arzo—like Gallese protected the Via Amerina link to the Adriatic,[64] and in controlling them Liutprand cut off whatever help might be expected from imperial or local Italian sources. The seizure of Blera, which was located well to the west of the other towns on the Via Clodia, gave the impression of a second front.[65] Already in control of the duchy of Spoleto, Liutprand was apparently in the process of isolating Rome. But the king did not actually begin a siege; instead, without yielding the four towns, he retired from the republic in August 739[66] and joined his associate Hildeprand in wasting ecclesiastical property around Ravenna.[67] It was perhaps at this juncture that Liutprand seized Ancona and Umana in the Pentapolis near Auximum.[68]

Gregory III did not shrink from the conflict, if that was the intention of the royal pressures. In 739 or 740 he received assurances of support from Duke Godescalc of Benevento,[69] who thus repudiated the submission to the monarchy which had been made by his predecessor, Duke Romoald, in 728.[70] The pope also solicited the assistance of Charles Martel, the celebrated Carolingian mayor of the Franks. Writing to Charles in both 739 and 740, the pope reported what he termed royal aggressions, urged him not to believe Liutprand's "lies," notified him of the Spoletan and Beneventan support, and implored him to succor St. Peter and his vicar.[71] But nothing came of the appeal to Francia. It is not difficult to understand why. In the first place, Liutprand and Charles enjoyed a kinship relationship, as both were married to daughters of the duke of Bavaria and were therefore brothers-in-law.[72] Moreover, Charles's son Pepin was the adopted son of the Lombard.[73] There were important political considerations as well. Liutprand had already served as a loyal Frankish ally against the Moslems in Septimania, and his help might be needed again.[74] Finally, Charles was under no illusions that his kinsman and friend was mercilessly abusing Rome like some pagan raider. The Frank knew better, for Liutprand communi-

---

[64] Specifically, Orte guarded the Amerina's Tiber crossing while Bomarzo, located a few miles west of the Amerina near the duchy's border with Lombard Tuscany, served as a support for Orte. Diehl *Études sur l'administration*, p. 70.

[65] That all four towns were fortified is clear from their description in a letter sent by Gregory III to Lombard bishops in 740. *Ep. Lang. Col.*, ep. 16, p. 708. See also *CC*, p. 478, n. 2.

[66] *VZ*, 3.426.

[67] *CC* #2, 477.

[68] Duchesne, *VZ*, 437, n. 14.

[69] Deduced from Gregory's reference to both Transamund and Godescalc as friends of the papacy. *CC* #2, 478.

[70] Godescalc became duke of Benevento about 739, succeeding Duke Gregory, a nephew of Liutprand whom the latter had appointed on the death of Romoald in 731 or 732. Paul, *Hist. Lang.*, 6.55, 184.

[71] *CC* #1 and 2, 476–479.

[72] Paul, *Hist Lang.*, 6.43.179–180; Hartmann, *Geschichte Italiens*, 2.125.

[73] Paul, *Hist. Lang.*, 6.53.183. Duchesne (*The Beginnings*, p. 9) says that the Lombard-Frankish relations "were too harmonious to be disturbed." See also Erich Caspar, *Das Papsttum unter Fränkischer Heerschaft*, p. 13.

[74] Norton Downs, "The Role of the Papacy in the Coronation of Charlemagne," pp. 7–22, 10.

cated his version of the crisis,[75] one which very likely pictured the trouble as neither his doing nor aimed at anything more than restoration of the dismembered kingdom. Denied aid from Francia, Gregory III tried to enlist the bishops of Lombard Tuscany, urging them to press Liutprand for peace and return of the four towns.[76] There is no indication that episcopal support had any effect upon Liutprand, if it was indeed forthcoming at all.

In late 739 or 740, events took a new turn. Still being sheltered in Rome by the pope, Duke Transamund pledged that he would seek to regain the four lost towns from Liutprand.[77] Apparently in exchange, he was given a Roman force to regain Spoleto from Hilderic, Liutprand's appointee.[78] By about late 740 Transamund had won decisively,[79] repossessing the ducal throne and killing Hilderic.[80] Once more, Spoleto was beyond Liutprand's grasp. It will be recalled that Benevento was also gone, its duke having allied with the pope some time before. A ray of hope appeared for Liutprand, however. Transamund and his Roman troops began to squabble,[81] and, more importantly, the duke refused to secure repossession of the four towns for the pope.[82] Why Transamund ignored his promise is unclear, but presumably he expected Liutprand to descend upon him forthwith and would therefore not risk dissipation of his strength outside Spoleto.[83] At any rate, Gregory III was outraged by the Spoletan betrayal. With Roman-Spoletan harmony thus fast disintegrating, Liutprand prepared to invade the holy republic for the second time in two years. Amid these circumstances Gregory III suddenly died and was succeeded by Zachary I (741–752).[84]

Liutprand could not have been grieved by Gregory's death; as far as he was concerned, Gregory was an implacable foe of the monarchy.[85] Without

---

[75] Gregory said as much. CC #2, p. 477. Duchesne (The Beginnings, p. 9) adds that Charles knew that the royal-papal conflict was the fault of the Romans. Partner (Lands of St. Peter, p. 16) asserts that Gregory's appeals lacked conviction in that Liutprand was acting primarily against the dukes, not the pope.

[76] Ep. Lang. Col., ep. 16, p. 708. See also CC, p. 478, n. 2. When Lombard bishops-elect were confirmed by the pope they swore to uphold the Lombard-imperial peace of 680 which specified permanent Lombard and imperial boundaries. Hartmann, "Italy Under the Lombards," p. 207. See also Caspar, Geschichte des Papsttums, 2, pp. 724–725. The episcopal oath may have been the basis of Gregory's appeal to the bishops, even though the pope was not defending Byzantine interests in seeking the release of the towns. See also Duchesne, VZ, 436, n. 4.

[77] Transamund's pledge is deduced from the fact that he is said later to have refused to fulfill it. VZ, 3.426.

[78] VZ, 4.426.

[79] Some scholars place the date of Transamund's reestablishment in late 739. See for example Carlrichard Bruhl, "Chronologie und Urkunden der Herzöge von Spoleto im 8. Jahrhundert," pp. 1–92, esp. pp. 20–21. See also Duchesne, VZ 436, n. 7, which sets December 740 as the date.

[80] VZ, 3.426; Paul, Hist. Lang. 6.55, 184.

[81] Or such appears to be the meaning of VZ 4.426, lines 16–17.

[82] Ibid., 4.426.

[83] Duchesne, The Beginnings, pp. 9–10.

[84] V.Z., 4.426–27.

[85] Macaigne, L'Église Merovingienne, p. 202. There are only vague intimations of the royal perspective elsewhere.

royal provocation Gregory III had allied with the dukes of Spoleto and Benevento. He had also summoned Frankish intervention against Liutprand which would have both ruined a valued friendship and left the king with an array of new problems had it materialized. Further, the pope had given Transamund Roman arms, thereby helping to disrupt the Kingdom of Italy when Transamund deposed and killed Hilderic. The Roman military intervention against the crown in Spoleto was firm testimony that Gregory's ultimate aim was destruction of the kingdom. The usual approach to this problem is that Liutprand was a menace and that the pope was simply doing what was necessary for Roman security.[86] Or, perhaps, Gregory was somehow dominated by Transamund and forced involuntarily to follow his lead. But Liutprand probably saw only a steady growth in pontifical hostility toward the monarchy. The first sign was Gregory's support of Eutychius, followed soon by his arrangement of the alliance with Transamund and his protection of the latter in Rome. Next came the association with Godescalc of Benevento and the effort to turn Charles Martel into a royal enemy, which, as Liutprand knew, involved considerable papal manipulation of the truth.[87] The culmination was Gregory's intervention for purposes of restoring Transamund in Spoleto, an action which made Gregory responsible for at least temporary dissolution of the Kingdom of Italy. Liutprand could only have hoped for a much more favorable performance by the next pope.

Analysis is also needed of Liutprand's ravaging in the holy republic and his seizure of the four towns there. The appropriation of the towns was apparently a preparation for a siege of Rome or was perhaps meant to persuade Gregory that one was imminent. But toward what end? Had Liutprand amid the tensions over Spoleto suddenly changed his mind, deciding that Rome and its duchy had to be incorporated into his kingdom? Perhaps, but even at the height of his trouble with Gregory the king did not go beyond ravaging and threat of a siege. The conclusion must be that the royal concern was to intimidate the pope, so threatening him that he would find the cost of opposing the monarchy so great that he would end his support of Transamund and other anti-royal activities in favor of returning to Gregory II's policy of cooperation with the crown. Presumably,

---

[86] See the following, for example. Gregory strengthened the walls of Rome because of "the renewed Lombard threat. . . ." Llewellyn, Rome in the Dark Ages, p. 201. He settled with Transamund over Gallese because of fear of Liutprand. Bertolini, Roma, p. 460 and idem, "Le relazioni politiche di Roma con i ducati," p. 687. Gregory and Roman noble leaders saw the Spoletan alliance as the means of defending Rome's independence against Liutprand. Bertolini, Roma, pp. 459-61; Diehl, p. 414. The Roman-Spoletan alliance was "the chief hope of Rome's preservation. . . ." Llewellyn, Rome in the Dark Ages, p. 201. Liutprand's aim in taking the four towns was to have a base of operation against Rome. Bertolini, Roma, p. 467. Liutprand's activity near Rome "seemed [to the pope] to announce the final Lombard victory in central Italy and the end of independent Rome." Partner, Lands of St. Peter, p. 16.
[87] Macaigne, L'Église Merovingienne, p. 203. Gregory said nothing of the seizure of the four towns, emphasized only ravaging of papal property, and gave the impression that the dukes of Spoleto and Benevento were being persecuted by the king.

too, that was the intention of the king's preparation of a second Roman invasion at the time of Gregory's death.[88] But Gregory III evidently found the royal pressure not too great to withstand, leaving it to be seen whether the next pontiff would bow, and what Liutprand would do if he did.

None of Gregory's activities were undertaken on behalf of the empire. The exarch was naturally delighted with the many problems raised for Liutprand by Gregory and Transamund, for they gave him some assurance that Ravenna would survive a little longer. But Gregory was no more an imperial associate than his predecessor. In fact, Gregory III persisted in the papal separation from the empire begun by Gregory II, both by neglecting to send notification of his election to Leo III at the outset of his reign, as was the custom, and by convening a Roman synod in or about 732 which excommunicated the emperor.[89] It is also clear that Gregory III also developed the earlier papal thinking that the duchy of Rome was a pontifical rather than imperial place. The pope's handling of foreign affairs advanced that perception, especially his protection of Gallese and his demands that the four towns be returned.[90] But more revealing is the new *sancta republica* terminology. The old imperial expression, *ducatus Romae* or duchy of Rome, was discarded. The new label was fashioned in the Lateran to reflect the growing reality of papal leadership—holy to indicate the presidency of the pope, and republic perhaps to reflect both the public as opposed to ecclesiastical nature of the papal position in the former duchy and its separation from imperial places, all of which except the exarchate bore the name of duchy. The republic's people were also being distinguished: in Gregory's 740 appeal to Charles Martel, the Romans are called "the special people of St. Peter,"[91] a phraseology altogether consistent with the emerging notion of a special papal territory. The appearance of the republican terminology was a most pregnant development, for Gregory's successors continued to use it, in time applying it to *all* former Byzantine territories in Italy, that is, to the central districts of Liutprand's Italian kingdom.

For the moment, in 741, the *sancta republica* was simply Rome and its old duchy. Whether Liutprand was aware of the new name or its accompanying perceptions is unknown, but in 741 he certainly believed that a crucial time was at hand. In recent years the general pacification and its attendant security for the Kingdom of Italy had both failed. The pope had proven

---

[88] Based upon source commentary, there is firm recognition that the royal actions were reprisals for Gregory III's collaboration with Transamund. *VZ*, 2.426 and *Pauli Cont. Tert.*, 14.207. The secondary opinions are Macaigne, *L'Église Merovingienne*, pp. 202–203; Llewellyn, *Rome in the Dark Ages*, p. 201; Hubert, "Étude," p. 31. The sense of reprisals for the sake of achieving papal neutrality toward the Lombard Kingdom of Italy is missing, however.

[89] See Miller, "The Roman Revolution," p. 111. It may have been about the time of the Roman synod that Emperor Leo removed the sees of Illyricum, Calabria, and Sicily from the jurisdiction of the pope and placed them under the patriarch of Constantinople. On this subject, see V. Grumel, "L'annexation de l'Illyricum Oriental, de la Sicile et de la Calabre au Patriarchat de Constantinople"; and Anastos, "Iconoclasm and Imperial Rule."

[90] Some scholars regard the Gallese settlement as the first step in the creation of the papal state. See for example, Bertolini, *Roma*, pp. 460–462.

[91] CC #2, 478. See also Miller, "The Roman Revolution," p. 112.

to be a great enemy, the dukes of Spoleto and Benevento had not been contained, and the turbulent Transamund had restored Spoletan autonomy. For the moment the Italian kingdom did not exist, and it appeared that it could not be revived until Transamund was deposed and the papal connection with the duchies definitively severed. If neither could be achieved, Pavia's great enterprise of creating an Italian rather than a regional kingdom would fail. Such were the stakes for Liutprand as he prepared to resume war in the papal republic and observed the election of Pope Zachary.

## THE KINGDOM RESTORED: LIUTPRAND, POPE ZACHARY, AND RENEWED ROYAL-PAPAL PEACE

Liutprand did not find it necessary to threaten the Roman territory again, for Zachary (741–752) immediately sought a rapprochement with the crown.[92] Soon after his election, Zachary sent envoys to Liutprand and a bargain was struck. If Liutprand would promise to restore the four Roman towns which he had taken earlier, the Roman army would assist him against Transamund. The king made the desired promise, and, at Zachary's direct order, Roman troops went forth to capture Transamund. The latter, learning of the royal-papal combination against him, gave up without a struggle, leaving the city of Spoleto and submitting to the king in person.[93] But Liutprand had had his fill of Transamund and refused to maintain him in the ducal office, forcing him to become a cleric, perhaps a monk. In his place as duke of Spoleto Liutprand appointed a nephew, Agiprand.[94] With the help of Pope Zachary a major step toward reconstruction of the Lombard Kingdom of Italy had been achieved.

There remained the problem of Benevento, for Duke Godescalc was still independent of Pavia. In Benevento there was partisan division between the followers of Godescalc and those of Gisulf. The latter was the son of Duke Romoald, who had been made to submit to Liutprand in 728, and Romoald's wife, Gumperga, a niece of Liutprand. Gisulf was thus Liutprand's grandnephew. When Romoald died in 732 or thereabouts, Gisulf was still young and, perhaps because he was of royal blood, was the object of a conspiracy against his life. After the conspiracy was thwarted, Liutprand took him from Benevento and raised him, as Paul the Deacon puts it, "with fatherly care. . . ." In 741, Liutprand moved into Benevento against Godescalc after ousting Transamund in Spoleto and replacing him with Agiprand. Godescalc attempted to flee to Greece, but he was killed by partisans of Gisulf, the royal protégé. Having arrived in the city of Bene-

---

[92] For what follows, see VZ, 5.427. A good secondary account is Llewellyn, *Rome in the Dark Ages*, pp. 202–205.

[93] Paul (*Hist. Lang.*, 6.56.185) asserts that a Roman-Spoletan force inflicted "great disasters" upon Liutprand's army when it entered Spoleto. This is difficult to understand with the switch of Roman support to Liutprand, but Duchesne (VZ, 436, n. 9) explains that the "Romans" involved were imperial forces from the exarchate and the Pentapolis. Duchesne here also characterizes the fighting as a rearguard action.

[94] Paul, *Hist. Lang.*, 6.57.185.

vento, Liutprand appointed Gisulf duke.[95] The installation of Agiprand and Gisulf, both royal relatives and appointees, meant that the Lombard south was once more in Pavia's grasp and the Kingdom of Italy therefore reconstituted.

Preoccupied with affairs in Benevento and Spoleto, Liutprand had not yet fulfilled his promise to return the four Roman towns.[96] Pope Zachary, evidently fearing that without his personal intervention the restitutions might never be made, left Rome in February 742 with a substantial retinue to negotiate with Liutprand, who was then at the Spoletan town of Terni, located just across the Roman border on the Via Flaminia. Liutprand was apparently determined to let Zachary know of his desire for harmony with Rome. A personal royal envoy and a party of leading Lombard nobles and officers were sent to greet the pope with honor and escort him on the final stages of his journey. When he arrived in Terni he was met before the basilica of St. Valentine by Liutprand himself and all his nobles and army. There followed warm exchanges of greeting and professions of mutual support and respect.

On the next day Liutprand and Zachary got to the business of the meeting. Zachary opened by calling for an end to hostility and the shedding of blood. Presumably the pope was speaking in general Christian terms, but he surely also referred to the violence between Liutprand and Gregory III. Peace, Zachary said, should always prevail. He then requested the return of the four towns. Without quibbling, Liutprand made the restitutions, apparently in the form of a donation to St. Peter.[97] There was evidently discussion about other places as well, patrimonial land over which Liutprand had some form of control, for he made several additional donations. What was termed the "Sabine patrimony," lands in the vicinity of the Roman-Spoletan frontier which had been seized some thirty years previously by Duke Faraold of Spoleto, were turned over. The same is true of patrimonies in the Pentapolis—Osimo, Ancona, and Umana.[98] It is doubtful that the three towns themselves were included in the donations, for they guarded Liutprand's access to the duchies of Spoleto and Benevento and were therefore vital to the maintenance of his kingdom.[99] Additional grants were Narni and the country around Sutri which Liutprand had kept in 727.[100] Then came what appears to have been the climax of the conference: Liutprand pledged to maintain peace with the duchy of Rome—*ducatus Romae* is specified, not *sancta republica*—for a period of twenty years.[101] Pope Zachary is not reported as having pledged peace with Pavia, but it may

---

[95] Ibid., 6.55–58.

[96] For what follows see *VZ*, 6.427–11.429. A shorter but similar account is *Pauli Cont. Tert.*, 20.208.

[97] See Duchesne, *VZ*, 436, n. 13.

[98] See Ibid., 437, n. 14.

[99] They were also later claimed by the papacy at the accession of King Desiderius in 757, indicating royal possession in 742. However, Llewellyn (*Rome in the Dark Ages*, p. 203) seems to argue that the towns as well as the patrimonies were turned over.

[100] See Duchesne, *VZ*, 437, n. 15.

[101] The Lombard source puts the donation at thirty years. *Pauli Cont. Tert.*, 20.208.

be assumed that he felt no less bound to the agreement than the Lombard since he was as interested in peace as the king. It is presumed that the return of the four towns, the patrimonial donations, and the promise of peace were all recorded in document form.

Upon completion of the conference, Zachary consecrated a bishop in celebration of the settlement with Liutprand and his court in attendance. There followed a jovial and sumptuous banquet. One should probably not make too much of it, but something of a personal fellowship seems to have arisen between Liutprand and Zachary at Terni. At least the papal source conveys a sense of genuine relaxation, trust, and conviviality between the two. The jubilations over, Zachary left Terni accompanied by a number of the highest royal associates, among them Agiprand, the newly-appointed duke of Spoleto. The pope and his Lombard company visited in turn each of the four towns just ceded by Liutprand, Zachary taking possession of them and Agiprand and his fellows probably serving as witnesses to royal consent for the transfer. Whatever Lombard forces were still in or near the towns were doubtless sent away at this point. Zachary and the Lombards proceeded to tour the frontiers of the papal republic—here *respublica*, not *ducatus* is used[102]—possibly a symbolic gesture to indicate that both Liutprand and Zachary understood and accepted the existing demarcations between royal and Roman territory. Upon the conclusion of the tour the Lombards departed while the pope went into Rome, there to be greeted by the assembled people and the whole city. Solemn prayers of thanksgiving were raised to St. Peter.

The Terni settlement and its antecedents were major developments in the royal-papal relationship and warrant careful analysis. As has been discerned by many scholars, in making peace with Liutprand Zachary completely reversed the anti-royal stance of his predecessor, Gregory III.[103] A determined foe of the crown, Gregory had fought Liutprand at every turn, even going to the point of consciously attempting to destroy the Kingdom of Italy. But immediately upon his accession, Zachary abandoned the Gregorian opposition. Where Gregory aided the exarch, Zachary ignored him. Where Gregory collaborated with the dukes of Spoleto and Benevento against the crown, Zachary put Roman arms at Liutprand's disposal against Transamund and remained neutral while Liutprand regained control of Benevento. Where Gregory tried to lure Charles Martel into Italy, Zachary left the initiative unrenewed. Where Gregory made conflict with Liutprand the preferred Roman technique—we hear of no attempt by Gregory to negotiate—Zachary pronounced it unacceptable and opted for negotiation and dialogue instead. Finally, where Gregory had accepted and even promoted a royal-papal rupture, Zachary sought to end such division in favor

[102] "fuisset itineris longitudo per circuitum finum reipublicae."

[103] Miller, "Papal-Lombard Relations During the Pontificate of Paul I," p. 360, n. 4; Partner, *Lands of St. Peter*, p. 16; Duchesne, *The Beginnings*, p. 10; Hubert, "Étude," p. 31; Bertolini, *Roma*, pp. 479–480; idem, "Le relazioni politiche di Roma con i ducati," p. 688; Pepe, *Il medio evo*, p. 202; Hartmann, "Italy Under the Lombards," pp. 213–214; Caspar, *Geschichte des Papsttums*, 2, pp. 732–733.

of agreement. In short, Pope Zachary repudiated the policy of his predecessor.

Why did he do so? Perhaps Zachary maintained a deep conviction that as pope he was bound to try to stop Christian bloodshed wherever he could, for his *Liber Pontificalis* biography seems to stress such a concern.[104] But, Zachary was no less the political leader of Rome than Gregory II and Gregory III. The harvest of Gregory III's belligerent policy is apt to have been decisive. In 741, just before Gregory's death and Zachary's accession, Liutprand was preparing a second attack upon the republic. Already having severely damaged the latter through ravaging, and already having threatened a siege of Rome through appropriation of the four towns, Liutprand might be able to attack and capture the city this time. No help could be expected from Transamund: he was too weak to do much good and had also proved to be a faithless ally by refusing to recover the four towns as promised. In brief, when Zachary became pope further hostility with Liutprand offered the prospect of grave danger for the papacy and Rome, leading him to end the problem by making peace with Pavia. The Gregorian belligerence was sacrificed principally because Zachary believed it to be politically untenable.[105]

Liutprand's speedy acceptance of both Zachary's overtures for peace in 741 and the subsequent formal peace settlement in 742 has been variously interpreted. One suggestion is that the king gave up the four towns in the expectation that Zachary would ignore future royal operations against the empire.[106] Another argument is that Liutprand decided to cooperate with the pope in the hope that the solidarity would be sufficient to keep Charles Martel from invading Italy on behalf of the pope.[107] A third estimate proposes that the change "stemmed from the powerful impression of Zachary's personality."[108] The first view is dubious since it postulates Zachary as an imperial surrogate. The second appears to be unfounded since, as observed, Charles Martel is most unlikely to have intended to attack Liutprand, and the third is too narrow to rest as the sole explanation.

It is thus necessary to search further for Liutprand's reasons for coming to terms with Zachary. As always, the king's primary concern was the well-being of his Italian kingdom and from the outset Zachary indicated that he was its friend: he both abandoned the dukes and made the Roman army available to Liutprand for his use in the deposition of Transamund. Nor did he stir when Liutprand restored Benevento to royal rule. Convinced

---

[104] See, for example *VZ* 8.427, lines 21–22.

[105] Hubert, "Étude," p. 31; Bertolini, *Roma*, pp. 479–480; idem, "Le relazioni politiche di Roma con i ducati," p. 688; Llewellyn, *Rome in the Dark Ages*, p. 203. Another view is that Zachary abandoned Transamund because he would not try to recover the four towns from Liutprand. Hartmann, "Italy Under the Lombards," pp. 231–214. Miller's opinion ("The Roman Revolution," p. 113) may confuse the issue: "When Zacharias became pope in 741, he began a new policy of seeking rapprochement with Liutprand, and due to the loss of Spoleto to the papal cause in the last years of Gregory III, and as a part of this policy, he abandoned the practice of siding with the king's Lombard enemies."

[106] Bertolini, *Roma*, p. 483; Hartmann, "Italy Under the Lombards," p. 214.

[107] See Bernard S. Bachrach, review in *CHR* 59, 3 (Oct. 1973), p. 534.

[108] Llewellyn, *Rome in the Dark Ages*, p. 205.

by these acts that Zachary, like Gregory II earlier, was prepared to co-exist with the Italian kingdom, he had no further difference with Rome and therefore met the pope's request for restoration of the four towns and the establishment of a formal peace.

This leads to the observation that the purpose of Liutprand's operations against the republic seems to have been to persuade the pope to accept peace with and tolerance for the kingdom. As soon as Zachary revealed an inclination for both, Liutprand ceased all warlike activities. The invasion in preparation was never executed; all ravaging of papal and Roman property ended; and the menacing Lombard possession of the four towns dissolved into royal transfer of those places to curial jurisdiction. It is notable that the king's policy was not only that of harassment for the sake of compelling papal acceptance of peace with Pavia, but also a policy which enjoyed success: as indicated above, the royal pressures seem likely to best explain why Zachary sought peace instead of the Gregorian opposition.

Turning to the Terni settlement itself, its highest importance appears to lie in its guarantees for Liutprand that the recently restored Kingdom of Italy would exist without disruption. In pledging peace with Rome for twenty years, Liutprand promised that he would not again harm that republic or threaten Rome. But, from his standpoint the more important consideration—since he had no interest in having the republic or the city— was that the pope pledged peace with Pavia, that is, in effect promised neither to interfere in the affairs of the Lombard kingdom, nor to assist the anti-royal elements in the duchies. The peace did not specify such a promise, but when Zachary accepted the settlement he also accepted the central Italian realities of the moment in which there was no connection between the papacy and the duchies and in which both of the latter were dependent upon the king.[109] A further guarantee for Liutprand's kingdom in the peace agreement was that both Pavia and Rome obligated themselves to peaceful settlement of differences, that is, avoidance of military action against one another which could easily bring forth more of the highly damaging ducal association with the papacy.

Liutprand's acceptance of the peace with Rome at Terni was a formalization of the rapprochement which the king had made with Gregory II in 728 when he and Eutychius were before the walls of Rome. On that occasion, it will be recalled, he had pledged that he meant no harm to Rome and clearly accepted Gregory II's request for peace. Therein lay a de facto peace agreement, one which involved papal acceptance of the Kingdom of Italy since the kingdom was extant by the time of the agreement. The Terni peace was different only in its formality and specification of duration: it was articulated in a written document and provided for twenty years of peace. But there was the same de facto recognition of the Italian kingdom. In this respect, Liutprand had evidently not altered his thinking in the

---

[109] Miller ("The Roman Revolution," p. 113) adds the important specification that "the peace involved recognition of Liutprand's conquests in the exarchate of Ravenna."

fourteen years since 728. Harmony with the pope and the Romans was still the best hope for the stability and prosperity of his kingdom.

What of Liutprand's donations to St. Peter at Terni? From the royal point of view they may be disposed of quickly in that they were all, especially the four towns, seen as harmless concessions to Zachary to win his acquiescence in peace and neutrality toward his kingdom. They were harmless in the sense that Liutprand had no use for the Roman towns in the first place, and to keep the patrimonies in question would, since the pope requested their donation, assure continuing trouble with Zachary, perhaps entailing delay or denial of the establishment of peace. For Zachary, however, the acquisitions had greater significance in two respects. First, as the principal political authority in the republic he was responsible for maintaining it intact and free of external occupation.[110] In gaining the four towns from Liutprand, that responsibility was squarely met. The same is true of his securing the Sutri and Sabine donations; Sutri had been in royal hands while the Sabine land had been held by the Spoletans. The second significance of the acquisitions was that they contributed to the growing understanding that Roman territory was under papal jurisdiction. It was the pope who won the towns back and gained the patrimonies. And, both were bestowed upon St. Peter, in whose name the pope presided in the republic. There were, then, considerable gains for the ideal of papal headship of an independent Roman state made by Zachary at Terni.

Some scholars are inclined to think that Zachary tried to restore Rome and the papacy to their former imperial constituency.[111] Certainly his dealings with Liutprand in 741–742 do not indicate such a concern, however. Like Gregory II and Gregory III he appears to be a formulator and executor of a specifically Roman foreign policy. The initiative to Liutprand immediately after his election, the dispatch of the Roman army against Transamund, and the conduct of negotiations with Liutprand at Terni over decidedly Roman concerns all suggest that imperial matters were not at issue. The exarch was not consulted, nor was anything reported to him. The donations were all to St. Peter alone. Finally, there may be something instructive in the pope's tour of the frontiers of the *republic* on the way back to Rome after Terni. The imperial *ducatus* term was not used, and the tour, coming after a time of uncertainty, clarified anew the limits of his jurisdiction, in this case evidently Roman rather than imperial.[112]

[110] Llewellyn, *Rome in the Dark Ages*, p. 203.
[111] See for example Bertolini, *Roma*, p. 486.
[112] These impressions of non-imperial orientation are confirmed by the point that when Zachary in 743 went to meet Liutprand for further talks, he left the government of Rome to the *patricius et dux*, Stephen: that is, the *dux*, whether he was a local officer or a Byzantine appointee, was seen by the pope as a papal subordinate. *VZ*, 12.429. Duchesne, *VZ*, 437, n. 25; Miller, "The Roman Revolution," p. 112 and n. 87; and especially A, Crivellucci, "Stefano patrizio e duca di Roma (727-754)," p. 123. Llewellyn (*Rome in the Dark Ages*, pp. 201-202) suggests that Stephen was the Roman duke elected during the Italian anti-imperial revolt of the 720s. On the question of Zachary's relationship to the empire, see also Bertolini, "I rapporti di Zaccaria con Costantino V e con Artavasdo," p. 21.

# III. THE PEACE HOLDS

The solidarity achieved at Terni between the Lombard monarchy and the papacy underwent its first test in 743 in major developments in Bavaria.[1] There Duke Odilo withdrew the duchy from the dependence upon the Carolingians which had been imposed by Charles Martel. King Liutprand, who was Odilo's brother-in-law, doubtless saw in the Bavarian pursuit of autonomy an opportunity for increased Lombard influence[2] and continuation of the long royal connections with Bavaria. Pepin and Carloman, who had succeeded Charles Martel as Frankish mayors, responded by marshaling their forces on the River Lech, Bavaria's western limit. At this juncture, a *missus* from Pope Zachary, Sergius, brought word to the Frankish leaders that they were neither to wage war nor invade Bavaria. But the papal commands went unheeded as the Carolingians soon entered Bavaria, badly defeated Odilo, and forced him back into submission. Pepin and Carloman thereby averted a serious loss. For our purposes the important point is that the Bavarian episode, following hard upon the Terni settlement, evidently reflected its spirit of cooperation in that Zachary's attempt to halt the Frankish invasion of the duchy was apparently his way of supporting Liutprand's interests there.[3] At least, the king could have legitimately regarded the action as such, even if the intention was really otherwise.[4] The Bavarian affair, it appears, points to continuing Pavian-Roman solidarity after Terni.

TROUBLE IN THE NORTH: ROYAL-PAPAL TENSION OVER RAVENNA
AND CESENA

A situation of a different hue arose when Liutprand sent his forces into the region around Ravenna and then began his third siege of the imperial capital.[5] Exarch Eutychius promptly turned to Pope Zachary. Together with Archbishop John of Ravenna and "the whole people of Ravenna and the Pentapolis and the Emilia," Eutychius begged the pope to show his concern for their freedom. Zachary quickly supported Eutychius, sending to Liutprand Bishop Benedict and the *primicerius notariorum* Ambrose, two high

---

[1] For what follows see *Annales Mettenses*, a. 743, 328; Hodgkin, *Italy and Her Invaders.*, 7.100–102.

[2] Robert Cutler, *Carolingian Italian Policies, 739–780*, p. 36.

[3] Ibid., p. 37.

[4] Zachary perhaps also remembered Charles Martel's exploitation of church land in Francia. Hodgkin, *Italy and Her Invaders*, 7.103.

[5] *VZ*, 12.429. The following is based upon ibid. 12–16.429–431. Good secondary accounts are Llewellyn, *Rome in the Dark Ages*, p. 205 and Hubert, "Étude," pp. 34–35.

officers of the *iudices de clero*, the body of clerical and lay officers who constituted a nascent curial bureaucracy in Rome. Presenting Liutprand with many gifts, Benedict and Ambrose begged that he cease his campaign. They also requested that he "restore" the fortress of Cesena, a stronghold located about fifteen miles south of Ravenna on the Via Aemilia which Liutprand had taken from the empire in the current hostilities and from which he threatened both Ravenna and Rimini.[6] But the king would not yield on either point. Once again Zachary resorted to personal intervention. Leaving the government of Rome in the hands of his deputy, the *patricius et dux* Stephen,[7] he proceeded into the exarchate with Ambrose and a Roman priest named Stephen, probably the future Pope Stephen III. At a town called Aquila, Zachary and his suite were met by Eutychius himself. From Aquila the pope went on to Ravenna with the exarch. What transpired between the two is not known, but specific papal support was evidently arranged, for Ambrose and Stephen were sent to meet Liutprand in person. They got as far as Imola on the Via Aemilia in Lombard territory, but their courage apparently left them there for they did their business with the king by letter. Zachary, not content with indirect contact, then left Ravenna and, having entered Lombard territory, came to Padua on June 28. The king was at Pavia and did not want to see the pope, but royal envoys were nevertheless sent to Padua to escort him to the Lombard capital. Zachary went on to Pavia, celebrated a mass in the cathedral of St. Peter there, and then entered the royal palace for negotiations with Liutprand.

The mood was far different from that of the meeting at Terni, for now the pope had forced himself upon the king in the name of a royal enemy. Liutprand should cease his oppressions of Ravenna and its district, Zachary said, and should return what he had taken from Ravenna, including the fortress of Cesena. The source is not entirely clear, but apparently the pope meant that the restoration was to be to the exarch, that is, to the empire. Liutprand was evidently furious, but he at length complied, at least in large measure. He agreed to "broaden the limits of the city of Ravenna, as they were originally"—an exceedingly vague specification which may mean either that Liutprand promised to restore to Eutychius everything which he had ever taken from the empire or that he would return a much smaller area, only the specifically Ravennese places which he had just seized in the 743 campaign. The terms regarding Cesena were somewhat clearer; the king "returned" two-thirds of Cesena's territory to the *republic*, that is, bestowed it upon the pope, not the empire.[8] The remaining third was to stay in Lombard hands until June 744, after the return of royal envoys from Constantinople, at which time the third in question would revert to the republic. Apparently, the approval of the emperor was to be solicited

---

[6] Diehl, *Étude sur l'administration*, p. 57.

[7] See above, Chapter 2, n. 111.

[8] Clear in the *VZ* phraseology ". . . et duas partes territorii castri Cesinae ad partem reipublice restituit;" return to the duchy would probably have been specified in the case of a restoration to the empire.

and obtained before the Cesena transfer was formally completed. Liutprand and "his dukes and principal men" being in compliance with these conventions, Pope Zachary returned to Rome where he was received with joyful thanksgiving. The citizens of Rome and the Pentapolis reportedly celebrated their liberation in extensive feasting and drinking.

Analyzing these developments, it is noted first that Zachary had greatly changed his attitude and policy toward the monarchy. In the 741–742 period which culminated in the Terni settlement, Zachary terminated Gregory III's opposition to the king, ceased papal intervention in the affairs of the kingdom of Italy, and entered into specifically peaceful relations with Pavia. Moreover, in 743 Zachary evidently supported royal interests in Bavaria. But now the pope clashed with Liutprand by collaboratig with and assisting his enemy Eutychius. He also intervened in the concerns of the Lombard kingdom by acting to prevent its annexation of Ravenna and attempting to deprive it of some of its territory. In brief, Zachary did not behave as though he had recently concluded a long-term peace with the king. War did not break out between the two, but the tensions were obviously serious. The directions taken by Zachary were clearly new and contrary to those which he had pursued through the Bavarian affair.

No certain answers account for this change. The evidence contradicts a sudden return of Zachary to papal and Roman membership in the empire; there was no papal payment of imperial taxes, no acceptance of Iconoclasm, and no envoy or letter to Rome or Ravenna defining the imperial constituency. Furthermore, imperial officers failed to reappear in Rome. Finally, when the transfer of Cesena took place Liutprand gave it to *the republic*, terminology which would not have been used had Zachary recognized dependence upon the emperor. In sum, Zachary maintained his leadership of an independent Roman state and pursued its interests at home and abroad.

The papal acquisition of the greater part of Cesena, granted by Liutprand to the republic, was no ordinary addition. A Byzantine fortress in the Emilia which had become a Lombard conquest, it was neither a patrimony nor within the limits of either the old duchy of Rome or the newer republic. For the first time the pope was asserting that the republic had rights *beyond* the former Byzantine *ducatus Romae*. It is also true that obtaining Cesena was on Zachary's mind from the outset of the trouble with Liutprand, for its cession to the papacy was requested in the first embassy which the pope sent to the king asking him to stop his war against Ravenna. The preoccupation with Cesena is also seen in the source description of the Pavia terms of 743. Therein the references to the exarchate are brief but the Cesena grant is treated with emphasis and in detail. The suggestion is that Zachary wanted Cesena badly, perhaps to the point of being willing to change his policy toward Pavia as the means to acquire it. The king would be most loath to surrender Cesena voluntarily, for the fortress, situated as it was on the Via Aemilia, was important to the crown in controlling communications between the northern portions of the kingdom and the duchies of Spoleto and Benevento and maintaining the monarchy's military access to both. What Zachary needed was a lever to pressure Liutprand into yielding Cesena involuntarily. He apparently found that lever in the exarch's appeal for aid against the royal encroachment around Ravenna. Nothing indicates that Zachary somehow generated the appeal, but there is no doubt that he quickly exploited the situation once it occurred, in the end gaining Cesena as desired. The pope ran the risk that Liutprand would respond by renewing the anti-Roman activity which he had inflicted upon Gregory III. But, as will be shown, there were factors which kept Liutprand from such action in 743, and, if the pope was aware of them he also knew there was little risk. There is thus good reason to think that Zachary altered his policy toward the Lombard crown in order to possess Cesena, and did so without much worry of the cost to Rome and its republic.

A second "Roman" explanation for Zachary's changed Lombard policy may pertain to possible Roman fears for the safety of Rome and its territories in the event of elimination of the imperial presence in the north. So long as Liutprand had to contend with the exarch and the remnants of imperial power in the exarchate, Rome was safe enough despite the growth of Liutprand's power and the proximity of his kingdom. The king and the exarch would engage one another in ceaseless struggle, in the meantime leaving Rome relatively secure. But, if Pavia took Ravenna and put an end to Byzantine Italy, Rome might be next to fall as the crown inevitably sought to round out the kingdom through acquisition of the last independent Italian place north of Apulia and Calabria. In brief, Rome was tactically much better off with at least some surviving imperial power in and around Ravenna. Judging from the great consternation aroused in the exarchate by Liutprand's 743 campaign, the effort was of major proportions,[9] threatening to extinguish the imperial presence, the very demise which the Romans are apt to have feared. It may have been that Zachary changed his policy toward Pavia: for the empire to survive in the north the pope had to aid Eutychius against Liutprand. If these assumptions are correct, Zachary's policy change of 743 was a function of papal protection of Roman security from potential royal threat. It is notable that Zachary's action in 743 and the culminating Pavia settlement obviously *did* preserve Ravenna's power, thereby assuring further royal-imperial difficulties well to the north of Rome. Assuming that perpetuation of such difficulties was the aim of the papal policy change toward the crown, the change had the desired effect.

There is some chance, however, that there was actually no papal change at all. This interpretation arises from the possibility that Liutprand and Zachary had different perceptions of the 742 Terni peace between Pavia and Rome. It may be supposed that the king believed that the peace applied only to his relations with Rome and its territories, leaving him free to make war upon the empire despite his convention with the pope. Indeed, some scholars think that Liutprand appreciated the Terni peace as a tacit papal

[9] Appreciated by Hubert, "Étude," p. 35.

authorization for the royal effort against the exarch.[10] But the pope may
have understood the peace in much different terms, seeing it as a general
Italian pacification in which Liutprand was obligated to remain in harmony
with Ravenna as well as Rome. In this reconstruction, while Liutprand
discerned no problems vis-a-vis Rome when he attacked the exarch in 743,
Pope Zachary found him in violation of the Terni peace—and sought to
return him to compliance with it by urging suspension of the campaign
and return of the territories which he had taken in 743. (Only such a limited
return, not restoration of all the territories which Liutprand had ever taken
from the empire, as the source may imply, can be envisioned in this reconstruction). In brief, Zachary's change of attitude toward the crown may
have been an attempt to bring the king back into conformity with the 742
peace; in the pope's sight, perhaps, it was the king who had changed.

Liutprand undoubtedly had his own perceptions of the 743 developments. In the overall sense the king was probably surprised by Zachary's
activities. At Terni and before, the pope had been a warm ally, seemingly
accepting the Kingdom of Italy and becoming its active friend. The same
understanding could have been gained from the pope's Bavarian intervention. Indeed, Zachary had in effect pledged neutrality toward the kingdom
through his arrangement of the twenty-year royal peace with Rome. Further, the pope had shown no concern for imperial interests at Terni. Now,
only a year later in 743, everything had changed. Pope Zachary had suddenly become an ally of the exarch, going to the most extraordinary lengths
to advance the imperial cause against the crown. High-ranking papal envoys had pressed Liutprand to suspend his war against the exarch; the pope
had personally collaborated with the exarch and accepted his company in
Ravenna, the very object of the campaign in 743; and finally, coming to
Pavia itself, Zachary forced Liutprand into suspension of the war, pledges
of restitution of territory to Byzantium, and bestowal of further territory
upon St. Peter.

Despite the absence of an open break between Pavia and Rome, there
can be little doubt that Liutprand believed in 743 that Zachary had suddenly
become a royal enemy. He was a foe in that his activities gave aid and
comfort to the exarch and clearly harmed the Italian kingdom. The harm
lay in the restitutions which Liutprand agreed to make to the empire. If
the restitutions were to be all the places which he had acquired from the
empire, the blow would be fatal to the kingdom since maintenance of
communications with and subordination of Spoleto and Benevento depended upon royal possession of the former imperial places and roads in
the exarchate and the Pentapolis. If the restitutions were to include only
those places which Liutprand had seized from Byzantium in 743 the damage
would be less, though still significant; security for the crucial Adriatic link

---

[10] For such views see Macaigne, L'Église Merovingienne, pp. 207–208 and 212; Llewellyn, Rome
in the Dark Ages, pp. 204–205; Partner, Lands of St. Peter, p. 17; Bertolini, Roma, pp. 483–485;
and Hubert, "Étude," p. 35.

to the Lombard south, surely one of the aims of the 743 campaign against Ravenna, would be denied. The Cesena transfer to the republic was not helpful either, for it placed a key stronghold on the Ameilia route to the south in papal hands, thereby raising the potential for the papacy to try to hinder royal control over the southern duchies. From Liutprand's perspective, then, the pope was in violation of the Terni settlement, for he was threatening the Italian kingdom which he had sanctioned and supported in 742.

When Gregory III had become a royal opponent, Liutprand had responded by ravaging the papal republic and raising the prospect of a siege of Rome. But there was no new round of royal retaliation in 743 to force Rome back into amity with Pavia. How does one account for the absence of renewed royal operation around Rome? Several factors working simultaneously may have restricted the king and caused him to accommodate the pope instead of harassing him. First, Liutprand in 743 was aging and was perhaps still weak from the 735 illness which had made Hildeprand co-ruler.[11] He therefore may have lacked the energy to oppose Zachary actively. Second, it has been suggested that by 743 there was within the kingdom a party of powerful Lombards revolving around Duke Ratchis of Friuli which held deep respect for Rome and wanted no trouble with the pope.[12] The supposition is that this group was influential enough to be able to restrain Liutprand. A number of scholars think that the king was also kept in check by pressure from Lombard bishops who responded to papal pleas and urged royal accommodation with the pope.[13] Finally, Liutprand was possibly distracted from action in the vicinity of Rome by the recent Carolingian repossession of Bavaria, which posed a threat to the northwest Lombard frontier despite Liutprand's earlier cordial relations with Charles Martel.[14] In some combination of these personal, internal, and external problems may lie adequate explanation for Liutprand's failure to attempt reprisals against Zachary as his method for restoring the pope to full compliance with the Terni peace. As it was, the king could only angrily and reluctantly do as the pontiff bid.

Such, then, were the complex ramifications of the 743 dealings between Pavia and Rome. Whatever the pope's motives, and despite the absence of an open royal-papal rupture, the bloom of Terni was gone. One may envision suspicion on the part of Liutprand, a sense that he had been misled by Zachary and forced into a settlement with Ravenna which he did not want and which would damage his kingdom were its terms to be fulfilled. And in Rome there was fear that Liutprand would engage in new reprisals, for divine mercy was invoked by the people of Rome and Ravenna for protection against the "insidious and vengeful King Liutprand."[15] Whether

---

[11] Bertolini, *Roma*, pp. 488–489; Hartmann, *Geschichte Italiens*, 2.2.144.
[12] Hartmann, *Geschichte Italiens*, 2.2.144; Bertolini, *Roma*, p. 488.
[13] Hartmann, *Geschichte Italiens*, 2.2.145–146; Haller, *Das Papsttum*, pp. 362–363.
[14] Bertolini, *Roma*, p. 488.
[15] *VZ*, 17.431.

the Roman anxiety was in response to real or imaginary plans or actions
by the king is beside the point. What matters is that royal ill-feeling had
entered into the royal papal relationship.

## THE INTERLUDE OF HILDEPRAND AND RATCHIS

What would have come of Liutprand's tension with Pope Zachary cannot
be known, for the king died in 744. Succeeding him was the little-known
co-king, Hildeprand,[16] who had been a vigorous opponent of the empire
but seems not to have renewed the war while he reigned. After several
months Hildeprand was overthrown by Duke Ratchis,[17] the powerful northern lord from Friuli about whom gathered the element sympathetic to
Rome. King Ratchis immediately promised Pope Zachary that he would
make no war in Italy for a period of twenty years.[18] He thereby abandoned
the monarchy's long struggle against the empire which Liutprand had been
made by Zachary to forego under duress. In further accord with the papacy,
Ratchis provided donations as frequently as they were requested.[19] Eventually Ratchis renewed the war with the empire, for in 749 he attacked the
city of Perugia and a number of towns in the Pentapolis.[20] Pope Zachary
again intervened, this time rushing to Perugia and urging Ratchis to end
the campaign. The king speedily complied and then abdicated several days
later. In June, 749, Ratchis became a monk at the monastery of Monte
Cassino,[21] perhaps influenced by the example of the Austrasian mayor,
Carloman, who had just entered the same house after renouncing his
throne.[22] Ratchis was followed at Pavia by his brother Aistulf, elected by
the aristocracy in early July.[23]

Interpreting these developments, it is clear that Ratchis intended to have
entirely cordial relations with the papacy and was inclined to permit the
pope to have a powerful voice in the crown's foreign relations. Ratchis's
first move as king was to pledge the twenty-year Italian peace–"because
of reverence for the prince of the apostles."[24] In other words, the Lombard
king decided on peace with the empire simply because he knew that it was
desired by Pope Zachary. Further, the pope requested patrimonial donations
and they were granted. Finally, when the struggle against the exarch was
resumed in 749, Ratchis was quick to end the campaign upon Zachary's
request. Why Ratchis was so partial to Rome is not clear. Perhaps his
Roman-born wife subjected him to powerful Roman influences,[25] or perhaps

---

[16] See VZ, 17.431. Pauli Cont. Rom. 1.200.
[17] VZ, 17.431; Pauli Cont. Rom , 1.200.
[18] VZ, 13.431.
[19] Benedicti Chronicon, 702.16, lines 35–36.
[20] VZ, 23.433–434. Several Lombard sources repeat the VZ statement practically verbatim.
[21] VZ, 23.434; Pauli Cont. Cas., 3.198–199; Chronicon Salernitanum, 1.471. See also Duchesne,
VZ, 439, n. 50.
[22] Bertolini, Roma, 498. On Carloman's retirement see VZ, 21.433; Pauli Cont. Tert., 21.208.
[23] Pauli Cont. Rom., 2.201; Pauli Cont. Tert., 23.208; Ben. Chron. 17.703.
[24] VZ, 17.431: "ob reverentiam principis apostolorum. . . ."
[25] Ben. Chron., 16.702.

he was independently sincere in his devotion to the papacy. Whatever the cause, Ratchis avoided conflict with the pope and permitted him to shape Pavia's basic attitude toward the empire. In the latter respect, the Lombard monarchy was coming under pontifical tutelage.

Ratchis's pro-Roman stance was strongly opposed within the kingdom and cost him the throne.[26] It was probably because of the opposition's pressure that the king at length resumed the war with the empire and broke the pledge of Italian peace. Later, having bowed to Zachary's demand at Perugia for peace after he had been forced to resume the imperial conquests, Ratchis found the opposition so strong that he could not continue to maintain the throne. The opposition's goals were logically threefold; restoration of royal Lombard freedom from the papacy in determining the crown's basic attitude toward the empire; resumption of war against the empire;[27] and a halt to the granting of donations to the papacy, at least on the scale practiced by Ratchis.[28] The men who advanced these goals were at least a portion of the Lombard nobles, a number of Lombard bishops, and Ratchis's brother Aistulf, who was seen as the leader of the malcontents.[29] Aistulf's election as king after Ratchis's abdication is presumed to have been the outcome of the successful opposition: to the factional victor belonged the throne.

### KING AISTULF'S EXPANSION OF THE KINGDOM OF ITALY

In 749, soon after his accession, Aistulf embarked upon the project which was expected of him, conquest of imperial Italy. He first seized Comacchio and Ferrara in the exarchate,[30] the former north of Ravenna on the coast and the latter inland near the northern border with the Lombard kingdom. By mid-751 Aistulf had taken Ravenna itself,[31] the object of royal war since early in the reign of Liutprand. But that was not all. Simultaneously Aistulf also took Forum Livii (Forli), Forum Populii (Forlimpopoli), and Cesena,[32] all of which were located on the Via Aemilia and, when joined with Liutprand's earlier acquisitions, gave the king control of that important road across the whole of the exarchate and linked his kingdom directly with the northeast corner of the Pentapolis. The Cesena appropriation appears to

---

[26] Hartmann, *Geschichte Italiens*, 2.146–148; Bertolini, *Roma*, 496–497; Miller, "Papal-Lombard Relations," pp. 360–361, n. 4.

[27] *Chron. Sal.*, 1.471. See also Miller, "Papal-Lombard Relations," pp. 360–361, n. 4.

[28] *Ben. Chron.*, 703.16. See also Drew, *The Lombard Laws*, p. 255, n. 2.

[29] Ibid.

[30] *Chron. Sal.*, 1.471–72.

[31] Clear from Aistulf's issuance of a charter in July 751. *Codice Diplomatico Longobardo*, ed. C. Troya 4, p. 382.

[32] The documentation here is indirect. The sources do not specify any such conquests, but in 756, after Aistulf failed to capture Rome, he was forced to surrender these places to the papacy. *Vita Stephani II, LP I,* 454. Since they were not royal territories at Aistulf's accession in 749, and since they were surrendered in 756, they were necessarily acquired by the king at some point in the period. The most likely time seems before or during 751, for thereafter Aistulf's attention was devoted to Rome and relations with the pope. See Duchesne, *VS II,* 460, n. 51.

have nullified the arrangements made by Liutprand and Zachary concerning the third not turned over to the papacy, and may have had the same effect upon the two-thirds supposedly already transferred. In the Pentapolis Aistulf took Rimini, Conca (La Cattolica), Pissaurum (Pesaro), Fano, and Sena Gallica (Sinigaglia)[33] along the Via Flaminia and the Old Flaminian Way. These conquests gave Aistulf clear passage from his kingdom through the Pentapolis to Liutprand's old territory in the Pentapoline southeast—and into Spoleto. In addition, the king pushed west and south along the Via Flaminia and the Via Amerina, seizing Cagli and Luceoli (Cantiano) on the former and Gubbio on the latter.[34] Aistulf now controlled movement to and from Rome as far as Perugia, but, more importantly, he had gained a second route of entry into Spoleto, this one by the Flaminian Way, which veered into Spoleto near Cagli. The territory and communications of both the exarchate and the Pentapolis were thus in Aistulf's hands, and he possessed at least two avenues into the Lombard south. Aistulf then went on to draw the duchies of Spoleto and Benevento into firm royal control. In Spoleto a royal officer evidently took military command[35] and when Duke Lupus, who had been appointed by Ratchis, died in 751 Aistulf designated no successor, apparently reserving the ducal powers for himself.[36] In Benevento there was potential disaster, however, for Duke Gisulf II, an ardent supporter of the monarchy who had been raised from childhood and installed by Liutprand, died and opened the prospect of Beneventan defection. But the pro-royal party held on, as the recognized duke was Gisulf's minor son, Liutprand, under the regency of the loyal mother, Scauniperga. Beneventan separatism was thus denied, and there is no sign that the duchy was significantly independent of the crown.[37] Quite clearly, Aistulf was as devoted as Liutprand to the restoration of the Lombard Kingdom of Italy.[38]

It has not been sufficiently stressed, however, that Aistulf had virtually achieved the royal goal. Benevento was open to steady royal influence in the hands of Scauniperga's government. Spoleto, normally the most autonomous of all the Lombard duchies, was now without a duke and evidently under direct royal authority. Much of the duchy of Perugia and all of the exarchate and the Pentapolis were now royal territories; the rest of northern Italy was under royal dominance, despite the continuing presence of powerful dukes; and the crown possessed the road communications nec-

---

[33] The same methodology and reference applies here. Away from the roads Aistulf seized a number of other places.

[34] Same methodology and reference.

[35] Or so it seems from the *Ben. Chron.* notice (17.703) that Aistulf immediately after his accession sent a count of the palace named Robert to Spoleto to hold the Sabine region.

[36] Donald A. Bullough, "The Writing Office of the Dukes of Spoleto in the Eighth Century." pp. 1-21, 13; Bertolini, *Roma*, p. 499. Bullough (p. 13) says that Aistulf ruled through local gastalds.

[37] Bertolini, *Roma*, p. 499; Hubert, "Étude," p. 39, n. 3; Oelsner, *Jahrbücher des fränkischen*, p. 144.

[38] As is widely recognized. Hubert, "Étude," p. 39; Gasquet "Le royaume lombard," p. 80; Halphen, *Charlemagne*, p. 29.

essary for strategic linkage of the northern, former imperial, and Spoletan-Beneventan regions of the kingdom. The great majority of Italy's territory was now under Pavia's auspices, with Byzantium retaining only Apulia, Calabria, the west coast enclaves of Naples and Gaeta and Venetia and Istria in the north. There was also the former imperial duchy of Rome, now the papal republic or in the process of becoming that. On every side except the sea the republic was surrounded by Lombard territory. Let there be no mistake. From the point of view of the monarchy a new era was at hand, for the Kingdom of Italy was in being again, more completely so than at any previous time in Lombard history. Henceforth the royal goal was naturally to protect the kingdom, to keep it together so that its artificial union might in time become real.

Those who had ousted Ratchis and elevated Aistulf to the Lombard throne must have been well pleased with him in the 749–751 period: in the process of forging the kingdom he had resumed the vigorous prosecution of the war against the empire and he had restored the royal freedom from Rome in dealing with it. That freedom from the papal dominance, which had threatened in the days of Ratchis, could not have been more complete under Aistulf, for as far as we know there was no papal effort to hamper or limit the 749–751 royal successes.[39] Zachary did not again travel to Ravenna, Pavia, or Perugia to halt royal attacks upon the Byzantines; nor did any papal diplomats collaborate with the beleaguered exarch. In 749 when Zachary persuaded Ratchis to suspend the campaign against Perugia, the monarchy seemed on the way to becoming a papal puppet, at least in the vital area of royal-imperial relations; under Aistulf's leadership in the next year and a half Zachary ceased to have any voice at all.

At least two plausible explanations exist for this development. First, Zachary was no doubt realistic about Aistulf. The pope was enough in touch with Lombard internal affairs to know that Aistulf won the throne on an anti-Roman platform and would reject out of hand any further papal efforts to direct Pavia's dealings with the empire.[40] Such activities were useless and could well be counter-productive in that they could provoke Aistulf into harassing and menacing Rome's territory, which so far had been spared a royal campaign. Second, the papacy and Rome were becoming increasingly isolated by Aistulf's formation of the Italian kingdom,[41] a new situation which suggested that the pope should re-examine his practice of intervening in the crown's affairs. The fall of the Byzantine territories on the Adriatic removed the exarch from Italy and deprived Rome of whatever benefit might be gained from that quarter; the advance into Perugia and the acquisition of the two great roads leading from the Adriatic to Rome

---

[39] "Zacharie ne semble pas avoir essayé de fléchir Astolphe par les prierès et les exhortations qui lui avait si bien réussi auprès de Liutprand et de Ratchis." Duchesne, VS II, 456, n. 9. See also Bertolini, Roma, pp. 515–516.

[40] Vaguely implied in Miller, "Papal-Lombard Relations," p. 361, n. 4.

[41] The isolation has been perceived by several authors. Miller, "Papal-Lombard Relations," pp. 360–361.

sealed the latter off from both the coast and the duchy of Spoleto; and the strengthening of the royal hand in the latter and Benevento meant that no Roman alignment with the duchies was possible.[42] The papacy and Rome were without Italian allies in a changing Italian world which was increasingly dominated by Pavia's king. It would thus be most unwise for Zachary to persist in actions which Aistulf would find obstructive of his Italian goals. Better to let him go unhindered, free of any papal efforts to mold the royal dealings with the failing empire.

Force perhaps won Aistulf freedom from Rome in the 749-751 period in the sense that it created conditions which produced Zachary's isolation, *but it was not brought to bear upon Rome or any of its territory*. No royal troops entered the republic, seized Roman fortifications, or shut off strategic roads within the republic; no royal army was brought before Rome's walls in a display of strength; and no papal territory was taken or harmed. The explanation for the royal restraint seems obvious: enjoying rapid and extensive successes in reestablishing the Lombard Kingdom of Italy and having the luxury of apparent papal indifference toward those successes, the king refrained from doing anything to stir Zachary into an intervention reminiscent of that which he had applied against Liutprand in 743. At least until the papal isolation was complete and the kingdom more firmly grounded, the pope should not be disturbed by royal use of force in the republic. In the meantime, any royal supporters who were unhappy with the king's lack of action against Rome would have to rest content with his restoration of the royal freedom from the papacy and the successful resumption and prosecution of the war against the empire.

The nine crowded years from the 742 Terni peace until Aistulf's triumph of 751 had seen extraordinary alterations in the royal-papal relationship. The Terni cordiality and concord, formalized in the royal-papal peace agreement, were followed in 743 by tension between Liutprand and Zachary as the latter opposed the war against the exarchate, thereby hindering progress toward a Lombard Italian kingdom. The trouble was ended by the strongly pro-Roman Ratchis, who twice let the pope dictate royal treatment of imperial Italy and made liberal proprietary grants to St. Peter. But there was more: Aistulf deposed Ratchis, ended the papal influence in royal-papal relations, and, in creating a Lombard Italian kingdom which surrounded the papal republic, made it clear that the papacy would run great risks if its treatment of the monarchy was hostile to the latter's interests. In 742 there had been formal peace between Pavia and Rome, voluntarily agreed to by both pope and king; in 751 there was de facto peace, in effect because Aistulf wanted it and Zachary had no choice but to accept it.

### AISTULF, POPE STEPHEN II, AND THE ROYAL-PAPAL PEACE OF 752

In the spring of 752, shortly after the death of Pope Zachary and the accession of Pope Stephen II (752-757), Aistulf menaced Rome without

---

[42] Bertolini, *Roma*, p. 499.

besieging it: he sent troops into the Roman republic and seized a number of unnamed towns and fortresses there.[43] Then, in June, 752, only a few weeks after commencing these hostilities, he accepted a formal pact with the papacy. The settlement may have begun taking shape as early as late May, for at that time Stephen referred to Aistulf in a bull as "the most excellent King Aistulf."[44] Then, in June, Pope Stephen sent his brother, the future Pope Paul I, and the *primicerius* Ambrose, who had earlier been sent by Zachary to deal with Liutprand, to negotiate with Aistulf.[45] The resulting agreement called for a forty-year period of peace between Pavia and Rome.

Reflecting first upon Aistulf's depredations in the papal republic, the king had apparently embarked upon the course of unprovoked war against the papacy which Pavia had last applied in 727 when Liutprand seized Sutri. It has already been noted that Pope Zachary had done nothing to threaten royal possession of the exarchate, the Pentapolis, and the Perugian districts, or to disrupt the enhanced royal position in Spoleto and Benevento. Nor was Stephen II any more menacing in the opening months of his pontificate. Even so, Aistulf attacked the papal republic. It thus appears that the royal operations during 752 were an unusual case of royal aggression, and as such represented a basic policy change by the monarchy.

This conclusion seems consistent with the modern scholarly opinion that Aistulf was a natural enemy of the papacy who automatically turned to conquest of Rome and its republic after annexing the exarchate.[46] The supporting rationale for this position is nowhere specified, but it may be summarized as follows. Aistulf, having taken the exarchate and the Pentapolis and strengthened his hand in the great duchies, was free to try to gain his most cherished objective—incorporation of both Rome and the papacy into his Kingdom of Italy. It was thus that he invaded Roman territory at his earliest convenience, the spring of 752, the intention of the campaign being to make the pope, Rome, and its surrounding republic dependent upon the Lombard crown.

This is apt to be an untenable interpretation, however, and consideration of Aistulf's possible or even probable domestic situation suggests one reason why. It seems conceivable that the 752 invasion of the republic was forced upon Aistulf by those anti-Roman nobles who had raised him to the throne in preference to Ratchis.[47] The following scenario may have obtained. The nobles, while they were doubtless pleased with Aistulf's conquest of By-

---

[43] *VS II*, 5.441; *Pauli Cont. Tert.*, 32.209; *Pauli Cont. Lombarda*, 217, lines 14–15.

[44] Troya, *Cod. Dip. Long.*, 4.414, #661.

[45] *VS II*, 5.441; *Pauli Cont. Tert.*, 32.209; *Pauli Cont. Lom.*, 217, lines 15–18.

[46] Duchesne, VS II, 456–57, n. 9: "C'était maintenenant le tour du duché de Rome. . . . Au bout de quelque temps, Astolphe, se sentant affermi dans la possession de Ravenne, commença a manifester ses prétentions sur Rome et son territoire." Halphen, *Charlemagne*, p. 31: "Ravenne était tombée aux mains d'Astolf au debut de l'été 751, et des l'année suivante Rome était menacée. . . . Astolf avait fait la sourde oreille." Miller, "Papal-Lombard Relations", 361, n. 5: "In this situation [the conquest of Ravenna] Rome was logically the next objective. . . ." And, most recently, Miller, "The Roman Revolution," p. 114; "The free papal enclave of Rome, then, was logically the next objective. Hence in 751, Aistulf began the offensive against Rome."

[47] Implied by Miller, "The Roman Revolution," pp. 113–114.

zantine places and liberation of royal policy toward the empire from papal control, were also perhaps unhappy with his maintenance of peace with Zachary and Stephen II, taking it as a sign that he was only somewhat less pro-Roman in attitude than the deposed Ratchis. They thus demanded that Aistulf undertake a Roman war in token of his worthiness as their leader. Not wanting to attack the papal republic for fear of jeopardizing the newly-expanded Lombard kingdom by arousing papal enmity, but also fearing that the malcontents were powerful enough to mount a successful coup, Aistulf reluctantly began the 752 invasion to protect his throne. If this view is correct, a party of dissident Lombard nobles rather than the king was responsible for the sudden renewal of royal hostility toward the papacy in 752.

But both of these views of the 752 campaign fail to consider that Aistulf made a specific and long-term peace agreement with the papacy shortly after he began the invasion. Given this important development, it seems most unlikely that the king was engaged in unprovoked aggression, for he quickly ended the war and pledged the monarchy to forty years of amity with Rome. Similarly, he was evidently not seeking to annex Rome and dominate the pope, for he accepted a convention which signified royal acquiescence in the reality of Roman and papal independence by establishing royal-papal peace. Finally, Aistulf was apparently not reacting to noble pressure in defense of his throne, for he would hardly have risked antagonizing the aristocrats further by ending the war which they had thrust upon him under conditions which were as favorable to Rome as Pavia.

Why, then, *did* Aistulf attack the Roman republic in 752? The apparent answer is that he launched the aggressions in order to force Stephen II to negotiate a specific treaty with him. Several considerations favor this argument.

It stands to reason that Aistulf wanted to have a firm accommodation with the pope. Having recently won the exarchate, the Pentapolis, and Perugia, and having recently strengthened the royal hand in the Lombard south, it was imperative that Stephen II forego the various interventions practiced by Gregory III and Zachary against Liutprand and Ratchis in the past nine years. If obtained, a peace treaty would naturally not assure papal neutrality toward the Lombard kingdom. But a treaty would nevertheless provide de facto papal recognition of that kingdom by specifying Pavian-Roman peace at a time when the kingdom was already in being. Such recognition would impose restraints upon anti-royal action by the pope and would discourage him from acknowledging any forthcoming Byzantine claims that the monarchy ruled the old imperial territories illegally. In sum, a treaty of concord with Rome was worth a good deal to Aistulf—enough for him to have posed as a Roman enemy to frighten Stephen II into negotiating one.

A second reason for believing that Aistulf commenced the 752 aggressions to obtain a peace treaty is that King Liutprand had utilized a similar tactic with success in 738 and 739 when royal troops invaded the duchy of Rome and appropriated the four fortresses after Gregory III attempted to keep Liutprand from acquiring the exarchate and absorbing the duchy of Spoleto. Gregory was unaffected by the pressures, but Zachary apparently gave in, negotiating the twenty-year peace agreement with the monarchy in 742 at Terni. The point is that Liutprand evidently had been able to gain a royal-papal accommodation by threatening Rome, and a decade later, in 752, Aistulf may have sought the same end by the same means.

The final argument favoring the view that Aistulf attacked the papacy in 752 to extract a peace with the pope is perhaps the most convincing. As noted earlier, the papacy in 752 was without allies because of Aistulf's successes in the 749–751 period. The direct papal connections with the exarch and the dukes of Spoleto and Benevento were no longer possible, leaving only imperial diplomacy and ties with the Franks as potential sources of aid. The papacy was largely defenseless, at Pavia's mercy. In these circumstances, Aistulf had only to manifest hostility toward the papacy for Stephen to agree to a royal-papal peace, whether the pope actually wanted to do so or not. Desiring a formal accord with the papacy, Aistulf apparently obtained it by threatening Rome at a time when the pope, who was bound to have been unsure of the royal war aims, could feel relatively secure only by arranging the very accord which Aistulf sought.

It thus seems fairly certain that Aistulf's hostility in 752 aimed at and gained a peace treaty between the monarchy and the papacy. The standard presumption that after mid-751 Aistulf set out to conquer Rome and its republic and place the pope in his power is thus open to question, for the apparent royal desire for peace and the conduct of a campaign which evidently sought and produced it, lead one to think that in 752, the king harbored no plan to seize Rome or win domination over the papacy. If so, Aistulf was no different from Liutprand in this regard: Liutprand was quite prepared to leave Rome, its territory, and the pope free of the Lombard Kingdom of Italy, and Aistulf may have exhibited the same attitude in the settlement of the 752 trouble. At minimum, it is far from certain that Aistulf was an intractable enemy of Rome out to alter basic royal policy toward the papacy; more persuasively, he continued the traditional lines laid down by Liutprand. Furthermore, rather than confirming the suspicion that Aistulf embarked upon a course of unprovoked aggression against the papacy in 752, the peace with Rome strongly suggests that despite the Roman campaign Aistulf was still holding to Liutprand's and his own basic theme of maintaining peace with the papacy—three years after his accession.

A brief consideration of the 752 developments from the papal perspective is in order, particularly since there is no modern commentary available. Hardly seated upon the chair of St. Peter after the death of Zachary, Stephen II may have been surprised by Aistulf's invasion since neither he nor Zachary had provoked the king by threatening his interests. Stephen must have also feared Aistulf; he did not know this new king, may have seen his sweeping 749–751 triumphs as awesome preludes to an attempt to conquer Rome for the Lombard kingdom, and was surely apprehensive about facing Aistulf without allies. But a measure of security amid the present uncertainties could be obtained through a peace settlement with the monarchy. Such a tactic had ended the crisis in 742 and might well work again, at least until a better solution could be reached. It was perhaps thus that Stephen II sent ambassadors to Aistulf and then entered the peace agreement. It should also be briefly noted that Stephen II conducted Rome's foreign relations on behalf of Rome alone, that is, in the manner of Gregory II, Gregory III, and Zachary. Nor did Stephen send notification of his election to the empire. Rome and the pope were both still going a way separate from that of the empire.

Returning to the royal side of the equation, circumstances as they stood after the conclusion of the June 752 accord were clearly favorable to the monarchy. The Italian kingdom was fully in being. Sometimes given to threatening and damaging that kingdom, the papacy was without allies, neutralized by the royal successes. And, most importantly, Stephen II had afforded de facto papal recognition to royal possession of the exarchate, the Pentapolis, and the Perugian places and to royal hegemony over Spoleto and Benevento by accepting a peace treaty with the monarchy. Stephen II had given a pledge of sorts that the monarchy would not attempt to reverse the crown's great victories of 749–751. One may surmise, of course, that Aistulf doubted that the peace would endure, for the Terni settlement had soured within a year and royal-papal amity had been anything but constant in the past. Nevertheless, Aistulf is apt to have been in a hopeful mood in June of 752, for conditions had rarely been so congenial to Pavia's interests

## FAILURE OF THE PEACE OF 752

During the summer the pope sent envoys to Emperor Constantine V, requesting him to send imperial forces to Italy against Aistulf.[48] The latter responded in October, 752, announcing that he intended to collect tribute from the Romans and compel them to accept his jurisdiction. One reads that Aistulf gathered his army before making these threats,[49] the implication being that both pope and Romans were to be made dependent upon the monarchy by force.[50] Presumably seeking to keep the June peace intact, Stephen sent two Lombard abbots to meet with Aistulf. But the papal biography asserts that their interview with the king was fruitless as the host refused any concessions and ordered them to return to their monasteries without stopping off in Rome on their way.[51] In the meantime, while

---

[48] Deduced from the fact that in the fall of 752 Stephen called on the emperor "as he [the pope] *had often done in writing,* to come to Italy with an army to liberate this city of Rome and all Italy from the clutches of this son of iniquity [Aistulf]." *VS II,* 9.442: "deprecans imperialem clementiam ut iuxta quod ei sepius exercitandis has Italiae in partes scripserat, modis omnibus adveniret et de iniquitatis filii morsibus Romanam hanc urbem vel cunctam Italiam provinciam liberaret."

[49] *VS II,* 6.441; *Pauli Cont. Cas.,* 4.199; *Pauli Cont. Tert.,* 209.32. The Cassino continuation says that Aistulf demanded one gold solidus from every Roman inhabitant.

[50] Duchesne, *VS II,* 457. n. 11

[51] *VS II,* 7.441–442; *Pauli Cont. Cas.,* 4.199.

the abbots were still dealing with the king, a Byzantine envoy, the *silentiarius* John, arrived in Rome with instructions from the emperor that the pope should attempt to persuade King Aistulf to restore the exarchate to the empire. Stephen was reportedly receptive to the request, having had the prior negotiations with the emperor on the subject. An embassy composed of John and the deacon Paul, the pope's brother, was sent to negotiate with Aistulf at Ravenna. Once more Aistulf refused accommodation. Instead, he appointed an ambassador of his own, persuaded John to accept his company, and sent them both back to Rome.[52] Learning of these developments, Stephen countered by forwarding papal emissaries to Constantine V along with John and the Lombard envoy. The pope's messengers were to beg the emperor "as he [the pope] had often done in writing, to come to Italy with an army to liberate this city of Rome and all Italy from the clutches of this son of iniquity [Aistulf]."[53] By the end of October, 752, Aistulf and Stephen II were virtually at war, the June accord forgotten.

Without much doubt, the collapse of the peace stemmed from Stephen II's effort to bring imperial troops into Italy against the Lombards. At a time in which the pope, by virtue of the peace with the crown which he himself had instituted, was expected to dwell in harmony with the king, he was instead soliciting Italian intervention by the empire, the royal enemy. If successful, that intervention would result in the empire's regaining of Ravenna, the exarchate, and the Pentapolis, thereby robbing Aistulf of his recently-gained territories, threatening if not eliminating the royal road access to Spoleto and Benevento, and inviting the separatist elements in those duchies to menace the royal hegemony there by turning to both the pope and the empire for support. The possibility of ruination of the Italian kingdom lay in Stephen's overtures to Constantine V, making it necessary that the pope halt his anti-royal action in favor of the neutrality demanded by the June accord. The tried and true method of winning the pope's compliance was by now the application of pressure in the form of royal threat to Roman and papal independence—and evidently such pressure was applied in October when Aistulf gathered his army and announced his intention of having the Romans pay him tribute and accept his jurisdiction. It was very likely a strategic maneuver, for the king surely wanted to end what he saw as Stephen's perfidy and the renewal of papal compliance with the June treaty. Nor would Aistulf be distracted either by Stephen's diplomatic persuasions or by the imperial envoy John. The king was probably interested in only one thing—maintenance of compulsion sufficient to push Stephen II away from the fresh imperial connection and back into conformity with the June peace.[54]

---

[52] *VS II*, 8.442.

[53] Ibid., 9.442. See n. 48 above for the Latin.

[54] One scholar holds that Aistulf was to blame for the failure of the peace by undertaking independent negotiations with the empire, the source words "agnito maligni regis consilio" being the proof. That is, Stephen II did not appeal for Byzantine aid against Aistulf until Aistulf deceived Stephen by secretly negotiating with the empire, presumably about the

Because the October threats were probably tactical in nature, they are not likely to have signaled a new concern on Aistulf's part to acquire political control over Rome and the surrounding country. As before, it appears, Aistulf had no plans to make the Roman district actually part of his Italian kingdom. It was rather a case of threatening Roman domination as a means of assuring the kingdom's unity without a Roman component. The threats are thus not likely to have posed real danger to Roman and papal independence. It is not known whether Stephen II saw things that way, but he surely understood that his machinations with Byzantium were the source of the rupture with Aistulf and that the threats from Aistulf might very well come to nothing if the machinations ceased.

---

exarchate etc. See O. Bertolini, "Il primo 'periuria' di Astolfo verso la Chiesa di Roma, 752-3." The interpretation seems dubious because of the unclear nature of the evidence and the fact that *Stephen's* negotiations could easily have pre-dated those of Aistulf.

# IV. CRISIS AND CONFLICT

Between October 752 and the spring of 753 there were dramatic new developments in the royal-papal relationship. During the fall Aistulf continued to threaten subjugation of the Romans, becoming increasingly vehement in his rhetoric and even going so far as to assert that he would massacre them all unless they yielded to his power.[1] Something approaching hysteria may have occurred in Rome, for the *Vita Stephani II* reports that crowds of Roman people and priests marched and begged for divine deliverance from the terrible Lombard king, with Pope Stephen himself apparently leading the demonstrations.[2] But Stephen did not neglect mundane support, for he continued to urge Byzantine aid, and when at length it became clear that the empire was powerless to mount an Italian campaign the pope turned instead to Francia.[3] There the papal solicitations fell upon King Pepin, the son of Charles Martel and the former mayor of the palace whom Pope Zachary had sanctioned as Frankish king in 751 when Pepin deposed and succeeded the last Merovingian ruler, Childeric III. Stephen's *Vita* puts it all very clearly: just as Gregory II, Gregory III, and Zachary had all appealed to Charles Martel (an inaccuracy since only Gregory III had done so), because of the oppressions and attacks being made by the Lombards in "this province of the Romans," Stephen sent letters to King Pepin informing him of the prevailing troubles and requesting that he send Frankish envoys to Rome so that the pope might be brought to the king.[4] While Stephen eagerly awaited the Frankish reply in the spring of 753, Aistulf began a new campaign in the papal republic, occupying towns, fortifications, and roads. Centucellensis (Civitavecchia) on the Aurelian Way northwest of Rome was taken from Lombard Tuscany. Nepete (Nepi) on the Via Amerina about twenty-five miles north of Rome fell; Aistulf himself seized Tibur, about ten miles east on the Valerian Way near the border with Spoleto; and Terracina on the Appian Way near the southern extremity of the republic was ordered to cease all land and sea communication with Rome.[5] Aistulf was advancing in a huge multi-pronged attack extending in an arc from Civitavecchia to Terracina. About half of the Roman republic was lost and Rome itself was severely threatened. In short, as Stephen II turned to King Pepin for aid against Aistulf,

---

[1] *VS II*, 10.442.

[2] Ibid., 10–11.442–443.

[3] Ibid., 15.444; *Pauli Cont. Tert.*, 32.209.

[4] *VS II*, 15.444.

[5] *Ben. Chron.*, 17.703. The *VS II* refers only in general terms to the new campaign. See 16.444, line 12. That the campaign occurred in the spring of 753 is based on *Cod. Dip. Long.*, 4.480–482, #678.

the latter launched what appears to have been a full-scale effort to conquer the republic.[6]

CHANGE IN ROYAL POLICY: AISTULF AND THE
CONQUEST OF ROME

In interpreting these developments one should first emphasize Stephen's solicitation of an interview with King Pepin as an act which was decidedly hostile to royal interests. As with Stephen's earlier unsuccessful negotiations with Byzantium, discussions between Stephen and Pepin could eventually lead to royal loss of the exarchate, the Pentapolis, and the southern duchies. To be sure, in requesting the talks with Pepin, the pope evidently made no specific mention of Carolingian aid against the Lombards and said nothing at all about the exarchate or the other places or of a Frankish invasion of Italy to force the monarchy to give them up. But, the nature of papal-Carolingian relations in 753 was such that Pepin might find himself campaigning in Italy if the pope pressed the issue forcefully enough. Papal claims upon the Carolingians were now much greater than they had been in Liutprand's day, certainly compelling enough to make a Carolingian war against Pavia not unthinkable. In deposing the Merovingian king and in seizing his throne, Pepin had received explicit support from Pope Zachary. Moreover, he had also been awarded both the Frankish crown and sacred anointing by Zachary's proxy in Francia, the great Bishop Boniface. In effect, the Carolingian family had become the legitimate and sacred ruling dynasty of the Franks through the recognition and anointing bestowed upon it by the vicar of St. Peter. Such conditions did not, of course, signify that Stephen II could automatically presume Pepin's service as advocate of papal interests. They did, however, mean that Pepin was in the papacy's debt and, more, that the Frankish monarchy was already engaged in a unique relationship with the holy see, as King Pepin was well aware.[7] If he could negotiate Pepin's acceptance of an explicit understanding of that relationship, and of his special role therein as the papacy's defender, Stephen might well be able to generate a Carolingian war against the Lombards, if that was his wish. It is not known to what degree Aistulf was cognizant of these possibilities implicit in Stephen's overtures to Pepin. But he is very apt to have seen the basic threat of Frankish intervention, making it likely that he perceived in the projected papal interview with Pepin an act which was at least as threatening to the Lombard kingdom as Stephen's recent negotiations with Byzantium.

In light of this judgment, and in view of Aistulf's treatment of the papacy in 752 and his apparent adherence to the Roman policy of King Liutprand,

[6] Bertolini, *Roma*, p. 521; Hodgkin, *Italy and Her Invaders.*, 7.180.

[7] For excellent discussions of various aspects of the development of the papal-Frankish association through 751 see Theodor Schieffer, "Angelsachsen und Franken, I: Bonifatius und Chrodegang;" idem., *Winifrid-Bonifatius und die christliche Grundlegung Europas*; H. Levison, *England and the Continent in the Eighth Century*, pp. 68–85; David Harry Miller, "The Motivation of Pepin's Italian Policy, 754–768," pp. 44–54, esp. pp. 50–53.

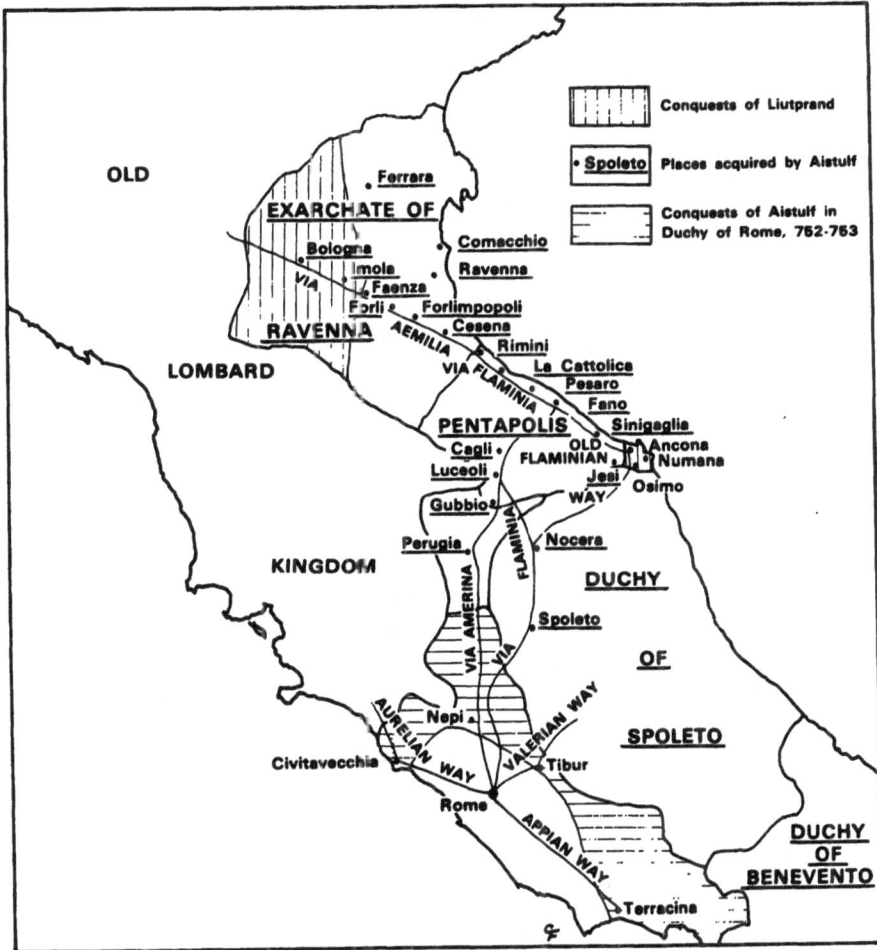

MAP. 4. The Lombard Kingdom of Italy in 751.

it may be suggested that the royal campaign of 753 was similar in motivation to the threats of October 752. In the latter instance Aistulf evidently had threatened to subject Rome and the papacy in order to bring about renewed papal acceptance of the 752 accord so that the Lombard Kingdom of Italy might be spared any disruptions stemming from the then-current papal negotiations with the empire. The Byzantine invasion never materialized, but a new danger arose when Stephen proposed a meeting with King Pepin. As Aistulf may well have viewed it, nothing had changed. The pope not only had not resumed adherence to the June accord but also had begun to arrange what he believed was another anti-royal combination. As a consequence, the need for him to harass the papacy in search of safety for his kingdom was still present. The only difference was that since the earlier hostility—the October threats—had not produced the desired papal neutrality, the royal menace would have to be intensified. The 753 campaign in the republic was perhaps the result. By taking Roman towns and by severing Roman contact with the rest of Italy through closure of several major roads, Aistulf evidently escalated the pressure in such a way that Stephen II could only believe that he was serious about the October threats. Specifically, the immediate royal objective was apparently to have the pope discontinue his negotiations with King Pepin. Thus it seems clear enough that Aistulf's treatment of the papacy in the spring of 753 was consistent with the Roman policy which the crown had apparently applied since the late 730s.

On closer examination, however, another interpretation may be more appropriate. The difficulty is that careful reflection upon the *nature* of the 753 campaign in comparison to those of previous apparent harassments administered by Aistulf and Liutprand leads to the conclusion that in 753 Aistulf abandoned the "traditional" Roman policy in favor of the new and radical course of trying to conquer Rome and win outright domination of the holy father. In sum, the royal policy toward the papacy was evidently transformed in 753.

The essential point in this connection is that the 753 campaign was of a different character from any of the previous eighth century royal aggressions. Prior to the 753 operation, neither Liutprand nor Aistulf had ever directly threatened the independence of Rome and its pontiff. Liutprand had wasted papal patrimonies, seized towns important to Rome's defense, and put on a brief show of force before the city's walls. These were partial measures which posed real dangers to Roman independence only in their presumed interpretation as such by the popes and in their potential for a siege had Liutprand been so inclined. The same was evidently true of Aistulf's two pre-753 hostilities, his seizures of the Roman towns in 752 and his threats of the following October. As with Liutprand's exercises, both menaces to Rome's autonomy were indirect and fairly distant, the one strategic and military and the other rhetorical. But, in contrast, the campaign of 753 had all the earmarks of a well-planned and systematic preparation for a real siege of Rome in that Aistulf was clearly trying to choke Rome off from all connection with Italy and the rest of the West. The closing of the Aurelian Way denied the Romans access to the western Alpine passes leading to Francia. The blockade of the Amerina and the Valerian Way prevented them from obtaining whatever help was available from the duchy of Spoleto or the exarchate, while the closing of the Appian Way kept them from enlisting support from the Byzantines in Naples. It thus seems entirely tenable that for the first time in the eighth century a Lombard king was preparing to besiege Rome and, hence, to conquer it and win some measure of domination over the pope.[8]

---

[8] A view close to this is offered by Hodgkin, *Italy and Her Invaders,* 7.180: "The old northward road by Perugia to the Exarchate, the *Via Flaminia,* was already closed. Now some stages on the southward road were occupied by the Lombards; the *ducatus Romae* was to be more effectively barred from all possible communication with the imperial governor at Naples; the pope might expect before long to see the Lombard standards on the southeastern horizon moving toward the Lateran itself."

Why did Aistulf take this unprecedented action? No answer may be certain, but several plausible ones may be offered. First, Aistulf had seen enough of Stephen II by early 753 to believe that he was his avowed and permanent enemy. In 752, in Aistulf's sight, he had faithlessly accepted the June accord. He then endeavored to incite the empire against the new Lombard kingdom. Failing in that, he had begun to maneuver himself into a position from which he could similarly try to activate the Carolingians. At no point after the breakdown of the 752 peace did Stephen seek its restoration, except briefly when he sent the Lombard abbots to Pavia while papal letters calling for Byzantine repossession of the exarchate were en route to Constantine V. The lone effort was thus insincere. Thus, it was probably clear to Aistulf that Stephen II would never accept peaceful relations with the monarchy as long as the Italian kingdom remained in place. The king apparently had to come to grips with reality: he had to recognize the pope as his lasting foe and treat him as such by making ready to besiege his city.

A related consideration which helps to account for the evident change in the nature of Aistulf's maltreatment of the papacy from harassment to conquest is that neither Liutprand's harassment nor that of Aistulf had produced permanent papal neutrality. At best, the previous antagonisms had led to only temporary curial impartiality such as that assumed by Zachary in 742 and by Stephen II in 752. The limitations of the harassment technique were especially evident in the period from the summer of 752 to the spring of 753. During this time, Pope Stephen urged imperial repossession of the exarchate and then sought to open presumably anti-royal negotiations with King Pepin in the wake and in the midst of royal harassments—first the Roman campaign of 752 and then the October threats of the same year. Contemplating this circumstance and its similar antecedents in Liutprand's reign, and given the likelihood of his conviction that Stephen was his permanent enemy, Aistulf is likely to have decided that new harassments designed to yield new curial neutrality would lead to nothing better than more temporary papal assumptions of that position. Thus, if he continued to maintain what appears to have been the standard eighth century royal policy toward the papacy, the future promised the necessity of repeated harassment of the holy see in defense of his kingdom. In short, it was clear by the winter of 752–753 that the apparent old technique of harassment had brought only limited success in the past and was not apt to achieve lasting papal neutrality in the future. The campaign of 753, with its systematic isolation of Rome, seems good evidence to the effect that he gave it up in favor of an actual conquest of the city.

The final explanation for Aistulf's movement from harassment to attempted conquest of Rome lies in appreciation of what the king stood to gain if the project were to succeed. If our previous estimates are reasonably precise, Aistulf wanted only one thing from the papacy—durable neutrality toward the Lombard Kingdom of Italy. Therefore, it seems logical to suppose that his principal objective in taking Rome was to force upon the pope the perpetual peace with Pavia which Stephen II had demonstrated he would not maintain voluntarily. Such a reality would be beneficial to Aistulf in several respects. It would free him from the troublesome burden of periodic harassment of the papacy, thus allowing him to proceed with the internal development of his realm. It would also liberate him from worry that the Byzantines or the Franks might descend upon Italy at papal urging to compel him to surrender the exarchate and thus ruin his kingdom. And finally, it would make the papacy his de facto ally rather than his autonomous enemy. There were of course dangers in a conquest of Rome to consider: the Franks might be speedily drawn into Italy and defeat him soundly; Stephen II might prove to be ungovernable, necessitating his removal, the appointment of another pontiff, and, consequently, very deep involvement in the tangled politics of Rome; and the Lombards might fail to capture Rome, leaving themselves weakened for retaliations which Stephen II would most likely essay, probably in conjunction with the powerful Carolingians. But successful conquest offered such promising rewards in contrast to the dismal failure and unattractive future of the policy of harassment that conquest may have been Aistulf's objective as he took the strategic Roman towns and controlled the republic's highways in the spring of 753.

In summary, reflection upon the events of early 753 strongly suggests that Aistulf at about that time transformed what appears to have been the monarchy's traditional eighth-century policy toward the papacy. Seeing that Stephen II was not inclined to agree to a resumption of the June accord, and fearing the papal appeal to the Carolingian monarchy, the king seems to have judged the old royal policy of harassment for the sake of gaining papal neutrality a failure and decided to pursue instead the novel course of capturing Rome. Only the initial stages of the project were visible in the campaign of 753 as Aistulf apparently isolated Rome in preparation for a siege. The king's ultimate goal in making the policy shift is uncertain, but it is likely to have been the acquisition of royal control over the papacy so that the pope could be made to live in steady peace with Pavia, that is, to maintain a constantly neutral policy toward the Lombard Kingdom of Italy. All in all, while a case may be made for interpreting the 753 campaign as a continuation of the crown's customary technique of harassment, it is much more likely that it was actually the first manifestation of a wholly new Roman policy.

What of the validity of the perception of Stephen II as a permanent enemy of the crown? Was it an accurate evaluation? One is inclined to conclude from his behavior up to the time of his Frankish initiative in early 753 the pope was indeed a consistent and determined royal foe. The proof lies in Stephen's activity after the establishment of the June 752 accord, arranged within a few months of his accession. First, although he was formally at peace with Aistulf, Stephen nevertheless worked hard to generate imperial military action designed to remove the exarchate and the other territories from Aistulf's grasp, thus threatening to destroy his Kingdom of Italy. Then the pope turned quickly to Pepin and the Franks when the empire proved unable to act. To Pepin, the initiative clearly resulted from the Lombard menance to Rome. But it would appear that Stephen II knew better, for the Lombard menace evidently arose because papal diplomacy had forced Aistulf into effecting it. Unprovoked by Aistulf, Pope Stephen by early 753 had spent most of the first year of his pontificate in activity which was obviously harmful to the Lombard kingdom.

### POPE STEPHEN II's CLAIM TO THE PAPAL REPUBLIC AND ESTABLISHMENT OF THE PAPAL-FRANKISH ASSOCIATION

As Aistulf continued his 753 spring campaign, the Frankish envoys solicited by Stephen II arrived at the Lateran, as the *Vita Stephani* puts it, "to fulfill all the wishes and petitions of the pope."[9] The envoys remained in Rome long enough to familiarize themselves with the Roman version of the Lombard-papal conflict,[10] and then returned to Francia bearing one papal letter addressed to Pepin and another to the Frankish nobility.[11] Both letters were phrased in general terms and carried essentially the same message: the papacy is in trouble and Pepin and his nobles ought to assist St. Peter and his vicar for the prosperity of their earthly lives and the welfare of their souls. Some time later, after the departure of the Frankish envoys, and amid continuing Lombard attack upon the Roman fortresses,[12] the Byzantine *silentiarius* John reappeared in Rome with the papal envoys who in 752 had accompanied him to Constantinople. John bore new imperial instructions for the pope, completely missing or ignoring the point that Stephen had lost all interest in political cooperation with the empire: the pope was to proceed in person to Aistulf and negotiate with him for the return of Ravenna and the other lost places to the empire. The pope had scarcely received the imperial directives when new Frankish *missi*, the important Bishop Chrodegang and Duke Autgarius, arrived with the welcome news that they were to bring the pope to King Pepin. Stephen thereupon assembled a suite composed of the Frankish envoys, the *silentiarius* John, some prominent Roman clerics, leading members of the curial or Lateran bureaucracy, and representatives of Rome's powerful military aristocracy. On October 14 the pope and this impressive body left for Pavia, where Stephen planned to talk to Aistulf.[13]

Arriving near Pavia, Stephen promptly sent envoys to the "most evil" king, asking him to restore the city of Ravenna and those of "the rest of the republic" which both he and his predecessors had taken.[14] Aistulf refused to discuss the matter with the envoys. Stephen countered by offering gifts and rewards if the king would cooperate, and even tried a personal interview with him. The Byzantine John also attempted to win the territorial concessions—for the emperor. But the angry Aistulf would yield

---

[9] *VS II*, 16.444: "omnem voluntatem ac petitionem praedicti sanctissimi papae adimplere." Dating of the embassy in the spring of 753 follows Duchesne, *VS II*, 457, n. 20.
[10] Ibid., 16.444.
[11] *CC*, #4 and 5, 487–88.
[12] *VS II*, 17.444; *Chron. Sal.* 3.472, lines 14–17.
[13] *VS II*. 18–19.445
[14] Ibid., 21.446, lines 1–8.

nothing to his unwanted guests. The Franks in Stephen's company thereupon persuaded Aistulf to let the pope proceed through Lombard territory
to Francia, and on 15 November Stephen left Pavia, now with a much
smaller suite limited to the two Franks, seven Roman clergy, and six high
curial administrators. The long winter journey to Francia occurred without
incident. Stephen crossed the Alps through the Mount Cenis pass and was
then escorted to the Carolingian winter court at Ponthion in Normandy
by Fulrad, the great abbot of St. Denis. At Ponthion Stephen was greeted
first by Pepin's young son, Charles, the future Charlemagne, and then by
King Pepin himself on 6 January 754.[15]

There is first a major point which appears to have gone unnoticed: in
asking that Aistulf restore the city of Ravenna and those of the exarchate
and "the rest of the republic" which both Aistulf and Liutprand had taken,
the pope was apparently claiming for the first time the existence of a papal
state which embraced not only the old imperial duchy of Rome but also
*all the former Byzantine territories in central Italy*. The source statement is
unclear, but it seems to yield the following understanding: the territory
rightfully belonged to the papacy, for it is all specified as belonging to the
"republic," which was the papal term for property belonging to the papacy
as distinct from the empire; the territory, although it was in Lombard hands
at the moment and had earlier belonged to the empire, was actually a
pontifical possession since it was to be *restored* to the papacy, implying that
the original ownership was papal; finally, the specific territory claimed by
Stephen must have been the exarchate, the Pentapolis, Perugia, and the
duchy of Rome, for those were the conquests of Aistulf and Liutprand—
apart from the duchies of Spoleto and Benevento, which were clearly not
at issue. While Stephen's assertion was obviously revolutionary in scope,
it was nevertheless an outgrowth of eighth-century papal traditions. As we
have seen, Gregory II and Gregory III began creation of the papal state by
viewing some non-patrimonial territory around Rome to be under papal
rather than imperial jurisdiction. Under Zachary the notion of a papal
republic became sharper as he received the four disputed towns from Liutprand in 742 and made a tour of the republic's "borders" after the Terni
settlement in 742. And, it was Zachary who first implied that the republic
was not confined to the limits of the old Byzantine duchy of Rome by
demanding Cesena in the exarchate from Liutprand and receiving part of
it. All the precedents were therefore established for Stephen II:[16] there was
a Roman state under papal auspices which was separate from Byzantium
and extended beyond the old imperial duchy. What Stephen did in 753 in
Pavia was to make an initial definition of the republic's limits, and indicate
that the bulk of its territory was the former imperial holdings in the exarchate and the Pentapolis, regions which were now possessed by the Lombard monarchy.

---

[15] These events are covered in the remarkably detailed *LP* recitation, *VS II*, 20.445–25.447.
[16] As perceived by Miller, "The Roman Revolution," p. 124.

The implications of the papal claim for the monarchy were very severe. If the republic which was envisioned by Stephen II actually came into being the Lombard Kingdom of Italy would cease to exist. The loss of the exarchate, the Pentapolis, and Perugia to the kingdom would rob it of its central districts, separate the Spoletan and Beneventan south from the north, and thereby invite renewed autonomy for the duchies and confine royal rule to the north. To Aistulf, Stephen planned nothing less than destruction of the Lombard kingdom through its dismemberment. The danger of the papal claim lay in the possibility that it would be actively supported by Pepin and the Franks, to whom Stephen was headed as he voiced the claim in Pavia. Aistulf could hardly accept the papal assertion and Stephen knew that, thus suggesting that the pope's negotiation with the king at Pavia was really an announcement to the king that there is a papal state in central Italy and the vicar of St. Peter is on his way to Francia to obtain Carolingian aid in bringing it to life; in the process, the Lombard Kingdom of Italy will have to be dissolved. It would appear that Aistulf must have been severely shaken by the revelation.

Stephen's mission to Pepin was most emphatically an independent papal enterprise,[17] even though John the *silentiarius* may have been under the impression that it was undertaken on behalf of the empire as the emperor had requested. But a papal embassy it was, for Stephen made the territorial claim in the name of the papacy, not the empire, and when he left Pavia to resume the journey to Francia, John was pointedly no longer in the papal suite. The embassy was thus an exclusively papal party, a fact which was underscored by the removal of even Roman nobles from it.[18]

Upon his arrival at Ponthion on 6 January 754, Pope Stephen was greeted by King Pepin, his wife and sons, and a number of nobles. The Frankish king dismounted, prostrated himself before the pope, arose and kissed the papal stirrup, and then led the pope's horse for some distance, thus symbolically serving as the papal groom. The entire group then moved on to the royal villa at Ponthion, where Stephen made it clear to Pepin why he had come to Francia.[19] According to the papal *Vita*, Stephen tearfully begged Pepin's assistance

so that the cause of St. Peter and the republic of the Romans might be aided by the making of a treaty of peace. At once the king promised the most blessed pope, under oath, that he would obey his orders and admonitions, and, as soon as he could convene a public assembly, would as much as he was able return the exarchate and the rights and places of the republic.[20]

[17] Most importantly, see Miller, Ibid., pp. 121–129.
[18] For views holding that Stephen II was acting on behalf of Byzantium, see C. Bayet, "Remarques sur la caractère et les conséquences du voyage d'Etienne III en France." pp. 89–94; H. Dannenbauer, "Das römische Reich und der Westen vom Tode Justinian bis zum Tode Karls des Grossen."
[19] VS II, 24–26.447.
[20] Ibid., 27.447–448: "ibidem b. papa praefatum christianissimum regem lacrimabiliter deprecatus est ut per pacis foedera causam b. Petri et reipublice Romanorum disponeret. Qui de praesenti iureiurando eundem beatissimum papam satisfecit omnibus eius mandatis et

Having received Pepin's assurance of Carolingian support, Stephen retired to the monastery of St. Denis near Paris to pass the winter. Then, in the spring or summer of 754 Stephen anointed Pepin and his two sons, Charles and Carloman, kings of the Franks, and gave all three the title *patricius Romanorum* in a great ceremony at St. Denis.[21] At some time after the coronation, Pepin held a public assembly at Quierzy where, wrote the papal biographer, Pepin

gathered all the nobility of his kingdom, informed them of the pope's holy commands, and, in agreement with them [the nobles], decided to accomplish with the help of Christ that which he had recently agreed to [at Ponthion] with the pope.[22]

In other words, the Ponthion agreement in which Pepin undertook to "return the exarchate and the rights and places of the republic," obey the pope's "orders and admonishments," and form a peace treaty or *pactum* with the papacy had been accepted by the Frankish nation.

In the meantime, diplomatic developments were under way. Perhaps even before the Quierzy assembly King Aistulf attempted to dissuade Pepin from advancing into Italy by sending him as a Lombard royal envoy his own brother, Carloman, who had abdicated in 747 as mayor of Austrasia and taken up the life of a monk at Monte Cassino; Carloman, who according to the *Vita Stephani* was acting under the direct orders of Aistulf,[23] implored Pepin not to assist the "redemption" of the holy republic. But thankfully, one reads, Pepin would not listen to his brother. Nor was Carloman permitted to return to Italy, instead being restricted to a monastery where he soon died.[24] At some point shortly after the Quierzy assembly, Pepin began an effort to persuade Aistulf to accept the pope's wishes without a Franco-Lombard war, that is, Pepin requested Aistulf to surrender "the exarchate and the rights and places of the republic" to St. Peter and live in peace with the pope. Three separate Frankish embassies were sent to Aistulf, each one offering heavy bribes if he would comply. Each time the overtures were rejected, however, leaving Pepin no choice but to move from diplomacy to military action.[25] In the spring of 755 Pepin convoked another public assembly, gathered the Frankish army, and prepared to set out for

---

ammonitionibus sese totis nisibus oboedire, et ut illi placitum fuerit exarchatum Ravennae et reipublice iura seu loca reddere modis omnibus." See also *Chron. Sal.*, 4.473.

[21] Stephen's *LP* biography says only that "hisdem christianissimus Pippinus rex ad eodem sanctissimo papa . . . cum duobus filiis suis reges uncti sunt." *VS II*, 27.448, lines 6–7. But Frankish sources record that the royal and *patricius* titles were bestowed simultaneously. *Chronicon Moissiacense*, p. 293, lines 15–18; *Annales Mettenses*, p. 332, lines 6–9 and *Clausula de Pippini in francorum regem consecratione, Recueil des historiens de Gaul et de la France*, 5.9–10. After 754 the Frankish rulers were addressed in the papal letters as *patricius Romanorum* as well as *rex Francorum*.

[22] *VS II*, 29.448.

[23] According to *Annales Laureshamenses* (p. 10), however, Carloman acted at the behest of his abbot. But, the *Ben. Chron.* (19.705) says that the abbot's action was a response to pressure from Aistulf so that Carloman might go to Pepin "ad dissipanda consilia Stephani pape, ut Francis in Italia ingredi non deberet."

[24] *VS II*, 30.448–449.

[25] Ibid., 31.449. See also *Fredegarii Chronicon*, 36.104 and *Chron. Sal.*, 5.473.

Italy. There was a last attempt to gain peaceful compliance by Aistulf. Piously asserting that he hoped to avoid the shedding of Christian blood, Pope Stephen urged Pepin to call once more upon Aistulf for a peaceful settlement. Pepin readily did so, but the effort was no more successful than the others. It was probably in March or April 755, that the Frankish host began to move across the Alpine passes into Italy.[26]

The foregoing events from the Ponthion meeting to the departure of the Frankish army for Italy more than a year later require some careful analysis. Preliminary remarks are in order, however. The events at issue have proven extraordinarily difficult to interpret in themselves, in relation to one another, and in conjunction with other mid-eighth century developments in both Francia and Italy. The 753–754 doings in Francia, often referred to as the papal-Frankish alliance or association of 754, have attracted the attention of many scholars working on various aspects of the problem,[27] such as the relationship between the Ponthion promise and the Quierzy assembly,[28] the nature and meaning of the papal republic,[29] the significances of the 754 coronation and the *patricius Romanorum* title,[30] and Pepin's motivations for accepting the alliance.[31] But little interpretive consensus has been reached on any aspect of the alliance subject, and no authority has yet ventured a comprehensive treatment of the problem in all its dimensions. The following analysis will not attempt that either, being as strictly confined as possible to those aspects of the alliance which have either direct or reasonably close bearing upon the relationship between the Lombard monarchy and the papacy.

The most noticeable development was that a treaty of peace, the *pactum*, had been established between two states, the Frankish monarchy and the papacy, or more appropriately, between Francia and Rome or the papal republic.[32] No specification of duration is found, but the implication of perpetuity is clear in the involvement of Pepin's heirs in the arrangements.

---

[26] *VS II*, 32–35.449–450.

[27] Noteworthy comprehensive treatments are Erich Caspar, *Pippin und die römische Kirche*; Johannes Haller, "Die Karolinger und das Papsttum" and Walter Ullmann, *Papal Government in the Middle Ages*, pp. 54–86.

[28] See especially Karl Heldmann, "Kommendation und Königschutz im Vertrage von Ponthion;" Percy Ernst Schramm, "Das Versprechen Pippins und Karls des Grossen für die römische Kirche."

[29] Levillain, "L'avènement de la dynastie carolingienne et les origines de l'état pontifical"; Caspar, *Pippin und die romische Kirche*. Miller, "The Roman Revolution," pp. 121–129; Ottorino Bertolini, "Il problema della origini del potere temporale dei papi nei suoi presupposti teoretici iniziali; il concetto di 'restituto' nelle prime cessioni territoriali (756–757) alla Chiesa di Roma."

[30] Miller, "The Roman Revolution", F. L. Ganshof, "Note sur les origines byzantines du titre 'patricius Romanorum;' " pp. 261–282; Ullmann, *Papal Government*, pp. 67–68; Léon Levillain, "De l'autenticité de la *clausula de unctione Pippini*;" Josef Déer, "Zum Patricius Romanorum Titel Karl des Grossen."

[31] See especially David Harry Miller, "The Motivation of Pepin's Italian Policy, 754–768," pp. 44–54; Johannes Haller, "Die Karolinger und das Papsttum"; Martin Lintzel, "Der *Codex Carolinus* und die Motive von Pippins Italienpolitik;" Karl Rodenberg, *Pippin, Karlmann und Pabst Stephan II*; Robert Holtzmann, *Die Italienpolitik der Merowinger und des König Pippins*.

[32] Very clear on the public aspect of the papal side of the relationship is Miller, "The Roman Revolution," p. 125.

The obligations of the *pactum* were evidently unwritten but are visible in the principles of the various agreements worked out during the year. On the one side, the pope, by anointing and crowning Pepin and his sons, indicated that henceforth Carolingian enemies were papal enemies,[33] and that the spiritual endowments of the Holy See would be applied to Carolingian projects which were presently in progress. The most notable of these were the reform of the Frankish church which contributed to strengthening of Carolingian rule in Francia, and establishment of the Christian church in the Germanic areas contiguous to Francia, areas which Pepin was attempting to conquer.[34] The Carolingian undertakings in the *pactum* are somewhat clearer than the papal. First, in accepting the *patricius Romanorum* title as an integral component of the royal title, Pepin accepted a patrician function as a royal function.[35] That function was to serve the papacy and Rome, that is, the papal republic, as its military protector.[36] In this context, what Stephen II envisioned, and what Pepin first promised to do at Ponthion, was to obtain for the republic the exarchate, the Pentapolis, and Perugia from the Lombards. As one scholar puts it, "The primary function of the alliance, and of Pepin within it, was to protect the Roman state and redeem the lands it claimed from the Lombards."[37] The peace treaty, more appropriately a papal-Frankish institutional association, thus offered King Aistulf the most difficult problem of his reign.

On the surface, at least, the papacy was the dominant partner in the new relationship, for Pepin accepted papal initiatives which made him and his institution in some way dependent upon the papacy.[38] For example, Pepin symbolically served as the pope's groom when Stephen arrived at Ponthion, thereby implying royal submission to the papacy at the outset. Much more significant was the coronation of Pepin and his sons. All three received their crowns from the pope, thereby in effect accepting them as a papal grant, an understanding which had its roots in Pepin's 751 request for and receipt of authorization for the deposition of Childeric III, and had an important anticipation in Pepin's coronation as Frankish king in 751 by Bishop Boniface, the papal agent in Francia. Further, the patrician protection service was to be undertaken *for* the papacy, a duty of a subordinate to a superior.[39] Finally, there is the Ponthion promise, made at the first conversation between Stephen and Pepin, that Pepin would in all things obey

---

[33] Miller, "Motivation of Pepin's Italian Policy," p. 52; Schieffer, "Angelsachsen und Franken, I," pp. 1446–1447.

[34] See especially Schieffer, "Angelsachsen," and idem., *Winfrid-Bonifatius und die Christliche Grundlegung Europas;* Miller, "Motivation of Pepin's Italian Policy," p. 50–52.

[35] Ullmann, *Papal Government,* pp. 67–69, 73–74.

[36] Miller, "The Roman Revolution," p. 127. Miller (p. 126) contends that as *patricius Romanorum* Pepin was an officer of the papal republic.

[37] Ibid., p. 127.

[38] This approach contrasts sharply with the argument, not widely held, that Stephen commended himself to Pepin, making him in some degree the king's feudal subordinate. See, for example, Peter Rassow, "Pippin und Stephan II."

[39] Miller, "The Roman Revolution," p. 126

the pope.[40] There was a clear theoretical dependence of the Frankish monarchy upon the papacy, or in reality upon St. Peter,[41] a condition which, as will become apparent, was both consistent with the general nature of the papal-Frankish relationship and a vital factor in shaping the future development of Lombard-papal relations in Italy.

The problem of motivations in the establishment of the papal-Frankish association is naturally difficult, but at least two paramount considerations seem to have confronted the papacy. First, Stephen II and his advisers had reached the point in 753–754 where practical realities had to conform to papal ideology.[42] As noted earlier, even before the eighth century the papacy had posited the Gelasian world view that the emperor is subordinate to the pope in the governance of Christian society, the pope commanding (always for Christendom's moral and spiritual welfare) while the emperor wields the secular sword for the maintenance of order and the enforcement of the pope's commands. The seventh and eighth-century Italian and papal revolts against the empire, Gregory III's excommunication of the emperor, the accompanying papal withdrawal from the empire, and the failure of Zachary or Stephen II to re-associate the papacy with Byzantium all presented the pope with a serious ideological dilemma: there was no emperor for proper assistance of the pope in the governance of Christendom. Stephen II came to Francia in part to rectify this shortcoming. In crowning Pepin as Frankish king and *patricius Romanorum*, Stephen transferred the ideological union of pope and emperor from Constantinople to Francia, making the Frankish king the pope's secular subordinate in the governance of Christian society in place of the Byzantine emperor.[43] The service function here bestowed may well explain the meaning of the *patricius Romanorum* office and title, if one may, as some have, presume that Roman = Christian.[44] *Patricius Romanorum* may thus carry the ideological inference of the Frankish king's being the executor of papal commands for Christian society. In sum, part of Stephen II's motivation for establishing the papal-Frankish association was to complete the papal dissociation from Byzantium and forge a new papal association with the Carolingian monarchy, thereby satisfying the highest requirements of the papacy's world view and accepting the actual historical rupture in papal-Byzantine relations.[45]

The second papal motivation was clearly to obtain possession of the exarchate, the Pentapolis, Perugia and the Roman countryside in its entirety.[46] Simply put, Stephen wanted Pepin's help in establishing a greatly

---

[40] See Karl Heldmann, "Kommendation und Konigschutz im Vertrage von Ponthion," passim; J. Haller, "Die Karolinger und das Papsttum," pp. 67–68.

[41] William M. Daly, "St. Peter: An Architect of the Carolingian Empire," pp. 55–69, esp. pp. 59–61 and 68–69.

[42] The following is based on Miller, "The Roman Revolution," esp. pp. 119–133. See also Ullmann, *Papal Government*, pp. 48–86.

[43] Miller, "The Roman Revolution," p. 128.

[44] Ullmann, *Papal Government*, pp. 64–65.

[45] Miller, "The Roman Revolution," pp. 131–132.

[46] Clearly seen in ibid., p. 124.

expanded papal state, a substantial republic, all of it land which had belonged to Byzantium prior to its conquest by the Lombard kings. Having articulated the claim to the expanded republic for the first time at Pavia just before going to Francia, Stephen made it part of the Ponthion promise at the outset, had Pepin refer to it in the public statement at Quierzy, and doubtless saw to it that Pepin's envoys pounded the theme home to Aistulf after the Quierzy commitment. Surely the foremost expectation of the pope when Pepin left for Italy in early 755 was that the exarchate and the other territories would all soon be taken from Aistulf and lodged in papal hands. The territorial motivation was consistent with the ideological concern, for the territory would be acquired by the papacy in the context of a war against the devil-inspired Aistulf, who was seeking to capture Rome. That is, the territorial gain would follow from Pepin's new ideological function as protector of the papal executive and executor of the pope's orders for Christian welfare. Moreover, there is reason to suppose that the former Byzantine territory involved, that is, the papal republic, was perceived in Rome as the Roman empire, the jurisdictional reality associated with the revolutionary papal ideology and Pepin's function as *patricius Romanorum*.[47] In terms of ideology, Stephen enlisted Pepin to restore the Roman empire.

It should be emphasized that the papal-Frankish association was an arrangement which was clearly hostile to the Lombard monarchy. From it the papacy derived a permanent military protector in Italy, a specifically anti-royal thrust in that Aistulf was the only papal enemy of the moment.[48] Moreover, the anti-royal protectorship was obviously meant to be long-term, for the same duty was assumed by Carloman and Charles, the royal sons, in their receipt of the patriciate. But most significantly, one of Stephen's principal objectives in the formation of the association was the acquisition of the exarchate, the Pentapolis, and Perugia, the loss of which would cause dissolution of Aistulf's Lombard Kingdom of Italy. And, if the kingdom was once dissolved by creation of an expanded papal republic from old royal territory, it would be most difficult for Pavia to reassemble it because of continuing Frankish obligation to protect the papacy, in this case meaning defense against any royal effort to regain the exarchate and the rest. For Aistulf's point of view, a more hostile and sinister arrangement could not have been devised by Stephen II and Pepin.

Why, given the previous Carolingian history of cooperation and peaceful relations with King Liutprand, did Pepin allow Stephen II to enmesh him in a set of agreements which promised to visit destruction upon the Lombard kingdom? A variety of answers have been given,[49] but one in particular

---

[47] Ibid., pp. 124–125.

[48] Two sources are very candid regarding the anti-Lombard character of the service as envisioned by the pope. *Fred. Chron.*, p. 104: ". . . Stephen asked for his [Pepin's] help against the Lombards and their king, Aistulf, so that he might thereby be freed from their oppressions and double dealing. An end might thus be put to the tribute or gifts which, contrary to every right, they had been demanding of the Romans." *Chron. Moissiac.*, p. 293: [Stephanus] Pippinum regem obsecrans ut se et populum Ramanum de manu Langobardorum et superbi Haistulphi servitio liberaret."

[49] See Miller, "Motivations of Pepin's Italian Policy," for discussion of the views.

seems most suitable.[50] In the 740s, while Pepin was mayor of Neustria and Carloman mayor in Austrasia, strong moral and practical bonds were formed between Francia and the papacy based upon the support of both rulers for the great Anglo-Saxon Benedictine mission in Germany and the reform of the Frankish church, both of which projects revolved around St. Boniface, the papal agent in Francia. By the late 740s, after Carloman's abdication, Pope Zachary and Pepin were in direct contact and when in 750 Pepin approached Zachary for papal sanction of Pepin's deposition of the Merovingian king and his own accession, both were readily granted. The 751 accession of Pepin was a matter of direct Carolingian-papal association, for Pepin was anointed Frankish king by Bishop Boniface. Thus, there was by 751 ingrained in Pepin and therefore in the Frankish monarchy an ultramontane or Rome-oriented perspective, rooted in royal commitment to the Rome-inspired German mission and ecclesiastical reform in Francia and consecrated by Boniface's anointing of the king. What happened in 753–754 during Stephen II's visit to Francia was simply the effecting of a number of logical extensions of the previously-developed Frankish ultramontane orientation, most importantly for our purposes in the matter of Pepin's *patricius Romanorum* office and service. Long devoted to serving St. Peter in Francia, and united with St. Peter by sacred bonds, Pepin now simply expanded his service to Italy, acting against Aistulf not really as his enemy but as military protector of St. Peter's republic. Pepin, in a word, could only place adherence to Stephen's request for Carolingian war against Aistulf, who was St. Peter's frightful enemy, far ahead of the previous Carolingian friendship with Pavia.

As Stephen presented the situation, of course, Aistulf was indeed a frightful enemy of St. Peter. Aistulf, Pepin was told, is on the verge of besieging Rome, something no Lombard king has ever done before, making him an especially insidious enemy. He has savagely attacked the republic, taken much of its Roman land, and utterly refuses to negotiate, as is clear from his recent refusal at Pavia to even discuss matters. He is pestiferous, evil. As observed, Aistulf in reality probably wanted no war with Rome, and attacked the republic and the city only because he felt that the safety of his Kingdom of Italy demanded capture of the city in order to compel the pope to accept peace with Pavia by direct and personal pressure. Also, as noted, it appears that by negotiating for imperial arms in Italy and then negotiating with Pepin in 753, Stephen II provoked Aistulf into this new and extreme position. The point is that Stephen II had a wretched situation to report to Pepin and play upon for aid at Ponthion. Pepin did not require it, but a terrible crisis was nevertheless available for his contemplation.

Some analysis of the Frankish-Lombard diplomatic exchanges of the period is also required. As for Aistulf's dispatch of Carloman to Francia, that is explained by Aistulf's realization during or just after Stephen II's stop at Pavia on the way to Pepin's court that Rome was suddenly claiming

---

possession of the center of his Italian kingdom—the exarchate and the other former Byzantine places—and that Stephen was going to Francia to enlist Pepin in making good the claim. Aistulf hoped that Carloman could dissuade him from his enterprise, perhaps in some form of cooperation with Austrasian nobles who had reason to be hostile toward Pepin.[51]

The other instance of diplomacy prior to Pepin's 755 invasion of Italy, the three Carolingian missions to Aistulf after Quierzy, is more difficult to understand. The embassies, it will be recalled, urged Aistulf to comply peacefully with Stephen's demand for papal possession of the exarchate and the other places. That Pepin sent envoys on three separate occasions, and had them offer substantial bribes to Aistulf, suggests something more than a perfunctory exercise as a prelude to an inevitable military campaign. Rather, Pepin seems to have wanted genuinely to avoid war in Italy if Aistulf would accommodate the papal concerns without it.[52] While the Frank was clearly anxious to cooperate with Rome for the reasons cited earlier, he was also doubtless apprehensive about a long campaign in Italy, perhaps unsure about Austrasian noble resistance,[53] and probably hopeful that he would not have to repudiate the heritage of his father's good relations with Liutprand.[54] Aistulf's reasons for refusing Pepin's diplomacy have not been determined, but it may be suggested that they lay in considering that even partial compliance with the papal territorial demands would do significant damage to the Lombard Kingdom of Italy. There was only one way to resolve the problem presented by the papal-Frankish association: force the papacy to abandon its claims, leaving Pavia in possession of the demanded territories. That resolution, of course, meant that Aistulf would have to risk both Frankish invasion of his kingdom and defeat the invasion if it occurred.

### Pepin's First Italian Campaign: Toward Creation of the Papal Republic and Dismemberment of the Kingdom of Italy

After April 755 there were no further Frankish envoys to Aistulf. Pepin took his army across the Alps and met first Lombard resistance at the Alpine *clusae* or pass mouths where Aistulf had stationed his forces after learning that the invasion had begun.[55] Presumably, as Pepin entered the north

---

[51] Holtzmann, *Die Italienpolitik*, pp. 37–38 contends that there was an alliance between Aistulf and Austrasian nobles who supported Carloman's sons in preference to Pepin. For criticism of this view see Miller, "Motivations of Pepin's Italian Policy," p. 50. See also Rodenberg, *Pippin, Karlmann*, pp. 22–23; Levellain, L'avènement de la dynastie," pp. 263–264. However, Pepin may have been frightened enough by the prospect of trouble from Carloman and his supporters to arrange the coronation of himself and his sons by Stephen II. David S. Sefton, *The Pontificate of Hadrian I (772–795): Papal Theory and Political Reality in the Reign of Charlemagne*, p. 18.
[52] Perceived by Norton Downs, "The Role of the Papacy in the Coronation of Charlemagne," p. 13.
[53] See above, n. 51.
[54] Miller, "Motivations of Pepin's Italian Policy," pp. 45–46; *Einhardi Vita Caroli*, p. 416.
[55] The most detailed contemporary account of the invasion is *Fred. Chron.*, 37.104–106. See also *VS II*, 35–36.450; *Chron. Sal.*, 474; *Ann. Ein.*, p. 13. An excellent secondary account is Levellain, "L'avènement de la dynastie," pp. 272–280.

Aistulf suspended his operations around Rome. The *clusae* fighting was over quickly, with the Lombard forces yielding the plain to Pepin and concentrating their strength in the stout fortress of Pavia. Pepin followed and put the city under siege, during which operation the pope arrived from Francia to keep the Frankish host company. In a fairly short time Aistulf indicated that he would discuss a settlement, and the pope urged Pepin to offer terms of surrender so that the flow of Christian blood might come to a speedy end. In the negotiations which followed, agreements were reached, as the papal *Vita* puts it, between Franks, Romans, and Lombards which were tantamount to a peace treaty. Aistulf and all of his nobles swore to maintain peace with both the Franks and the Romans and "restore the city of Ravenna with its various cities."[56] No statement specifies to whom the restoration was to be made, but given the recent developments in Francia and the campaign as a service of the *patricius Romanorum* to the republic, the restoration could only have been to the papacy. To insure that Aistulf would actually effect the pledged return, Pepin took a number of Lombard hostages, presumably important nobles.[57] Pepin may also have required Aistulf to pay an indemnity as well as annual tribute,[58] suggesting that the Lombard was being made to recognize dependence of the Lombard kingdom upon the Frankish.[59] In the expectation that Aistulf would soon comply with the territorial requirements, Pepin gathered his army and returned to Francia.

For Aistulf, the 755 treaty revolved around the central requirement that he restore Ravenna and its dependencies to the papacy. If he did that, the other two treaty components would be fulfilled: there would be peace between all parties—Lombard, papal, and Frankish—and Aistulf would be demonstrating his dependence upon Pepin by obeying Pepin's order to surrender the territories. By the same token, if Aistulf refused to give them up, he would both repudiate the tripartite peace and deny the required Frankish suzerainty over Pavia.

As Aistulf reflected upon the territorial demand of the treaty, he knew very well that compliance would mean destruction of the Lombard Kingdom of Italy. At issue were the exarchate, the Pentapolis, and Perugia. If he gave up these places to the pope as he had promised, the integrity of the Lombard kingdom would end as its central districts would become the expanded republic of St. Peter and the rest split into two parts. Of these, the ducal portion—the duchies of Spoleto and Benevento—would naturally again become independent of Pavia, for the crown, having lost the direct access to them furnished by the highways of the central districts, would be unable to suppress the autonomist powers which would naturally surface anew in the duchies. If Aistulf accepted the treaty terms his kingdom would

---

[56] *VS II*, 37–38.450–451: "reditturum civitatem Ravennantium cum diversis civitatibus." Similar language is *Pauli Cont. Tert.*, 39.210.

[57] *VS II*, 37.451. See also *Ann. Ein.*, 13; *Ann. Lauriss.*, p. 12.

[58] *Chron. Moissiac.*, p. 293.

[59] *Fred. Chron.*, 37.106. According to this source Aistulf recognized the Franks as having overlordship over him.

shrink to its former dimensions, the northern regions only, the same area held by Liutprand before he began the royal project to create the Italian kingdom in 726–727. The long-term prospect was no better, for once the kingdom was dismembered it would be difficult if not impossible to reassemble. Reconstitution would require Lombard military action to force the papacy from its new republic and that action would logically prompt new Frankish intervention against Pavia to protect the republic—and deny reunification of the Lombard kingdom. In sum, Aistulf knew that if he complied with the 755 Pavia treaty he would pull apart the very kingdom which he himself had done so much to establish.

Between October 752 and the spring of 755 there had been a fundamental Italian change. The relationship between the Lombard monarchy and the papacy, which had been basically pacific since the reign of Agilulf in the early seventh century, became a matter of intense hostility. Supporting the papacy was the Frankish monarchy, uninvolved in Italian affairs since the late sixth century but now committed in Italy as military protector of the papacy and an officer of the papal state. The latter, embracing the duchies of Rome, Perugia, and the Pentapolis and the exarchate, may have been the most striking novelty, linked as it was with the complex process of Stephen II's ideological disengagement of the papacy from the Byzantine empire, association with the Carolingians, and formation of the papal-Frankish alliance. For Aistulf, each of these novelties presented another, prospective failure of the Lombard Kingdom of Italy, which, despite problems, had been an Italian feature for a quarter century. A set of new conditions was thus taking shape, pointing toward the eventual establishment of a new Italian *modus vivendi*. The latter had not yet jelled, and until it did, Aistulf would naturally do what he could to assure a place within it for the Lombard Kingdom of Italy.

# V. FROM NADIR TO RECOVERY

L ate in 755, without having turned over a bit of territory to Stephen
II,[1] Aistulf unleashed a fierce attack upon the papal republic and
then in January, 756, put Rome itself under siege.[2] Pope Stephen,
writing to King Pepin requesting aid against these aggressions, reported
both operations in vivid detail. Homes, churches, and monasteries around
Rome were looted and burned. Tenants of the *domus cultae*, the papacy's
agricultural estates on the patrimony, were taken captive or put to death.
The stronghold of Narni and several other Roman outposts were seized.
Soon, Rome was surrounded from every quarter. Tuscan troops assaulted
the Porta Portuensis and the gate of St. Pancratius along the Tiber. Con-
tingents under Aistulf himself beset the northwestern walls. Beneventan
units completed the encirclement, besieging the gates of St. John and St.
Paul and seeking penetration of the southern fortifications. Rome's only
connection with the outside was the Tiber, upon whose waters papal envoys
set out in late February to Francia in search of relief from King Pepin. Day
after day, night after night for nearly three months, Aistulf pressed the
attack. Then, in April, Pepin answered the pope's pleas, bringing an army
to Italy for a second time and causing Aistulf to retreat from Rome to try
to protect the northern districts of his kingdom.

### AISTULF'S 756 SIEGE OF ROME: A DESPERATE GAMBLE

Although it was unsuccessful, Aistulf's siege was a major event in that
it was the first royal siege of the holy city ever undertaken and was obviously an important matter in the royal-papal relationship. In the modern
scholarship one finds only a vague assumption that Aistulf besieged Rome
in order to annex it to his kingdom or at least establish some sort of protectorate over it.[3] Let us investigate this and other explanations of the 756
siege of Rome.

---

[1] One scholar (Bertolini, *Roma,* p. 554) suggests that Aistulf interpreted the 755 treaty to
mean that he was to maintain peace with the empire, giving him freedom under the treaty
to wage war against independent Rome. This may have given Aistulf an excuse for not yielding
the exarchate and the other places—the treaty was not yet ratified by the emperor, and until
it was, no territory had to be transferred. Ibid. The view seems dubious owing to disagreement
with demonstrable political realities.

[2] CC, # 8, 494–496. Other accounts of the siege and its corollary ravaging of the republic are
*VS II*, 61.451–452; *Chron. Sal.*, 474. For secondary accounts see Bertolini, *Roma*, pp. 558–568;
Hodgkin, *Italy and Her Invaders*, 7.209–215; Llewellyn, *Rome in the Dark Ages*, pp. 213–215.

[3] See the quotations in n. 46 of Ch. 3 above. See also Duchesne, *VS II*, n. 11, 457; Miller,
"The Roman Revolution," p. 114.

The argument that Aistulf was attempting to conquer Rome so that he could include it in the Lombard kingdom or exercise protectorate over it has appeal in that it seems to represent a logical culmination of the royal treatment of Rome from October 752 onward. In October 752, it will be recalled, Aistulf issued the threats to exact tribute from the Romans and to make them his subjects. A few months later he threatened to massacre them all and then proceeded to overrun much of the papal republic and seize the various fortresses, an action which blockaded Rome and made a siege appear both imminent and inevitable. Against this background, the 756 siege appears to have been simply the final step, the fulfillment of 752 threats after the interruption of Pepin's invasion and the Pavia treaty. In sum, Aistulf's aim in attempting the 756 siege may have been Rome's incorporation into the Lombard kingdom or her reduction to the status of a Lombard client, for either one seems implicit in the nature of the king's dealing with Rome since late 752.

But, Aistulf's threats and subsequent operations against Rome evidently aimed to give Pavia control of Rome so that the king could force Stephen II into abandoning his collaboration with the Byzantines and the Franks which he saw as lethal to his continued maintenance of the Kingdom of Italy. Neither annexation nor protectorate seems visible in this objective. Thus, the interpretation that the 756 siege was motivated by Lombard desires to render Rome in some way dependent on Pavia because such desires were a natural outgrowth of a long-term interest seems untenable. If the annexation-protectorship motivation applied in 756, it must have been new at that time.

Is it likely that Aistulf suddenly in 755–756 adopted the novel aim of wanting to have Rome in his kingdom or establishing a protectorship over it? It might have been very possible for him to capture Rome and declare it to be part of his kingdom or to make it in some way dependent upon him. But, there was a good chance that such a situation, whichever it was, would not last. In all probability Stephen II would be able to generate a new campaign by Pepin, particularly given the Lombard failure to fulfill any of the 755 treaty obligations—which Pepin *had* to see fulfilled by virtue of his *patricius Romanorum* status. Pepin would come again, and in the end Aistulf would have to relinquish his victory over Rome and surrender the territories to the pope as originally demanded. In sum, it was doubtful that Aistulf could maintain Roman conquest or protectorate because of the Frankish support of Rome which was inherent in the papal-Frankish alliance, making it unlikely that either annexation or protectorate was a new royal interest in 756 leading to the siege of that year.[4]

Further objection to the view that the siege was generated by royal annexation or protectorate interests arises from its ignorance of the central

---

[4] Aistulf clearly dreaded Pepin's reappearance; when he besieged Rome he did so in January, when the snow in the Alpine passes would both block Roman communication with Francia and prevent passage of Frankish troops into Italy. Bertolini, *Roma*, p. 558. On Lombard military weaknesses in relation to the Franks, see Katherine Fischer Drew, "The Carolingian Military Frontier in Italy," pp. 439–440.

problem which faced Aistulf in 755 and early 756 during the planning and execution of the siege. At this time, the king's concern was obviously to preserve his kingdom from the dismemberment demanded by the 755 Pavia treaty and to find some way of counteracting the new reality of Frankish interference with Lombard freedom of action in Italy which flowed from the papal-Frankish alliance. In these circumstances, the likelihood that Aistulf in 756 besieged Rome to secure rule or suzerainty over it seems remote indeed. The royal interest was the salvation of the Lombard Kingdom of Italy, not the augmentation of its territory.

The true motivation for Aistulf's siege of Rome resembles the probable explanation for his military operations in the Roman republic subsequent to his October 752 threats. The contention is that Aistulf in 756 sought to capture Rome so that he would be in a position to have Stephen II in some way alter the unfavorable circumstances which confronted the crown in 756, thereby preventing the dissolution of the Lombard Kingdom of Italy demanded by the 755 Pavia treaty. In more detail, with both Rome and the pope in his hands, Aistulf would perhaps have Stephen modify the papacy's alliance with the Franks so as to remove its anti-Lombard features, conceivably by having Stephen restrict Pepin's military activity to defense of the papal republic as it stood in 754. He would also perhaps have Stephen terminate his claim that the exarchate, the Pentapolis, and Perugia belonged to the papacy. Or, he might recognize the regions as St. Peter's territory but insist upon having right of passage through them for purposes of maintaining royal control over the dukes of Spoleto and Benevento, an arrangement which both the pope and Pepin eventually accepted in the reign of the next Lombard king, Desiderius. Finally, Aistulf would perhaps have Stephen agree to a Lombard-Roman treaty calling for a long-term peace between Pavia and Rome. Such a treaty could constitute both a substitute for the disastrous 755 treaty and public commitment of both parties to the alterations which might result from a successful siege. But, we may suppose that permanent Lombard occupation of Rome was not a royal goal. The city and the papacy were to have freedom from the monarchy in the new conditions. In those conditions would lie what Aistulf desired most: preservation of the Lombard Kingdom of Italy.[5] Beyond these suggestions arising from circumstantial considerations one cannot go with any certainty, for the sources are completely silent about the motives for the siege, whose failure kept its intentions hidden.

### PEPIN'S SECOND ITALIAN CAMPAIGN: CREATION OF THE PAPAL REPUBLIC AND DISMEMBERMENT OF THE KINGDOM OF ITALY

Aistulf had to lift his siege when King Pepin invaded the Lombard kingdom in April 756 in response to the papal pleas.[6] As in the first cam-

---

[5] The foregoing views are explored at length in Jan T. Hallenbeck, "Rome Under Attack: An Estimation of King Aistulf's Motives for the Lombard Siege of 756," pp. 190–222.

[6] Aistulf reacted even before Pepin was across the Alps. *Fred. Chron.*, p. 107: "At this news [of Pepin's gathering his army] King Aistulf again brought the Lombard army to the passes, there to halt King Pepin and his Franks and to deny them entry into Italy."

paign the year before, the Alpine *clusae* could not be held and the Lombard stand was made at Pavia.[7] During the early stages of the second campaign Pepin received ambassadors from Constantinople, who, after holding fruitless conversations with Stephen II, urged Pepin to turn over the exarchate and its territories to the emperor—obviously looking forward to the fall of Pavia and Aistulf's being forced to disgorge the disputed places. But Pepin would not hear of denying what he had once promised to St. Peter, thereby again making it clear that the papal-Frankish association existed entirely apart from Byzantium and its Italian interests.[8] Aistulf and Pavia were able to hold out for several months this time, but finally the beleaguered Lombard asked for terms in the autumn of 756. The treaty which followed is characterized in Stephen II's *Vita* as an enforcement of the 755 terms rather than a new pact, a perception which is apparently valid.[9] Once more Aistulf accepted peace with the papacy and the Franks. He also again recognized the latter's suzerainty, agreeing to pay an immediate heavy indemnity and annually send representatives to Pepin with payment of tribute. He was also made to swear a new oath that he would restore the previously-promised territories—the exarchate and the rest. This time Aistulf had to sign and turn over to the papal archives a document which specifically listed the places which were transferred from Lombard to papal possession. Erroneously and unfortunately known as the "Donation of Pepin," the deed was as specific as early medieval documents ever became. Given to the papacy from the exarchate was Ravenna, Cesena, Forlimpopoli, Forli, with its castle of Sussubium, Montefeltro, and Comacchio; from the Pentapolis came Rimini, Pesaro, La Cattolica, Fano, Sinigaglia, Jesi, San Marino, Urbino, Cagli, Gubbio, and Luceoli; and in the Roman district—Narni, which had been taken by the Spoletans, presumably during the recent siege of Aistulf.[10] For unknown reasons Perugia was not on the list. Nevertheless, the duchy and city of Perugia were surely in papal hands, for all the roads to and from Perugia were in papal control. Pepin soon took his army home, but to be sure that the ceded places actually became papal possessions, he had Abbot Fulrad tour them one by one with Frankish and Lombard representatives, receive the keys of the towns in token of submission to the papacy, take hostages from the local aristocracies, and place both the keys and the donation document in the *confessio* of St. Peter.[11]

---

[7] *VS II*, 43.452; *Fred. Chron.*, p. 108.

[8] *VS II*, 44–45.452–453. See also David Harry Miller, "Byzantine-Papal Relations During the Pontificate of Pope Paul I: Confirmation and Completion of the Roman Revolution of the Eighth Century," pp. 49–50.

[9] For what follows, see *VS II*, 46–47.453–454.

[10] As listed in *VS II*, 47.454: "Ravenna, Arimino, Pensauro, Conca, Fano, Cesinas, Sinogalias, Esis, Forumpopuli, Forumolivi cum castro Sussubio, Montefeletri, Acerreagio, Montelucati, Serra, castellum sancti Marini, Vobio, Orbino, Callis, Luciolis, Egubio, seu Comiaclo; necnon et civitatem Narniensem, quae a ducato Spolitino parti Romanorum per evoluta annorum spatia fuerat invasa." Acerreagia, Serra, Montelucati and Vobio are not identifiable. A similar listing is *Pauli Cont. Tert.*, 42.211.

[11] *VS II*, 47.454; *Pauli Cont. Casinensis*, 4.199.

Stephen II had been able to prevail upon the Franks to return to Italy, Pepin's arms had proved irresistible, and Aistulf had been compelled to live up to the terms of the 755 treaty, surrendering all he had taken from Byzantium to the pope, thereby bringing into existence the expanded papal republic which assured the destruction of the Kingdom of Italy. With the exception of the limited conquests of Liutprand, which Pavia was not required to surrender, the exarchate and the Pentapolis were now papal territories, the roads leading from Pavia to Spoleto and Benevento were now papal roads, and the great power of the Carolingian monarchy stood by the changed situation. It was only a matter of time before Spoleto and Benevento, removed from royal control, reverted to their traditional independence. The Lombard monarchy had lost its Italian kingdom, suffered humiliation at Frankish hands, and accepted dependence upon the Carolingian crown. The collapse of Aistulf's and Liutprand's plans for a Lombard Kingdom of Italy could not have been more complete. The apparent gamble of the siege of 751 had failed and the great process of change and movement toward a new Italian *modus vivendi* begun in 752 was nearer completion.[12]

### THE ACCESSION OF KING DESIDERIUS: ROYAL ACCEPTANCE OF A NEW ITALIAN *Modus Vivendi*

Much to the relief of Stephen II, Aistulf died in 756, the victim of a hunting accident.[13] Immediately the Lombard crown was claimed by Desiderius, who was duke of the Lombards and count of the stables,[14] the latter post making him a royal official. Desiderius was also clearly an associate of Aistulf, for the latter had made him army commander in Lombard Tuscany.[15] But Desiderius evidently enjoyed little support beyond the army in Tuscany, for another claimant soon appeared—Ratchis, the former king and brother of Aistulf who had been deposed in 749. Emerging from his monastery to contest Desiderius and seek the crown for himself, Ratchis commanded powerful noble and army support, especially from the northern regions of the kingdom.[16] Ratchis soon confronted Desiderius with an army, and to overcome his weakness the Tuscan turned to Pope Stephen II for aid, promising that he would respect Rome and restore to St. Peter the "cities that remained"[17]—the places in the exarchate and the Pentapolis which had been conquered by Liutprand and not demanded by Stephen II of Aistulf in 755 or 756.[18] Stephen quickly snapped at the opportunity,

---

[12] Clearly perceived in such works as Miller, "Byzantine-Papal Relations During the Pontificate of Paul I"; idem., "Papal-Lombard Relations During the Pontificate of Pope Paul I"; Bertolini, "Il problema della origini del potere dei papi"; idem., "Le prime manifestazioni concrete del potere temporale dei papi nell' esarcato di Ravenna, (756–757)."

[13] VS II, 48.454; Pauli Cont. Cas., 4.199.

[14] VS II, 48.454; Ann. Ein. a. 756, p. 15.

[15] VS II, 48.454; Pauli Cont. Rom., 4.201.

[16] VS II, 48.454–455; Pauli Cont. Rom., 5.201; Pauli Cont. Tert., 44.211; Pauli Cont. Lom., p. 217.

[17] VS II, 49.455: "civitates quae remanserant . . ." See also CC #11, 505. There the expression is "civitates reliquas."

[18] Duchesne, VS II, p. 461, n. 57; Miller, "Papal-Lombard Relations," pp. 362–363.

sending his brother Paul, the *primicerius* Christopher, and Pepin's agent Fulrad, who was still in Rome following the details of the Lombard-papal relationship after the 756 treaty, to Tuscany to deal with Desiderius and receive his promise. The latter was given, although without enumeration of the places to be ceded. Envoys from the pope thereupon pressed Ratchis to return to his monastery, which he did with no resistance, and a Roman army was put at Desiderius' disposal. Desiderius then finalized his territorial pledge, swearing before Fulrad that he would turn over Faenza, Imola, and Ferrara from the northwest corner of the exarchate and Ancona, Umana, and Osimo from the southeast corner of the Pentapolis, on the Old Flaminian Way into Spoleto. Desiderius also begged assurance of peace between the Lombards, Romans, and Franks.[19] With Ratchis back in his cloister, his army and adherents apparently unwilling to resist further, and the pope and the Franks clearly supporting Desiderius, the issue was settled: by April 757 Desiderius was king of the Lombards.

Reflecting upon these developments, one should first consider the opposition evoked by Desiderius.[20] The situation is a complex one, and there is much that remains obscure, but the problem was apparently whether or not Desiderius should be permitted by his peers to succeed. That is, the earlier foreign policy considerations vis-a-vis Rome which had figured in the disputes surrounding the abdication of Ratchis and the accession of Aistulf seem not to have played a part here. Simply put, Desiderius seems to have inspired little loyalty and trust in the kingdom and Ratchis, for lack of a better candidate, was supported as preferable once he made his intentions known. It is possible to see dynastic forces at work, for Ratchis had once been king, would succeed his brother, and would deny the throne to a man many must have thought was an upstart usurper. Further, it may be that support for Ratchis was simply renewal of his former strength, which was perhaps in some way cultivated while Ratchis was cloistered. In this speculation, Ratchis simply moved for the throne after Aistulf's death, his adherents being old advocates and new ones dismayed at the prospect of accession by Desiderius.

Whatever its cause, the opposition was sufficiently strong to explain why Desiderius so readily promised to give up the additional places to the papacy, acknowledged dependence upon Pepin, and cooperated so thoroughly with both Rome and the Franks: being the weaker of the two competitors, Desiderius required Roman and Frankish support to win the Lombard throne.[21] The point is that Desiderius was not naturally pro-Roman and pro-Frankish in his political outlook. The concessions were his timely and

---

[19] *VS II*, 49–51.455; CC #11, 506; *Pauli Cont. Tert.*, 45.211.

[20] Comparatively little attention has been devoted to the contest between Desiderius and Ratchis. However, see Miller, "Papal-Lombard Relations," pp. 363–366; Gasquet, "Le royaume lombard," p. 86; G. Romano, *Le dominazioni barbariche in Italia*, p. 362; Hartmann, *Geschichte Italiens*, 2.2.206–208; Llewellyn, *Rome in the Dark Ages*, p. 215; Hodgkin, *Italy and Her Invaders*, 7.238–242.

[21] Ibid., 7.240; Miller, "Papal-Lombard Relations," p. 364.

clever devices to neutralize Ratchis and his supporters, thereby gaining Pavia's crown.

But the concessions also signify that Desiderius had an acute perception of the new conditions prevailing in Italy and in Lombard-papal relations. The Lombard monarchy had been defeated and humiliated by Stephen II and Pepin; Desiderius approached both as a docile and compliant subordinate. The monarchy was already dependent upon the Frankish crown; Desiderius acknowledged that dependence by swearing his oaths before Fulrad, the Frankish agent. Between the Frankish monarchy and the papacy there were now strong bonds of mutual attachment; Desiderius played to that situation by making territorial concessions which would please both. And the papacy had recently shown great concern for the establishment of an expanded papal republic through surrender of Lombard territory; Desiderius addressed that concern by offering to augment the republic through another contribution of royal territory. In brief, while Desiderius made his concessions to Pepin and Stephen with the limited objective of gaining the Lombard throne for himself, he did so apparently in an astute grasp of the new political realities obtaining in 756.

One should dwell for a moment upon the nature of the territorial concession promised by Desiderius. The lands in question—in the northwest portion of the exarchate and in the southeast portion of the Pentapolis— were the conquests of Liutprand from the empire, and when they were possessed by the papacy they would make the papal republic exactly the same as the old imperial territorial belt which ran from Ravenna to Rome. In the papal sources for the events of 756 one finds for the first time the expression *plenaria iustitiae sancti Petri*[22]—"the full rights of St. Peter"—and one sees the statement that Desiderius promised to return to St. Peter "the places which remained."[23] The implication is that in papal thinking the lands which had been returned by Aistulf in 755 and 756 (his own conquests from the empire) were only part of a larger territorial bloc belonging to St. Peter, namely the old imperial Ravenna-to-Rome belt, and that in returning Liutprand's conquests Desiderius would be placing the remainder of the bloc in papal hands, that is, providing "the places which remained" and satisfying the full rights of St. Peter, the *plenaria iustitiae*.[24] Stephen II, in short, saw Desiderius' promised concessions as completion of the papal state, effecting its final transmutation from imperial provinces to Petrine republic. One notes in passing that if Desiderius was in some degree able to perceive these papal perspectives, his promise to concede the two regions to Stephen was even more sensitive than suggested earlier.

The reasons for the papal support of Desiderius instead of Ratchis also

---

[22] See CC #11, 505, lines 28–29 and 506, lines 21–22. More directly in CC #14, 512, line 6.

[23] Miller, "Papal-Lombard Relations," p. 363, n. 15.

[24] Here it is important to recall that Stephen II, under whom the concept of the papal republic reached maturity, envisioned the republic as *all* of the exarchate, the Pentapolis, Perugia and Rome. See above, note 46 of ch. IV.

deserve discussion. In part, Stephen was drawn to Desiderius because of his *plenaria iustitiae* promise and his general inclination to abide by the changed circumstances as a new status quo. Surely, Stephen was aware that Desiderius gave no sign of worrying about the recent royal loss of Aistulf's conquests or of control over Spoleto and Benevento. But there were other reasons as well. For example, because Ratchis apparently enjoyed the majority of Lombard noble support, he might if he became king have to follow *national* Lombard inclinations instead of the narrow pro-Roman attitudes of his earlier reign. He might now reflect the inevitably anti-Roman views of the Lombard aristocracy, making it impossible for him to enjoy papal support as he had in the past.[25] But the weakness of Desiderius was perhaps definitive:[26] with significant strength only in Tuscany, and with decided hostility everywhere else, Stephen II was bound to have seen Desiderius as an ideal choice to assume the Lombard throne, for he might have difficulty holding it and thus would not be able to cause the papacy and the Franks the military problems which Aistulf had presented.

That Stephen II could act in royal Lombard affairs to the point of virtually deciding the accession is worthy of comment. Such intervention was previously unknown in the eighth century and is indicative of the defeat suffered by Aistulf at papal and Frankish hands. In the 749 accession dispute between Aistulf and Ratchis, the papacy had played no active role and Ratchis had lost his throne precisely because he was too closely identified with papal interests to suit the aristocracy. But now in 757 the situation was exactly the opposite: Desiderius *gained* the Lombard throne because of papal support, and those in the kingdom who would have preferred Lombard freedom of action in relation to Rome were powerless to act. No more complete reversal is imaginable, a sharp indication of the disarray and vulnerability facing the Lombard crown at the time of Desiderius' accession. One is struck by the particular point that Desiderius was effectively a client of the pope,[27] neither in theory nor in fact independent of Rome.

As Desiderius contended with Ratchis for the throne, the duchies of Spoleto and Benevento slipped from Pavia's control. Apparently after Aistulf's death, a duke, a certain Alboin, appeared in Spoleto,[28] thereby resuming the normal Spoletan practice of maintaining a native duke after Aistulf's exercise of the ducal powers in his own name. In Benevento, ducal rule was now held by Liutprand, the son of the pro-royal Scauniperga who had kept Benevento in Pavia's orbit during Aistulf's reign.[29] During the 757 division between Desiderius and Ratchis, Stephen II, in ways not made clear in the sources, arranged for the dukes to commend themselves and their duchies to King Pepin, thereby acknowledging Frankish suzerainty over them.[30] Alboin and Liutprand had withdrawn Spoleto and Benevento

[25] Hartmann, *Geschichte Italiens*, 2.2.206.
[26] For example, Miller, "Papal-Lombard Relations," p. 364.
[27] Recognized by ibid., p. 366.
[28] Nothing is provided on the circumstances of his accession. CC #17, 515.
[29] Hodgkin, *Italy and Her Invaders*, 7.256–257.
[30] CC, #11, 506; *Chron. Sal.*, 9.475.

from the Lombard royal obedience, in both cases with the help of the papacy.

As Aistulf had probably expected, once the papal state had been expanded to include the exarchate and the Pentapolis, and the monarchy thus deprived of its central districts needed for maintenance of royal power in the duchies, those duchies renounced their dependence in favor of the traditional ducal separatism. This development was of course encouraged by the two military defeats suffered by Aistulf, by the tense division between Desiderius and Ratchis, and finally by the weaker of the two becoming king. But as the anticipated ducal treason occurred,[31] there was a new element, that of the ducal recognition of Frankish suzerainty. In part the recognition was probably a device by which the dukes tried to assure themselves permanent aid against Pavia, should the latter one day attempt to reimpose its hegemony in the duchies: having commended themselves to Pepin, Frankish aid against the crown might be expected. It turned out that Pepin did not take the commendations seriously,[32] but at the time the dukes were likely to have been optimistic about Frankish help, especially in view of the aid which Pepin had brought to another ally, the papacy. But the dukes no doubt saw acceptance of Carolingian dependence as more than a source of aid against Desiderius, for it was their way of declaring independence of Pavia and acting to weaken the crown. The former point is obvious and the latter easily delineated: by separating their duchies from Pavia the dukes would lessen any royal danger to Rome and its republic and contribute to royal abasement by leaving only the north in royal hands.[33]

The papal role in the Spoletan-Beneventan defection is unclear in detail but obvious in outline. Apparently Stephen forwarded the dukes' desires for submission to King Pepin, and it is not impossible that he put the notion of submission into their heads. In any event, Stephen aided and abetted the defection. He thereby returned to the papal policy of collaboration with the dukes against the crown which had been practiced to perfection by Gregory III. In a world dominated by revolutionary novelty it is interesting to see this recurrence of an old pattern. Papal motives are not difficult to discern: loss of the duchies would further weaken the monarchy, much to be desired so that the papal-Frankish association and the papal republic might be afforded a period of peaceful development. In particular, the monarchy would no longer be able to utilize Spoletan power against Rome or the republic in the future, as it had in 755. Instead, both Alboin and Liutprand would be allies of Rome, perhaps an added element of protection against Pavia. Stephen's collaboration with the dukes was adroit, undertaken at the very time in which his envoys were arranging for the

---

[31] Miller ("Papal-Lombard Relations," p. 368) calls the ducal action "open treason."

[32] Pepin apparently took no steps to claim or protect his ascendance in the duchies and evidently had no legal association with them. Wilhelm Martens, *Die römische Frage unter Pippin und Karl dem Grossen*, pp. 92–93. See also Miller, "Papal-Lombard Relations," p. 370; Baumont, "Le pontificat de Paul I<sup>er</sup>," pp. 16–17.

[33] Appreciated by Hodgkin, *Italy and Her Invaders*, 7.255–256.

weak Desiderius to take the Lombard throne. He had seized just the right moment for deft exploitation of the traditional ducal policy of separatism for papal interests.

In Aistulf's gamble to save the Kingdom of Italy after the first Pavia treaty of 755 there was perhaps some hope for success, but in Desiderius's accession and very early reign there was only confirmation of the kingdom's demise and the promise, in the full defection of Spoleto and Benevento, that the demise could easily be permanent. It was as if the developing new Italian *modus vivendi* had room only for a Lombard kingdom which was confined to northern Italy.

### DESIDERIUS, POPE PAUL I, AND THE *Plenaria Iustitiae*: TOWARD RECONSTRUCTION OF THE KINGDOM OF ITALY

By the end of 757, within a few months of his accession, Desiderius was at odds with Pope Paul I (757–767), the brother and successor of Stephen II. Long an intimate and adviser of Stephen, Paul proved to be a persistent advocate of the papal-Frankish alliance, unswerving in adherence to the papal separation from the empire, and determined to develop and protect the papal republic.[34] Despite his promises to Stephen and Fulrad, Desiderius would not transfer the *plenaria iustitiae* to St. Peter.[35] Paul complained of this to Pepin,[36] but there was evidently no reply.

Perhaps a belief that Pepin would not soon return to Italy governed Desiderius's refusal, but more likely internal considerations were paramount.[37] Desiderius, knowing that he was weak at the time of his accession and that he was opposed by many aristocrats, probably sought to win their favor by holding back on transfer of Liutprand's conquests to Rome. Many nobles were bound to have been aroused by the recent Lombard defeats at papal hands, and perhaps also by the re-emergence of Ratchis, who had once been the object of anti-Roman feeling. In short, to fulfill the *plenaria iustitiae* promise would invite open opposition or even deposition.[38]

Refusal to transfer the *plenaria iustitiae* may have strengthened Desiderius's hand in the kingdom, but it was very risky business coming as it did after Aistulf's disaster and in the context of the monarchy's weakest eighth-century moment to date. The action was insulting to Pope Paul and King Pepin: the humiliated Lombard monarch was repudiating not only a peace treaty with Rome and Francia to which he had personally sworn obedience but also his dependence upon Pepin. In consequence, new papal-Frankish pressures might be applied, making the Lombard plight worse

---

[34] It is difficult to study Paul I because his *LP* biography contains little of use to the historian and the *CC* letters pertinent to his reign present numerous problems of dating. See especially Miller, "Papal-Lombard Relations"; idem., "Byzantine-Papal Relations"; and Baumont, "Paul Iᵉʳ." In general, the chronology followed in this chapter is that of the two Miller studies.

[35] CC #14, 512.

[36] Ibid.

[37] As recognized by Miller, "Papal-Lombard Relations," p. 368.

[38] Ibid.

than it was at Desiderius's accession. But Pepin did not respond to Paul's complaints, perhaps because in 757 he was involved in a successful effort to bring Duke Tassilo of Bavaria under his suzerainty.[39] Whatever the reason, Desiderius was at least for the moment unscathed.

Major developments followed Desiderius's refusal to accommodate Paul on the *iustitiae*. In 758, the next year, the king marched forces through the Pentapolis, presumably along the Old Flaminian Way route into Spoleto via Osimo, thereby violating a portion of the papal republic.[40] Desiderius proceeded to visit destruction upon both Spoleto and Benevento, capture Duke Alboin of Spoleto, drive Duke Liutprand of Benevento into flight,[41] and replace him with a new duke, Arichis,[42] to whom Desiderius gave in marriage his daughter, Adelperga.[43] Quite surprisingly, the Lombard Kingdom of Italy was evidently on its way to restoration despite the highly unfavorable circumstances of 756. Apparently after the repossession of Spoleto and Benevento, Desiderius negotiated an alliance with the imperial *missus* Gregory, who was resident in Naples. Byzantine assistance would be forthcoming to help Desiderius capture Liutprand of Benevento and Desiderius would join the empire in an attack upon Rome, Ravenna, and the Pentapolis.[44] But Desiderius never made an attack and before long was in Rome for dealings with the pope. He either persuaded or forced Paul to inform Pepin that the Lombards wanted only peace with Rome and would transfer Imola to the republic if Pepin would return the hostages, presumably those taken in 755 and 756.[45] But Paul managed to provide Pepin with a second letter, asking him to ignore the first since it was a royal dictation.[46] Paul went on to report Desiderius's violation of the Pentapolis, his subsequent repossession of Spoleto and Benevento, the Lombard-imperial coalition, and Desiderius's visit to Rome. Paul further noted that Desiderius was still withholding the *plenaria iustitiae*,[47] and urged Pepin to hold firm to his obligations to Rome and the papacy, especially regarding Desiderius and the Lombards.[48]

Obviously, the events of 758 showed that Desiderius had achieved a partial reconstitution of the Lombard Kingdom of Italy through reimposition of royal control over the dukes of Spoleto and Benevento.[49] That success ended the 756 regional confinement of the Lombard kingdom and restored to it a considerable measure of the nearly universal Italian scope

[39] *ARF*, a. 757, pp. 14–16.
[40] *CC* #17, 515.
[41] Ibid.
[42] Ibid.
[43] *Chron. Sal.*, 9.476.
[44] *Codicis Carolini Epistolae*, #15, 4.74–75. This letter is not in the *CC*. See also *CC* #17, p. 515. A fairly detailed treatment of the recovery of Spoleto and Benevento is Hodgkin, *Italy and Her Invaders*, 7.256–258.
[45] *CC* #16, 513–514. See Miller, "Papal-Lombard Relations," 368–369.
[46] *CC* #17, 514–517.
[47] Ibid., pp. 515–516.
[48] Ibid.
[49] See Baumont, "Paul Ier," p. 16.

which it had known under Aistulf. The latter's conquests in the exarchate, the Pentapolis, and Perugia were not included in the reconstruction, for Desiderius had not attacked them but merely marched his troops through them en route to Spoleto. But the march made it clear that the partially restored kingdom would be maintained by transit of royal strength from the northern districts of the kingdom to Spoleto and Benevento via papal territory. That is, temporary penetrations of the papal state were visualized as the means of holding Spoleto and Benevento obedient, thereby maintaining the Italian character of the kingdom. In 758 Desiderius did not know whether Pepin would tolerate either loss of Frankish dominion over the dukes or the violation of the republic necessary to hold Spoleto and Benevento, that is, whether he would condone the partial restoration of the Lombard Kingdom of Italy. But, such a restoration was plainly in being and was therefore a distinct royal aspiration. This arose from occupancy of the throne: being king, Desiderius inevitably sooner or later had to do what he could to pursue the monarchy's now-venerable commitment to make Pavia's kingdom an Italian realm.

It is apparent that while the Lombard did act boldly in 757–758, he also exercised considerable restraint.[50] Thus, while he refused to give up the *plenaria iustitiae*, he did not attempt to redeem the places surrendered by Aistulf to Stephen II. While he penetrated the Pentapolis en route to Spoleto, he did not try to occupy it. While he allied with Byzantium to apprehend Liutprand of Benevento so that his duchy might be secured, he did not actually campaign with the empire against the papal republic. And, while he did come to Rome and manipulate Pope Paul into accepting a royal dictation, he did not attack Rome or generate some sort of Lombard fifth-column in the city. The meaning of the restraint seems fairly clear: Desiderius was evidently signaling Pope Paul, and perhaps King Pepin as well, that his refusal to yield the *plenaria iustitiae*, his repossession of Spoleto and Benevento, his collaboration with the empire, and his pressure in Rome did not preview a repudiation of the basic alterations which had been imposed by Pepin and Stephen II in 756—the expanded papal state and the papal-Frankish alliance. Desiderius seems to have avoided a clear, decisive threat to either.

The king did chafe against his dependence upon Francia, however. The refusal to concede the *plenaria iustitiae* in 757 implied rejection of Frankish overlordship, but the deposition of Alboin and Liutprand in Spoleto and Benevento was even more specific: Desiderius was dispatching two sworn vassals of Pepin and in so doing was disregarding both their Frankish dependence and his own. Finally, when Desiderius confronted Pope Paul in Rome he sought a return of the Lombard hostages held by Pepin in guarantee of Pavia's subordination to Francia. This can be best construed as a corollary to Desiderius's other apparent steps to resume the royal autonomy which had been enjoyed by Liutprand and Aistulf.

---

[50] Miller, "Papal-Lombard Relations," p. 376.

In Rome, Pope Paul was greatly disturbed by Desiderius's behavior in 758. His violation of the Pentapolis naturally aroused papal doubts about his intentions regarding the papal state. Would he merely violate it occasionally en route to Spoleto, or would conquest efforts follow? The royal subordination of the duchies of Spoleto and Benevento was offensive in the extreme, for in that action Desiderius again, as he had in the *plenaria iustitiae* denial, flouted Frankish supremacy in Italy, ruined the papal reorganization of the ducal region carried out just as Desiderius became king, and, worst of all, renewed the old problem of Rome's territory being encircled by that of Pavia. It must have been most difficult for Paul to witness the reappearance of the Lombard Kingdom of Italy, even in its partial form, for nothing seemed more certain in 756 than Pavia's containment in the north. But there was more, for Desiderius had been willing to engage with Byzantium against the papal republic. While the collaboration had come to nothing, it revealed to Paul that Desiderius would not hesitate to work with the empire against the papacy to achieve his ends. Finally, the Lombard's application of pressure upon Pope Paul in Rome itself was disconcerting; Desiderius was both willing and able to act as though the pope was a creature of Pavia. To Paul, it would seem, Desiderius was disregarding the restrictions which had been placed upon the Lombard monarchy by the treaties of 755 and 756 and by the new conditions generated at that time, not to mention the limitations which were implicit in his own accession.

But Pope Paul probably believed that Pepin would determine Lombard fortunes more than Desiderius, making the Frank's reaction to the 758 developments crucial. In the secret letter, sent to Pepin in contradiction of the first, which had been dictated by Desiderius, Paul pressed the patrician to resume his supervision of the Italian scene—and took care to bring him up to date on the king's misdeeds. Pepin was exhorted not to forget his duties to St. Peter, and was specifically told that his aid was expected. The pope implied that Desiderius was an unrelieved malignancy. He was a deceitful withholder of papal territory, an intolerable disrupter of Frankish suzerainty in Spoleto and Benevento, a hateful ally of Rome's dangerous imperial enemy, and an insidious manipulator of the pope himself. Pepin should not accede to Desiderius's request for return of the hostages, nor should he believe that Imola alone was to be surrendered to the papacy. Instead, Desiderius had again been asked to give up the *plenaria iustitiae* which he had promised at the outset of his reign; again, however, he had refused them. Pepin should see to it that what had once been promised before Fulrad by Desiderius was actually received by the republic. The letter was long, vituperative, and agitated—probably a good reflection of the angry and apprehensive mood in which Pope Paul found himself in late 758.[51]

---

[51] The language is reminiscent of that generally applied by Stephen II, although more restrained.

As had been the case in 757, Pepin did not act or even reply to Paul, no matter how concerned the latter was. Once more it is not clear why, unless it was new business on the Frankish frontiers—this time wars with the Saxons, beginning in 758.[52] Like the Bavarian project of 757, the Saxon war was a vital Carolingian concern, perhaps sufficient to account for Pepin's disinterest in Italy.[53] By 760 Pepin revealed that he still maintained his *patricius Romanorum* duty, but in 758 he was evidently prepared to let Desiderius move toward autonomy and restoration of the Lombard Kingdom of Italy with impunity. Perhaps, too, Pepin saw that Desiderius was acting with restraint, not trying to overturn the traditional settlement of 756 and leaving Rome, the pope, and the papal-Frankish alliance all undamaged. That Pepin failed to respond to Desiderius's ouster of Alboin of Spoleto and Liutprand of Benevento seems good evidence that the Frank did not regard their submission as valid. Pepin, pressed by domestic business and not inclined to accept the papally-inspired ducal subordinations, was evidently tolerating Desiderius's attempt to limit the papal state to Aistulf's conquests, restore the Lombard kingdom of Italy at least partially, and regain autonomy relative to Francia.

It remains to consider Desiderius's alliance with the empire. Its inception lay in the Byzantine loss of the exarchate, the Pentapolis, and Perugia to Aistulf in 751.[54] After these losses, the emperor attempted to retrieve them by engaging the papacy in his behalf, as is visible in the imperial diplomacy surrounding Stephen II's departure for Francia in 753. But that effort failed in the definitive repudiation of the empire made by Stephen II in forming the papal-Frankish association, which involved exclusion of the empire from any sort of connection with the papacy, and in creating the papal state, which placed imperial territory under independent papal rule. Henceforth, the papacy was an imperial foe, from whom the exarchate and the other territories had to be taken. Not for nothing did the papal chroniclers begin to refer to the imperialists as "most wicked Greeks,"[55] refusing to use any longer the normal imperial terminology. The empire, of course, had only negligible military power in Italy, none of it north of Naples. There were forces in the east and Sicily, but difficulties in both areas made it unlikely that imperial troops could be imported into Italy. The empire was therefore compelled to rely upon diplomacy, seeking both to persuade Pepin to turn over the exarchate and the Pentapolis to the emperor and gain Lombard arms to win the region from the papacy by force. Thus was Pepin approached in 756 by imperial envoys, during his second campaign against Aistulf, requesting restoration of the exarchate and its territories to the empire.[56] But the *patricius Romanorum* had remained loyal to the papacy

[52] *ARF*, a. 758, p. 16.
[53] Miller, "Motivations of Pepin's Italian policy," pp. 53–54.
[54] The most important work on this subject is Miller, "Byzantine-Papal Relations," esp. pp. 49–53.
[55] See for example CC #30, 536, line 14.
[56] Miller, "Byzantine-Papal Relations," p. 51.

only, and when some subsequent Frankish-imperial negotiations in Francia came to nothing, Emperor Constantine's last hope was the Lombard crown, just battered into defeat and humiliation by the Franks.[57] Thus, as Desiderius was busy trying to regain control over Spoleto and Benevento, imperial envoys promised to help apprehend Liutprand of Benevento in exchange for royal help in attacking "Ravenna, Rome, and the Pentapolis," the understanding being that an imperial army from Sicily would assist the enterprise. Desiderius was glad to have the Byzantine help in Benevento— but he is not apt to have taken the imperial project against the papal republic seriously: his collaboration with the empire was aimed at the fleeing Liutprand, and he certainly doubted that the Sicilian force was more than bait to get him to attack the republic on his own.[58] Such an attack, *or* an attack in conjunction with an imperial unit, was excessively provocative, perhaps enough to draw Pepin into Italy against him. As observed, Desiderius exercised restraint, showing respect for the safety of the papal state. He thus abandoned the Byzantine coalition before it became a significant factor. For Constantine V, it was simply another bitter failure in the fruitless imperial effort to repossess the central Italian districts.

### MODIFICATION OF THE *Modus Vivendi* OF 755–756

In the broadest sense, the events of 758 showed that the 756 papal-Frankish-Lombard settlement, the *modus vivendi* apparent after Pepin's second campaign against Aistulf, was undergoing significant change. While Stephen II's expanded papal republic remained intact, and while Pavia remained bereft of its former Ravennese, Pentapoline, and Perugian districts, the Lombard Kingdom of Italy, dissolved in 755–756 and thus not part of the *modus vivendi*, was once more in being. Moreover, Lombard royal transit of the papal republic, certainly not envisioned in 756, was in 758 an accomplished fact. In addition, Pavia's subordination to Pepin, a major part of the 756 scheme of things, was on the verge of disappearing, and limitation upon the Lombard crown's freedom of action in Italy, which was implicit in the restrictive conditions of 756, was being countered as Desiderius refused the *plenaria iustitiae* transfer, marched through the republic, restored royal power in Spoleto and Benevento, allied with Byzantium, and intervened in Rome. Finally, the thoroughgoing Carolingian commitment to the papacy, vital in the 756 *modus vivendi*, was now in question as Pepin refrained from either new military or diplomatic activity in Italy. To contend that the 756 settlement was a thing of the past would be presumptuous. Desiderius was careful not to harm the papal state or disrupt the papal-Frankish association, and it remained to be seen whether and how Pepin would react. But it was nevertheless plain by 758 that new conditions, largely favorable to Pavia, were taking shape. The question was, would the change last, and if so, how far would it go? Would the 756 settlement

---

[57] Ibid., p. 52.
[58] Ibid., p. 53.

somehow be restored, or would it and the changes evident by 758 be merged into a new Italian *modus vivendi*?

An appraisal of King Desiderius's performance from 757 to 758, the first year and a half of his reign, is also in order. Desiderius was clearly proving to be a sensitive and effective leader. He adroitly mixed force, diplomacy, and restraint, pursuing the risky and sophisticated effort to discover what the royal potentials were in the decidedly hostile conditions which prevailed at the end of Aistulf's reign. Throughout the period he had shown himself to be deft and vigorous, essentially a master of the Italian scene, perhaps even its predominant personality. He was emerging as a strong and able leader, apparently acceptable to those in his kingdom who desired a strong posture vis-a-vis Rome, the papacy, and the Franks, those who hoped for a recovery of the monarchy, and those who wanted peace with Rome, the pope, and the papal republic. By the end of 758 Desiderius was an experienced participant in the complex and changing Italian environment, and, having learned a great deal of the realities affecting him and his monarchy and enjoying considerable success, was a confident leader ready to explore the situation further.

# VI. EQUILIBRIUM AND NEW DIRECTIONS

The Italian situation was clarified greatly in 759 and 760 in the context of a new and apparently significant Byzantine threat to the papal republic. At some point in 759 Pope Paul began to hear of an impending attack by "the most wicked Greeks, the enemies of the church," against Ravenna and Rome.[1] Before long Paul asserted that he had hard information that Rome, Ravenna, and the maritime cities of the Pentapolis (presumably Rimini, La Cattolica, Pesaro, Fano, Sinigaglia, and Ancona) would be attacked.[2] Despite inevitable misgivings, Paul asked Desiderius to help repel the invasion.[3] To bring about a joint Lombard-imperial defense of Rome and its territory, Paul wrote, Pepin should send *missi* in the coming March (of 760) to negotiate with Desiderius.[4] Replying to Paul apparently for the first time in his pontificate, Pepin said that Paul should seriously consider accommodating Desiderius (presumably, as we shall see, regarding the *plenaria iustitiae*) in the interests of peace.[5] Paul replied that he would be pleased to have peace with Desiderius if the king would have it with Rome.[6] Meanwhile, rumors of an imminent Greek attack upon Ravenna continued to circulate daily.[7] Then, with Lombard-papal negotiations apparently already in progress, Pepin's *missi* arrived in March as requested by the pope and in their presence Desiderius swore that before the end of April he would return all rights, all patrimonies, and the rights, places, borders, and various territories of the republic of the Romans.[8] A survey would determine exactly which lands were papal or Lombard. As usual, although this time with some surprise, the imperial attack failed to materialize, but its threat had had the effect of drawing Desiderius and Paul together.[9]

### A Revised *Modus Vivendi*: Preservation of Royal Autonomy, Restoration of the Kingdom, and Royal-Papal Peace

One notices first in these 759–760 developments that Pepin was again taking his *patricius Romanorum* duties seriously: he was finally looking after

---

[1] CC #30, 536.
[2] The information came from a letter from Constantine passed on to the pope by the archbishop of Ravenna, and from another letter from papal friends in Venice. CC #31, p. 537.
[3] Ibid., #30, 536, and #31, p. 537.
[4] Ibid., #30, 536.
[5] Ibid., #38, 551, lines 1–2.
[6] Ibid., lines 3–6.
[7] Ibid., 551.
[8] Ibid., #19, 519–520.
[9] For a good secondary account of these developments see Miller, "Papal-Lombard Relations," pp. 371–372.

the interests of the papacy, protecting it and its republic. Thus, did he press Desiderius into effecting a new territorial promise to the papacy in March 760. Furthermore, Pepin insisted that the tension between Pavia and Rome be lessened: pope and king were made to engage in dialogue and were led away from conflict. As Paul had requested, the *patricius Romanorum* made Lombard-papal collaboration against the projected Byzantine attack possible. Finally, when Desiderius gave the new promise of territorial cession to the papacy, he did so in the presence of the Frankish *missi*—in acknowledgment of dependence upon Pepin. Desiderius's earlier movement away from Frankish suzerainty was thus cut short. In brief, by responding to Paul's territorial demands, encouraging amicable settlement of Lombard-papal differences, assuring Paul of an ally against Byzantium, and resuming insistence upon Lombard dependence upon Francia, Pepin signified that he was still Roman patrician committed to the papacy's service.

But the Frank also revealed that he was willing to accommodate the Lombard king when he could, probably because his commitments in Francia made steady management of Italian politics exclusively or largely in papal favor impossible. Most importantly in this regard, Desiderius in 760 was not ordered to restore the *plenaria iustitiae*, the conquests of Liutprand in the exarchate and the Pentapolis, but rather only territories given by Aistulf in the 755–756 treaty which had evidently not yet been turned over to the papacy.[10] As the leading authority on the problem puts it, "the agreements made in the spring of 757 [during Desiderius's struggle for the Lombard throne] were considered to be of no standing and Pepin seems to have felt that he was not committed by them in spite of the fact that his agent Fulrad had negotiated them."[11] In brief, Pepin accepted Desiderius's refusal of the 757–760 period to fulfill his promise to enlarge the papal state beyond the 756 borders assented to by Pepin himself in the treaty with Aistulf. Miller summarizes the situation well: "Desiderius was able to retrieve his promise of 757 . . . and make good the idea that the treaties of 755 and 756 were the limits to which Rome might expand."[12] With this the *plenaria iustitiae* issue was settled, a considerable victory for Desiderius, a serious and ultimately unacceptable setback for the papacy. It is emphasized that King Pepin was the deciding factor in Desiderius's favor.

There were other suggestions in 760 that Pepin was trying to accommodate Desiderius. For example, despite ample opportunity to order the Lombard to withdraw from the duchies of Spoleto and Benevento, and restore them to independence from Pavia, he did not do so. Nor did he reimpose the previous vassalage of the dukes.[13] Thus, by leaving the issue unaddressed Pepin seems to have effectively sanctioned Desiderius's res-

---

[10] Ibid., p. 372.

[11] Ibid.

[12] Ibid. A similar view is Baumont, "Paul I^er," pp. 17–18. Here the 760 treaty is seen as a defeat of Stephen II's territorial ambitions.

[13] As noticed by Miller, "Papal-Lombard Relations," p. 370, and Baumont, "Paul I^er," p. 17.

toration of royal power in Spoleto and Benevento.[14] But he perhaps allowed more than that, for the broader tacit authorization was evidently for the partial reassembly of the Lombard Kingdom of Italy achieved by the ducal suppressions. By permitting the partial renewal of the kingdom Pepin apparently accepted the means of its maintenance: occasional Lombard passage through the papal republic for movement of royal strength from north to south. Finally, Pepin's approval of Pavia's partially restored kingdom implies that Pepin also tolerated the encirclement of the papal state by royal Lombard territory. As in the concession to Desiderius on the *iustitiae* matter, Pepin in these respects was evidently finding ways to support Pavia's perspective.

In general terms, the developments of the 759–760 period defined vital details of Italy's emerging political organization, clarifying the outlines of the 756–758 period. It was to be a stable environment, the Lombard and papal principals dwelling in harmony, cooperating to defend themselves against the empire and mutually satisfied that their interests were met. On the one hand, the papacy was to have possession of its republic, according to the limits prescribed by the 756 Pavia treaty. The republic, Rome, and the papacy were to be free of any danger from Pavia, its king kept in check by the Carolingians' *patricius Romanorum* service, exercised on behalf of the papacy through the medium of diplomacy, direct Frankish dealing with the royal and papal courts, with military intervention apparently being reserved for extreme situations only.[15] The Lombard monarchy would also find its interests met. Through control of the duke of Spoleto and Benevento it would have a limited version of the Italian realm long desired. It would also have a means of joining the northern and southern districts in spite of their geographic separation. The pope would be constrained by the Frankish patrician to stay in harmony with the king, but the latter could expect Frankish pressure until the territories in question in 760 were actually in papal hands. The Lombard monarchy was to be subservient to the Franks, but the traditional Lombard royal autonomy would be respected in both the considerable latitude given to royal action throughout Italy and Pepin's relinquishment or refusal of Frankish suzerainty over Spoleto and Benevento. Such was the Italian *modus vivendi* which had been developed by 760. It marked the limit of the change initiated in 757–758 period, and reflected a blend of the post-756 change and the fundamental conditions arrived at in 756.

For the relationship between the Lombard monarchy and the papacy in particular, the basic hope arising from the 760 *modus vivendi* was for peaceful interaction, an end to the tensions which had marred the relationship since the Terni peace of 742. Desiderius had discovered the limits of his power and potential, and both Pavia and Rome had received territorial satisfaction, although the *plenaria iustitiae* had not been granted to the republic. More-

---

[14] Baumont, p. "Paul I<sup>er</sup>," p. 17.
[15] Miller, "Motivations of Pepin's Italian Policy," pp. 53–54.

over, the Frankish moderation would both prohibit blatant disruptions by either side and defuse dangerous situations by forced negotiations. Byzantium might remain something of a menace, but the expectation was that it would draw Desiderius and Paul together, as had been the case in 759–760. A calm future dialogue and cooperation between Pavia and Rome was a reasonable prospect.

Part of the reason for the hopeful future in 760 was the recovery of the Lombard monarchy under Desiderius. While the monarchy was officially dependent upon King Pepin, it was now strong enough to have a relatively independent and significant role in Italian political life. In 756–757 the royal defeat and humiliation seemed total, the Italian kingdom lost, Frankish arms triumphant, the king twice humiliated, and a candidate for the throne bargaining to win support of the pope. The future was grim—royal rule in the north only, haughty dukes ignoring the crown in Spoleto and Benevento, papal officials ruling Aistulf's great imperial conquest, and the king letting Rome and Francia dictate Italian affairs without reference to Pavia. But Desiderius in 757–758 explored this wasteland with energy and sensitivity and in so doing rebuilt the monarchy's Italian kingdom to a considerable degree, somewhat lessened Pavia's dependence upon the Franks, and replaced the papal dominance with royal-papal parity. Pepin's acceptance of the royal recovery in 759–760 was vital to it, of course, for had Pepin been willing and able to commit force to Italy he could have prevented it. But what mattered was they by the end of 760 the recovery was a fact, enabling Desiderius to contemplate the future with a certain amount of confidence.

## THE *Modus Vivendi* ENDURES

For the remainder of Paul's pontificate, from 760 to 767, the focus of relations between Pavia and Rome was upon Desiderius's fulfillment of his 760 territorial promise, that concerning adjustments within the lands taken from Aistulf in 756. Before long, Paul informed Pepin, it was clear that Desiderius was no more inclined to surrender the places involved than he had previously been willing to give up the *plenaria iustitiae*. Pepin responded by sending a delegation to Italy to verify the pope's allegation and discovered that Desiderius was in fact hesitant in fulfilling his promise.[16] Apparently nothing came of this intervention, for another occurred at some point in 761 or 762. This time Pepin meant business. Frankish envoys came to Rome and conducted a thorough inquiry into the territorial problem, at which representatives of King Desiderius and other places at issue were in attendance.[17] Evidently, border places were in dispute, for it was alleged that Desiderius retained or otherwise violated "the frontiers of our cities

---

[16] CC #22, 526. For a good secondary account see Miller, "Papal-Lombard Relations," pp. 372–375.

[17] CC #34, 541.

and the patrimonies of St. Peter."[18] The statement is very ambiguous, but the implication is that while Desiderius had given up the principal places which he had promised in 760 he was still retaining or somehow interfering with the lands which surrounded them.[19] In any event, the inquiry proceeded to find sufficient grounds for supporting the papal claim, for it was arranged that the Frankish investigators, papal representatives, and the witnesses from the disputed places should all go to Pavia to have Desiderius attest before the Franks and their associates to his originally promised boundaries, having him by implication renounce his present violations and reaffirm the promise.[20] Pope Paul was skeptical that Desiderius would comply even under such pressure, and as it turned out he was quite right. The source puts it simply: the delegation was unable to achieve anything at all.[21] The implication is that Desiderius probably did negotiate with his guests, although he would not agree to unequivocally fulfill the promise of 760.

The failure of this attempt to enlist Desiderius's compliance was followed by mounting tension between Pavia and Rome. By 762 or 763 Desiderius was perpetrating "devastations" in unspecified papal territory and was harassing the pope with threatening letters.[22] Paul promptly reminded Pepin again of his *patricius Romanorum* responsibilities and told him that Frankish *missi* should be sent to both Pavia for conversation with Desiderius and to Rome for support of the pope.[23] Paul was clearly alarmed, but not to the point that he requested Frankish military intervention. The trouble went on for some time despite efforts of Frankish delegations to get Desiderius to desist. He would in no way comply and envoys came away convinced that Desiderius alone was at fault.[24] In the meantime, in 763 and 764, Desiderius continued his military operations, attacking the Pentapoline town of Sinigaglia and a fortress in Campania, the former ceded by Aistulf to the papacy in 756 and the latter located in the papal state.[25] But by the fall of 765 Desiderius came to terms with the papacy. Having traveled to Rome ostensibly to discuss another matter with the pope, Desiderius agreed to carry out his promised cession of 760. Toward that end he sent a joint Lombard-papal legation to the various cities in question, where their rights were turned over to the papacy.[26] There followed a general Lombard confirmation of the transfer, for Tuscan, Spoletan, and Beneventan representatives as well as the Lombard legation all supported it. The totality of the lands gained by the papacy in 756 was evidently finally in papal possession.

---

[18] Ibid., lines 39–41: "Nam de finibus civitatum et partimoniis b. Petri ab eisdem Langobardis retentis atque invasis nihil usque hactenus recepimus. . . ."

[19] Miller, "Papal-Lombard Relations," p. 373.

[20] CC #34, 541–542.

[21] Ibid., #20, 521.

[22] Ibid., 520.

[23] Ibid., lines 13–18.

[24] Ibid., #21, 524, lines 2–8.

[25] Ibid., 524–525.

[26] Ibid., #37, 549, lines 35–37.

MAP. 5. Basic Italian settlement accepted by Desiderius by 765.

What is more, the Lombard-papal tension, which as late as 764 had threat-ened to become open war, had been replaced by a return to amity.

In analyzing the 760–765 developments, one notices first that relations between Pavia and Rome apparently did not experience the calm, dialogue, and cooperation hoped for in 760. Instead, royal-papal tension seems to have been predominant. Desiderius would not concede territorial satisfac-tion until the end of the period, deflecting every Frankish-papal effort to secure his obedience and coming to terms only after resort to violence. This placed him in defiance of his overlord and in conflict with the pope. Fur-thermore, for the better part of the period Desiderius was at war with the papacy, carrying out various ravagings of the papal state and conducting specific campaigns against Sinigaglia and the Campanian fortress. For the first time since the end of Aistulf's 756 siege of Rome the Lombard monarchy was in active conflict with the papacy. It would seem that the 760–765 period was anything but a time of Lombard-papal concord.

That there was considerable tension between the king and the pope from 760–765 is indeed true, but more importantly the trouble never approached a general deterioration of the relationship or of conflict on a wide or irreconcilable scale.[27] At no point in the period does one feel that passions similar to those visible in the struggle between Liutprand and Gregory III or between Aistulf and Stephen II obtained in the territorial controversy. The mood was more one of essentially coexistent powers attempting to settle a serious technical disagreement than one of fundamentally divided enemies. The rhetoric in Paul's letters was very mild, even after Desiderius had attacked the papal territory. Furthermore, Paul asked Pepin to send envoys, not armies. For his part, when Desiderius could have ordered more extensive attacks he confined his operations to only a few places which were apparently quite some distance from Rome. The latter he was careful not to threaten or attack, and Paul never intimated to Pepin that he feared for his capital. Finally, even as Desiderius was engaged in military activity within the republic he was open to discussing the territorial problem with the Franks and the papacy and he did at last voluntarily end the difficulty by complying in 765. Neither Desiderius nor Paul had threatened the other's basic interests, and both had been inclined to let the essential peace between Pavia and Rome prevail. Thus, the anticipated period of calm, dialogue, and cooperation had materialized in basic respects in spite of the tension and strife.[28]

This point leads to the related one that the Italian *modus vivendi* achieved by 760 was not seriously disturbed by the 760–765 territorial dispute. The general Italian environment had remained relatively stable, the tensions and even fighting never approximating the crisis periods of the 730s and the 750s. Negotiation had played a much more important role than war. The papacy remained in possession of the republic and Rome was not troubled. Pepin as *patricius Romanorum* pressed Desiderius for settlement with the papacy, always via diplomacy rather than force, the threat of which Pepin did not raise. Further, Pavia continued to hold Spoleto and Benevento, keeping the partially restored Lombard Kingdom of Italy in being, but never seeking to enlarge it. Pope Paul avoided any manipulation in the duchies, accepting whatever violation of the papal state was necessary to keep them dependent upon Pavia. By steadily trying to hold Desiderius to the 760 oath taken before Frankish *missi*, Pepin would not let Desiderius forget that he was a Frankish vassal. But he did not seek any further royal subjection, either, thereby continuing to recognize wide latitude for Desiderius in Italian affairs. This was particularly evident in Pepin's failure to

---

[27] This and the following points seem generally recognized in Miller, "Papal-Lombard Relations," p. 376.

[28] The trouble was less than it seemed because Paul may have overstated the problems to Pepin. Ibid., p. 374.

admonish Desiderius for his taking up arms against St. Peter. In short, the essential political realities which were in effect in 760 were still present in 767, unchanged by the Lombard-papal territorial problems. The *modus vivendi* of 760 was proving durable.

Perhaps one reason that the territorial issue did not disturb that order is the relative marginality of the issue itself between 760 and 765. Desiderius perhaps saw it as having importance, for nothing else seems to have occupied him so much. But after 760 neither King Pepin nor Pope Paul is apt to have thought it central. For Pepin the more important concerns were the long and difficult effort to subdue Aquitaine and its duke, Waifar, the defection of Duke Tassilo of Bavaria,[29] and the resolution of the new and complex Frankish negotiations with the empire regarding Iconoclasm.[30] In the pope's sight, papal participation in the Frankish-imperial deliberations was surely more vital than the territorial debate, for if the emperor was able to convince Pepin that Iconoclasm was orthodox belief the solidarity between Rome and Francia might well end with the papal state being returned to Byzantium.[31] Also demanding the pope's attention ahead of the territorial question were three other concerns, the problem of bringing Archbishop Sergius of Ravenna to heel,[32] the development of bona fide papal rule in the republic,[33] and the nurturing of the papal central administration in Rome, the *iudices de clero*.[34] In brief, while all parties devoted considerable attention to the territorial matter, and while it was unquestionably the principal focus of the Lombard-papal relationship in the 760–765 period, it was probably a secondary concern in the general sense to all but Desiderius.

Perhaps that is why Pepin was not lured into using force to bring Desiderius into compliance with his 760 oath. Given the relatively limited significance of the issue, use of force was simply uncalled for. But, it is doubtful that Pepin could have brought force to bear even if he had deemed it necessary.[35] As Frankish sources plainly indicate,[36] after 760 the subjection of Duke Waifar was an all-consuming Frankish royal business, and the lack of decisive victory over him gave army commitment in Aquitaine priority over its use anywhere else. Additionally, Pepin is likely to have understood that Desiderius was no great menace to the pope or his republic: the Lom-

---

[29] On these two matters see Hodgkin, *Italy and Her Invaders*, 7.270–273.

[30] See Miller, "Byzantine-Papal Relations," pp. 59–60.

[31] See ibid., pp. 58–60.

[32] For a description of the background of the problem see Llewellyn, *Rome in the Dark Ages*, pp. 215–217. But see especially Bertolini, "Le prime manifestazioni concrete del potere temporale," and idem, "Sergio, arcivescovo di Ravenna, 744–769"; also Baumont, "Paul I$^{er}$," pp. 12–13.

[33] See the two Bertolini articles in n. 32 above.

[34] The only attempt at thorough consideration of the curial administration in the mid-eighth century is Bertolini, *Roma*, pp. 614–622.

[35] Archibald R. Lewis, *The Development of Southern French and Catalan Society, 718–1050*, pp. 30–31.

[36] See for example, ARF, pp. 20–24. The Aquitanian war dominates in the Frankish sources of the period.

bard's restricted use of force, avoidance of war against Rome, and willingness to keep dialogue going were all sufficient to show Pepin that Pavia
was keeping well within the bounds of the 760 *modus vivendi*. There was
therefore no need for military intervention. Finally, as noted, Paul did not
request armed assistance from Pepin. Limited importance of the territorial
issue, the Aquitaine problem, the lack of a real Lombard danger, and papal
restraint collectively explain why Frankish force was not introduced into
Italy in the 760–765 period.

One is left to consider why Desiderius would not fulfill his 760 promise,
why he turned to force during the controversy, and why he finally transferred the disputed places to the papacy. No source tells us why the king
reneged on his 760 promise, but two considerations were apt to have been
important. First, as before, to give up the territories, at least without first
going through strong resistance, might seriously offend Lombard nobles.
And second, Desiderius must have asked himself why he should yield the
places if he did not have to do so. Paul could not force his hand alone, and
Pepin was in no position to exercise other than diplomatic pressure. One
suspects that this circumstance was most persuasive. The royal switch from
dialogue to military and literary threats seems easily explained. By 762 or
763 Paul was mounting steady and relentless pressure to secure the complete
return of the territories, and Pepin was supporting him at every turn.
Desiderius evidently felt that the time had come to persuade Paul to reduce
his pressure and to secure a lessening of Frankish intervention. It was
probably thus that force was applied—enough to frighten the pope into
worrying about the safety of the papal state at a time in which Pepin could
not act in arms for Rome. The implication was that if Paul refused to tolerate
the royal non-compliance in the territorial affair Lombard forces might
increase their activity and overrun the republic. An escalation of sorts
apparently did occur, for Paul spoke first of devastations and next of attacks
upon Sinigaglia and in Campania, suggesting two stages, the second more
serious than the first. Desiderius was evidently trying to browbeat Paul
into abandoning or lessening the pressure on the territorial question, a
repeat on a small scale of the tactics which were apparently employed by
Liutprand and Aistulf to seek royal-papal peace and papal neutrality toward
the Lombard Kingdom of Italy.[37] Paul was seemingly not gravely disturbed
by the royal depredations, however, and that in itself may explain why
Desiderius gave up the same game of force and finally turned over the
territories. The solution was not to return to simple non-compliance, for
Frankish and papal *missi*, not to mention hordes of witnesses from the
disputed places, would hound him endlessly; rather, he would end the
problem by complying, as he did in the settlement of 765.[38] Lombard nobles
might fume, but they would be few in view of Desiderius's eight-year
resistance on various territorial matters and recent warning to Paul and his

---

[37] Appreciated by Miller, "Papal-Lombard Relations," p. 374.
[38] Miller (Ibid.) asserts that it was Pepin's pressure which secured his cooperation.

Romans that Pavia was not without the capacity to wage war in the papal state. Desiderius had again shown that Pavia had considerable room for pursuit of its Italian objectives; but he also had learned again that there were limits to that action.

For the remainder of Paul's pontificate, the year and a half from late 765 until June 767, there were no notable developments in the royal-papal relationship and no important changes on the Italian political scene. The sources are devoid of information bearing upon either, suggesting a normal situation. Most importantly, nothing seems to have disturbed Desiderius's settlement of 765, for there is not a hint of non-compliance or any other form of trouble. The *modus vivendi* was evidently fully operative, with Pavia and Rome apparently at last reaching a balanced relationship.[39]

## UPHEAVAL IN ROME AND DESIDERIUS'S ATTEMPT TO CONTROL THE PAPACY

In the city of Rome in mid-767, however, there began a train of events wherein the royal-papal relationship was subjected to new strains and threatened with utter breakdown. Before the end of June, 768 it became known that Pope Paul was very ill.[40] As the news spread, a conspiracy took shape. The leaders were rural Roman aristocrats from Nepi in Roman Tuscany, four brothers named Toto, Constantine, Passivo, and Pasquale. They had numerous followers in Roman Tuscany. At first they apparently planned to break into Rome, assassinate Paul, terrorize the city, and impose election of Constantine as pope, even though he was a layman. The energetic and experienced *primicerius* Christopher discovered the plot and tried to thwart it. Summoning Toto and his associates to his house, Christopher persuaded them to desist from their plans and had them swear not to bring armed men into the city. This was enough to deter Toto for the moment, but when it was learned late in June 767 that Paul's death was imminent, Toto and his brothers brought armed peasants and Tuscan militia into Rome, occupying the city with such ease that connivance of the urban military leadership is suspected. The city's commander or *dux*, Gregory, who was a supporter of Christopher, was apparently neutralized. Controlling Rome, Toto gathered his followers at his house and had that group proclaim Constantine as pope when Paul died. Constantine was thereupon rushed to the Lateran, where a terrified bishop successively ordained the pope-elect subdeacon and then deacon without heed to canonical regulations. The Roman populace was then summoned to swear fidelity to Constantine, and on 5 July 767 he was consecrated Pope Constantine II.

The new pope hastened to enlist the support the King Pepin. Writing a few days after his coup and then again in September,[41] Constantine argued

---

[39] Miller (Ibid., pp. 375–376) terms the *modus vivendi* "a political equilibrium" and sees its accomplishment as the chief accomplishment of the post-756 period.

[40] The following events from Paul's illness through the election of Stephen III are described in *Vita Stephani III, LP* I, 2.468–11.471. See also the deposition given by Christopher in 769 at the Lateran council of that year in *VS III*, 480–481, n. 3.

[41] *CC* #98 and 99, 649–653.

that he had been thrust into office by the will of others,[42] justified the usurpation on the ground that Paul had been an excessively harsh and unjust pope,[43] and called upon Pepin to maintain the special relationship which had prevailed between him and Constantine's two predecessors, Stephen II and Paul I.[44] Constantine also begged Pepin to ignore any hostile rumors which he might hear about him,[45] probably a reference to his fear that Christopher had been or would be in touch with the *patricius Romanorum*. Pepin did not respond to Constantine, possibly a sign that he did not recognize the new regime.

In the meantime, the usurpers tried to acquire permanent military ascendance. Toto secured the death of Duke Gregory and made himself duke in his place while his followers terrorized Roman Campania, a region which seems to have been much opposed to the Tuscan regime. Christopher apparently resisted openly for a while, but eventually, in early 768, had to take refuge in the basilica of St. Peter with his son, the high-ranking curialist Sergius. Constantine tried to lure them out, but they would not be fooled, begging instead to be permitted to retire to a monastery of their own selection. Constantine consented, and in April 768 Christopher and Sergius went to the monastery of St. Salvador near Rieti in the duchy of Spoleto. But before reaching the monastery they went to Duke Theodicius of Spoleto, imploring him to take them to the court of King Desiderius, whose intervention in Rome they desired to free the city of Toto and Constantine. Theodicius did as he was bid, and Desiderius personally authorized Christopher to direct Spoletan soldiers for the overthrow of Toto and the deposition of Constantine. Christopher and Sergius thereupon took up headquarters at Rieti and there made the necessary contacts in Rome with high military and curial personnel opposed to the Tuscans and gathered in the Spoletan forces. Also present in Rieti was Waldipert, a Lombard priest who was to be Desiderius's representative in the enterprise.

In late July 768 Sergius and Waldipert led the operation against Rome while Christopher stayed behind in Rieti. Friends let them into the city, but Toto, who seems to have been completely taken by surprise, put up effective resistance for a time. The duke was killed, however, and on the last day of July Constantine and his brother Passivo were arrested by Roman collaborators of Christopher after being hounded from one church to another. At this juncture, there was a major unexpected development.

Without any prior consultation with Christopher and Sergius, Waldipert went with some Romans (no Lombard troops are mentioned) to the monastery of St. Vitus, seized the monastery chaplain, a certain priest named Philip, and acclaimed him pope. The dazed Philip was then carried into the Lateran where he was made to host a banquet for some members of the high clerical administration and the Roman military aristocracy. But

---

[42] Ibid., #99, 650–651.
[43] Ibid., 651.
[44] For example, Ibid., 651–652.
[45] Ibid., 652.

Christopher, who by now had come over to Rome from Rieti, stood outside the city loudly insisting that Philip had to be expelled from the Lateran. Waldipert's coup thereupon collapsed as prominent Romans, responding to Christopher's pronouncement, quietly took possession of Philip and led him back to his monastery. With Toto dead, Constantine II under arrest, and Waldipert's coup suppressed, Christopher was in command and promptly set about restoring legitimacy to the papacy. Selected as the best man to fill the special needs of the moment was the priest Stephen, a cleric of impeccable clerical credentials, an intimate of Stephen II and Paul I, an experienced papal diplomat, and a long-term member of the *iudices de clero*.[46] On 1 August 768 the day after Philip's deposition, Christopher gathered an assembly of Roman clergy, aristocrats and people which unanimously raised Stephen to St. Peter's chair as Pope Stephen III (768–772). The dynasty of Stephen II and Paul I had been restored.

In the meantime, terrible deeds of violence occurred after Constantine's deposition and Philip's ouster. Constantine's brother, Passivus, and his *vicedominus*, Theodore, were both seized and blinded.[47] An ally of Toto, a certain Grachilis, was blinded and deprived of his tongue, while Constantine himself suffered the same fate.[48] Waldipert was no luckier. He is reported to have plotted with the duke of Spoleto and a number of Romans to kill Christopher and other Roman leaders and to hand Rome over to the Lombards.[49] Once this charge was known, he was arrested, pulled violently from the church where he had taken refuge, hiding vainly behind an image of the Virgin. He was subsequently imprisoned in a Lateran cell and then had his tongue and eyes ripped out by unnamed people, but surely at the order of Christopher. A few days later Waldipert died of his wounds.[50]

Why, did Christopher turn to Desiderius for help in deposing Constantine? At first sight the choice seems to be an odd one, for Christopher was an architect of the papal-Frankish alliance, which, as has been noted, was pointedly anti-Lombard in its original vision in the mind of Stephen II. But there was nevertheless considerable sense in Christopher's action. Pepin would of course have been preferred as *patricius Romanorum*, but the Frank was still sunk in the Aquitanian quagmire, and had not been disposed to direct military intervention in Italy since 756, leaving aid to be sought elsewhere. The empire was both powerless and heretical, and the dukes of Spoleto and Benevento could not be approached for that would be apt to provoke Desiderius, only adding to Rome's problems. The alternative was Desiderius, approached *through* the duke of Spoleto, a nice touch of protocol which Desiderius would be bound to notice and appreciate. But Desiderius was no last and worst choice, for Christopher knew better than

[46] On the selection of Stephen III see Jan T. Hallenbeck, "Pope Stephen III: Why was He Elected?" pp. 287–299.

[47] *VS III*, 12.471. For a good description of the post-election violence see Llewellyn, *Rome in the Dark Ages*, pp. 223–224.

[48] *VS III*, 13–14.472.

[49] Ibid., 15.472.

[50] Ibid., 15–16.472–73.

most that the king in his reign had never been a serious enemy of Rome or the papacy and had in 765 granted the papacy at least limited satisfaction in the territorial disputes in which the *primicerius* had been involved since their inception. It is also possible that by 768 Desiderius was understood by Christopher and the Romans to be Pepin's agent in Italy,[51] a view which was apt to have arisen from Pepin's insistence that Pope Paul move into full and frank cooperation with Pavia in defending Italy against the Byzantines. If so, it is not unthinkable that while Christopher was in Pavia seeking Desiderius's help there were contacts with Pepin through which the Frank authorized Desiderius to intervene in Rome for the sake of the papacy.[52] What seems likely from all this is that even though Christopher knew that allowing Desiderius to act in Rome entailed certain risks, there were good reasons for trusting him to do no more than help depose Constantine.

The other side of the problem is equally important: why did Desiderius assure Christopher of his assistance against Constantine? A possibility is that Pepin ordered him to do so as Francia's Italian agent. Such an order may have been given, but there were surely other reasons as well. First, the cooperation was not out of character with the apparently constructive royal-papal relationship after the resolution of the territorial differences in 765. In brief, it may have been only a function of the currently harmonious nature of the royal-papal relationship. But, that is probably too limited a view, for Rome was in terrible disorder and Desiderius was doubtless invited to reflect upon the options open to him if he should intervene to depose Constantine, and use that intervention to give Rome a pope who would follow the lead of Pavia in Italian affairs.[53] Among other things, Desiderius could contemplate such a pontiff allowing him to have back much or all of the papal state which Stephen II had gouged from Aistulf in 755-756. In such circumstances, the Lombard Kingdom of Italy as Aistulf had known it might be restored.

Desiderius may have been thinking in such cosmic terms for several reasons. Pepin was mired in Aquitaine, unable to act in Italy, and was evidently suggesting that Pavia was being delegated management of Italy for Francia. In both respects the implication to Desiderius was that he was coming to have an increasingly free hand in Italy, despite the limits shown him by Pepin in 765. This prospective freedom, combined with his successes from his accession to 765, perhaps emboldened him in 767 to think in extreme terms about what he might be able to accomplish if his aid to Christopher were converted to royal selection and domination of Constantine II's successor.

One cannot prove the scope and details of Desiderius's thinking, for Christopher was able to oust Philip; but the king apparently helped Chris-

---

[51] Miller, "Papal-Lombard Relations," pp. 374-375.

[52] Bertolini, *Roma*, p. 628.

[53] See for example Ibid., p. 630 and Kleinclausz, *Charlemagne*, p. 7. One scholar asserts that Desiderius's aim was to gain direct control of the papal state. Sefton, *The Pontificate of Hadrian*, p. 31. The view cannot be substantiated.

topher so that he would be in a position to install a puppet. That seems clear in that Waldipert took steps to elevate the priest Philip. Waldipert did not act on behalf of Christopher and Sergius, for they knew nothing of his stroke when it occurred and were opposed to it after it happened. Nor was the coup attempted as a seizure by some party of Romans, for such of the latter who were involved were clearly in Waldipert's service, not he in theirs.[54] And Waldipert was obviously not working on his own behalf, for attempted domination of the papacy by a lone Lombard priest makes no sense at all. This leaves only Desiderius as Waldipert's sponsor, and since Waldipert's interest was installation of a weak figure who could be easily controlled, it follows that it was Desiderius's aim as well. Philip was an ideal figurehead. He had no control over his installation, had no power in Rome or anywhere else, and would not ever be apt to assert himself. Philip was to be Desiderius's route to domination of the papacy, whatever the particular objectives of that domination might have been.

Christopher knew that there were risks, and one was the prospect just raised. It would be interesting to know what understandings were reached in Pavia in private negotiation before Desiderius agreed to let Christopher have the Spoletan strength requested for deposition of Constantine. Only one thing is sure to have been specified: the Lombard military aid was for use against Constantine. But very likely Christopher did not in any respect sanction Desiderius to appoint the next pope—which, since Desiderius *did* aim to do that, leaves little doubt that the king deceived the Romans once the expedition was in progress. If for no other reason, Christopher would have vetoed a royal dictation because he had his own choice in Stephen III and was determined to have him both as the means of restoring clerical rule in Rome and perpetuating his own powerful influence.[55] But, Desiderius gave Christopher something important, the Spoletan aid, and unless Desiderius was acting only by order of Pepin, Christopher must have promised *something* in order to secure it. If it was not the right to select the next pope, what was it? Perhaps Waldipert's role as the co-leader of the enterprise was Christopher's concession, for Waldipert's presence was no small worry to him in that it built a royal role into an enterprise that was actually more ducal than royal.

What of the statement that after the collapse of his attempt to elevate Philip Waldipert plotted with the duke of Spoleto to kill Christopher and other leaders and hand Rome over to the Lombard? There are at least three possibilities here. First, Desiderius may have ordered such plotting by Waldipert before the intervention as part of the effort to elevate a puppet pope. For successful puppetry, the argument runs, the Lateran had to be clear of enemies, and such clearance could be quickly achieved by assas-

---

[54] Bertolini, *Roma*, p. 630. Here Philip is viewed as simply Waldipert's instrument, not at all representative of a point of view in Rome. It is doubtful that there was ever a Lombard party in Rome. On this question, see Jan T. Hallenbeck, "The Lombard Party in Eighth-Century Rome: A Case of Mistaken Identity," pp. 951–966.

[55] On Christopher's reasons for selecting Stephen III, see Hallenbeck, "Pope Stephen III," pp. 296–299.

sinations carried out by Waldipert in conspiracy with the duke. But this view appears dubious because it ascribes to Desiderius violent outlooks and methods which seem inconsistent with his past treatment of the papacy. Second, Waldipert may have been acting on his own. Desperate after the failure of the coup, he was perhaps driven to the extreme of wildly planning to murder Christopher in cooperation with Duke Theodicius. One finds this argument too speculative to be credible, however. Finally, it is possible that Waldipert actually did no plotting at all, but was merely *said* by Christopher and his party to be doing so, the purpose being to vilify him. It is important to realize that the alleged conspiracy occurred amid the brutalization of Constantine and his associates, which was without doubt ordered by Christopher.[56] The brutalizations were obviously a purge of Christopher's foes, and one of these was Waldipert, for by trying to place Philip upon the papal throne he had clearly betrayed the action to depose Toto and Constantine. Simply put, Christopher had Waldipert mutilated, making the charge that the Lombard was conspiring to kill Christopher and hand Rome over to the Lombards the most likely justification for the mutilation.

Who were the Romans who are said to have assisted Waldipert in the elevation of Philip? They are not specified as other than members of the curial administration and the military aristocracy, and they were apparently few because the great part of both groups obviously remained loyal, the coup in which they participated failed quickly and decisively, and they apparently felt too weak to risk violence. Why these people cooperated with Waldipert is unclear. Perhaps they were members of a pro-Lombard party, a Lombard fifth-column in Rome devoted to serving Desiderius's interests from within. That seems unlikely, however, for no such group had existed before and one is not likely to have grown up overnight in the 768 disturbances.[57] Rather, the partisans of Waldipert were probably enemies of Constantine *and* Christopher, important Romans who were pleased to see an end to the Tuscan regime but also unhappy with the prospect of renewed dominance by Christopher and his son. Wanting to deny the latter, they sided with Waldipert, who offered the only available means of resisting Christopher although he was a foreigner and servant of Desiderius. In this respect, the crushing of Waldipert by Christopher may also have broken what little internal resistance there was to his return to power.

It is not possible to speak with certainty about the developments of 768, but the following reconstruction may represent the most tenable interpretation. Embarking upon his project to oust Constantine and Toto in 768, Christopher knew that he needed external help. Pepin as *patricius Romanorum* was preferred, but only Desiderius was available, an acceptable selection since the Lombard had never been a serious enemy of Rome, had three years earlier satisfied the papal territorial demands, and was perhaps by this time understood in Rome as Pepin's agent. Desiderius, deceiving Christopher from the start, agreed to provide the requested help so that

---

[56] Ibid.
[57] See Hallenbeck, "The Lombard Party in Eighth Century Rome," pp. 961–962.

he could intervene in Rome and appoint a pope who would be dominated by the crown in his Italian activities. Desiderius could think in such radical terms because Pepin was evidently turning management of Italy over to him and could no longer act in Italy against Pavia. The royal agent for procurement of a Lombard figurehead pope was the priest Waldipert, and the confused Philip was the intended figurehead. In the negotiations between Desiderius and Christopher before the beginning of the intervention, Desiderius told Christopher nothing of his real plans. To enlist Desiderius's help against Constantine, Christopher probably accepted Waldipert as the leader or co-leader of the project. Waldipert was guilty of trying to place the papacy under Desiderius's control, but not conspiring to kill Christopher and present Rome to the Lombards: that was a false charge of Christopher as part of his effort to purge enemies and consolidate his power in Rome after the fall of Constantine. Finally, although there were Romans who participated in Desiderius's attempted coup, they represented not a pro-Lombard faction in Rome but enemies of Christopher who were opposing him by exploiting the coup. They failed, as did Waldipert and Desiderius, leaving only Christopher and Stephen III as the beneficiaries of the fall of Constantine and the Lombard intervention.

These developments had serious implications for the relationship between the Lombard monarchy and the papacy. For example, Christopher could have had nothing but distrust for Desiderius. To the *primicerius*, now dominant in Rome, the king had engaged in perfidious treachery, using the promised support to attempt to steal the papacy for Pavia. But Desiderius was also unquestionably bound to have been estranged from Christopher: the coup had failed because of Christopher, and Waldipert had been brutalized at his behest. For Desiderius, Christopher was an enemy, to be punished for his insults. Whereas in 767 there was and had been for some time an essential condition of amity and cooperation between Pavia and Rome, now in 768 that harmony was suddenly gone, replaced by a stormy gulf between Desiderius and Christopher, who was the dominant personality within the new regime of Stephen III. There was, of course, potential here for the breakdown of the 760–767 Italian *modus vivendi*, for the latter was in large measure predicated upon the peaceful co-existence of the monarchy and the papacy. Worrisome also was Desiderius's attempt to impose Pavia's will upon the papacy through royal appointment of a figurehead pontiff, hardly the kind of behavior necessary for continuation of status quo equilibrium. The implication was that Desiderius no longer felt bound by the limits of the 760–767 political organization, but was coming to believe that he had enough strength to step beyond it, for royal interests alone. For both the royal-papal relationship and Italian politics at large, then, a new stage was evidently in the making by August 768, one characterized by renewed Lombard-papal tension and royal efforts toward aggrandizement at Rome's expense. But for the moment the most visible thing was the impending dissolution of the status quo.

# VII. REALIGNMENT AND ACCOMMODATION

Late in September 768, about two months after the deposition of Constantine II and the election of Stephen III, King Pepin died. There
followed a division of the Frankish kingdom into two realms, one
for his elder son Charles, and the other for his younger son, Carloman.[1]
The latter received the larger of the two inheritances, the most settled and
developed areas of Pepin's kingdom: Provence, Septimania, eastern Aquitaine, Burgundy, eastern Neustria, and Alemannia. This was a compact
territory allowing ready access to Italy. Charles's kingdom formed an arc
around Carloman's inheritance from the Pyrenees to Bavaria and was composed of newer Frankish territories, some of which were only nominally
obedient: western Aquitaine, western Neustria, most of Austrasia, Frisia,
Hesse, and Thuringia. There was no natural integration of these places, and
they did not touch Italy, being blocked from it completely by the kingdom
of Carloman.

### ROYAL TENSIONS IN FRANCIA AND THEIR RELATION TO DESIDERIUS AND THE PAPACY

Charles and Carloman viewed one another with hostility. The root of
the difficulty is not really discernible,[2] but in 769 the two were said to have
reached the brink of war[3] as Charles was outraged when Carloman de-
clined to aid him in a military campaign in Aquitaine.[4] The tension was
only exacerbated by certain considerations arising from Pepin's division.
On the one hand, Charles resented both Carloman's possession of the better
parts of Francia and his exclusive control of direct communication with
Italy, especially with the papacy.[5] On the other hand, Carloman saw himself

---

[1] The *divisio* is fully delineated in *Fred. Chron.* 121. For modern maps see Kleinclausz, *Charlemagne*, p. 5 and Jacques Boussard, *The Civilization of Charlemagne*, pp. 40–41. See also L.
Oelsner, *Jahrbücher*, pp. 523–526. The principal modern treatment of Charles and Carloman
is still Martin Lintzel, "Karl der Grosse und Karlmann," pp. 1–22.

[2] Some authorities trace the trouble to the circumstances of the birth of Charles as opposed
to those of Carloman. When Charles was born, his mother, Bertrada, was no more than Pepin's
concubine, but by the time of Carloman's birth Pepin and Bertrada were man and wife in a
canonic marriage. Carloman could therefore look upon his brother as illegitimate and expect
to have Pepin's entire inheritance. See for example Winston, *Charlemagne: From the Hammer
to the Cross*, pp. 4–5.

[3] *Vita Karoli Magni*, 3.4–5.

[4] *Ann. Ein.*, a. 769, p. 29. But Einhard asserts that the high tension was caused by associates
of Carloman who deliberately sought to undermine good relations between the two kings.
*Vita Karoli Magni*, 3.5. See also Kleinclausz, *Charlemagne*, pp. 4–6; Lintzel, "Karl der Grosse,"
pp. 1–6.

[5] Bertolini, *Roma*, p. 648.

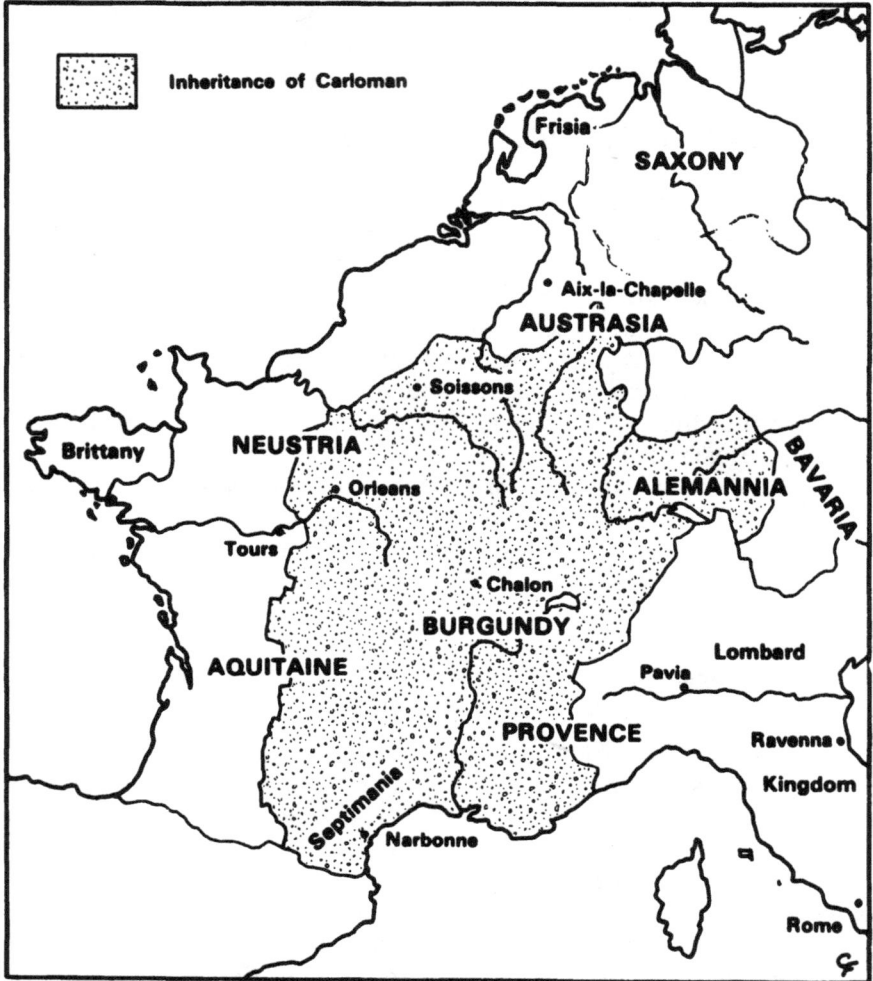

MAP. 6. Pepin's division of the Frankish kingdom, 768: Jacques Boussard, *The Civilization of Charlemagne*, 1968: pp. 40–41.

surrounded by Charles's territories, menaced on three sides and free from danger only on the Italian and Bavarian frontiers. Francia was poised for dynastic war in which personal animosity and dissatisfaction with Pepin's division were central factors.

Curiously, there has been little consideration of King Desiderius's perspectives upon these developments. The Frankish situation had direct implications for royal interests, the monarchy's relations with the papacy, and Italian political affairs at large. First, the tension between the two Franks suggested that neither might be inclined or able to have significant interest or involvement in Italy as war in Francia might occupy and devour them. In this case, the increased freedom in Italy which Pavia had begun to enjoy in the later stage of Pepin's reign, especially visible in the episode of the fall of Constantine II, would be greatly enhanced. Desiderius might reach the point of being virtually unrestricted in what he could do in Italy, for neither Rome nor the empire could curb him. But there was another possibility: Charles, already surrounding Carloman on three sides, could effect complete geographic encirclement by forming an alliance with the Lombard monarchy. Like the first prospect, that development could encourage rather full royal freedom of action in Italy, for one *patricius Romanorum* would be a Lombard ally and the other would be apt to be neutralized in Francia by the alignment between Charles and Desiderius, leaving Rome without any Frankish support at all. As long as Carloman and Charles remained divided the time might soon be at hand wherein the Lombard crown would be at liberty to work its ends in Italy freely.

As Charles and Carloman fumed at one another, Pope Stephen III sent forth envoys announcing a church council in Rome for 769. Italian bishops were enlisted, and to Francia went Sergius, the practiced son of Christopher, to have Pepin provide Frankish bishops.[6] Learning that Pepin had died, Sergius called upon first one son and then the other to furnish the bishops. Warmly received by both Charles and Carloman, Sergius was given to know at both courts that the bishops would attend.[7] Moreover, Sergius was able to report to Stephen when he returned to Rome by the end of 768 or early 769 that Carloman and Charles alike viewed the *pactum* between Stephen II, Paul I, and Pepin as the basis of their dealing with the papacy.[8] When the council convened in April 769 there were twelve Frankish bishops present, several of them being veteran diplomats who had been utilized by Pepin in maintenance of the Papal-Frankish association.[9] The council itself, known as the Lateran council of 769, provided for formal removal and punishment of Constantine II, procedural guidance for proper conduct of papal election—especially prohibition of lay succession—review of the clerical appointments and promotions which had been made by Constantine, and new rejection of the imperial Iconoclastic heresy.[10] From the lack of any comment to the contrary, it appears that the Frankish bishops supported these measures without dissent.

Despite their differences in other areas, Carloman and Charles in 768–769 became one in their adherence to the papacy. They both informed Stephen III that they subscribed to the arrangements made by Pepin with the papacy, that is, that they supported the papal-Frankish association. They further promised to provide the bishops requested by Sergius for the

---

[6] *VS III*, 16.473. See also Duchesne, *VS III*, p. 482, n. 27.

[7] Ibid., pp. 16–17.473–474.

[8] The apparent meaning of CC #45, 562, lines 23–35.

[9] The bishops are listed by name. *VS III*, 17.473–474. See also Duchesne, *VS III*, p. 482, notes 28–32.

[10] The *LP* recitation of the council is *VS III*, 17–24.474–477. For the council's decree on papal elections see *Concilium Romanum, a. 769*, 1.1.86–89. Of the secondary discussions see Charles Hefele, *History of the Councils of the Church*, 5.473–476; Bertolini, *Roma*, pp. 635–640.

Roman council, and saw to it that they attended. They may also have instructed the bishops to follow the papal lead at the council, for they apparently did not oppose any of the measures brought forth by Christopher and Stephen. In both the episcopal attendance at the council and support of its resolutions was implicit Carolingian endorsement of the pontificate of Stephen III as legitimate, purged of the stain of Constantine's lay usurpation. For the time being both Charles and Carloman were firm in their allegiance to the papacy and committed to their *patricius Romanorum* duties.[11]

The mutual solidarity of Charles and Carloman with Rome despite their severe personal tensions is explicable on several counts. First, the two kings had both grown up within the papal-Frankish association. Having been crowned *patricius Romanorum* long before in 754, and having for years seen Pepin's military and diplomatic service, the devotion of each king to the papacy was only natural. Further, conscious that trouble could result if the kings were to ignore Italy, or if Charles decided to ally with Desiderius against Carloman, the papacy deliberately stressed the *patricius Romanorum* duty of *both* rulers. Sergius evidently impressed that upon the two when he circulated in Francia in 768, or so it would seem in his report to Stephen that both monarchs subscribed to Pepin's arrangements with the papacy. Additional papal emphasis upon the necessity of unified Carolingian support is visible in the insistence of Sergius that both kings send representatives to the Lateran council. Finally, Charles and Carloman may have mutually supported Rome because of their tensions. Carloman perhaps assured loyalty to Rome in part because he feared that if he did not do so Charles would be able to monopolize Pepin's former patrician relationship with the papacy. Charles may have supported Rome to prevent Carloman from enjoying the same sort of monopoly. In this view, the solidarity of the Carolingians with Rome was to some extent an artificial matter, a case of preemptive politics.

With the two kings firmly adhering to the papal-Frankish alliance, Stephen III told them probably before the end of 769 that they should assist the papacy to gain a return of the *plenaria iustitiae* from King Desiderius; he received word from them that they would do so with all their strength.[12] Probably early in 770 the pope responded, giving his thanks, underscoring the *iustitiae* problem again, once more calling for aid from both kings, and stressing that they should not believe anyone who claimed that the *iustitiae* were already in papal possession.[13] The *plenaria iustitiae* issue, which had presumably been settled in 760 when Pepin prevailed upon Pope Paul to drop the claim,[14] was suddenly again a central concern. The renewal was a major development, worthy of careful reflection.

---

[11] Seen indistinctly by Bertolini, *Roma*, p. 640.
[12] The exchange is visible in CC #44, 559, lines 1–20.
[13] Ibid., 559–560.
[14] See above, ch. 6, p. 98.

The explanation for the return to the *plenaria iustitiae* claim in 769 must begin with recognition that it appears to have been a contrivance of the *primicerius* Christopher. He was one of the original architects of the *iustitiae* claim,[15] he, not Stephen III, was the dominant figure in papal circles in 769,[16] and Stephen soon abandoned it when he decided to end Christopher's dominance. As *primicerius* Christopher was chief among the *proceres ecclesiae*, the Lateran bureaucracy, whose hand in Rome was immeasurably strengthened by the fall of Constantine and the success of Christopher's coup generally.[17] The *primicerius* post also gave Christopher primacy in Rome's legal class, the most important lay group in the city apart from the military aristocracy. But Christopher had military leadership as well, for his protégé Gratiosus—who had performed great feats in the deposition of Constantine—was made duke of Rome, or commander of the army and head of the military nobles.[18] Christopher furthermore had Gratiosus marry his daughter. Army and Lateran were therefore in concert, with Christopher presiding over both.[19] Dominant in Rome, Christopher was in 769 also fiercely anti-Lombard, or at least violently opposed to the Lombard king, Desiderius.[20] The trouble between Christopher and Desiderius stemmed from Desiderius's 768 attempt to elevate Philip as a pro-Lombard puppet in the context of the Lombard aid in the deposition of Constantine: Christopher regarded this as a royal betrayal of the papacy, an insidious perversion of a friendly act. Desiderius to Christopher was a perfidious enemy, never to be trusted and always to be feared. Having sufficient power in Rome to decide its foreign policy alone, and being intensely hostile to Desiderius, Christopher, it is argued here, renewed the *iustitiae* claim through the medium of Stephen III to damage his royal enemy by redeeming the most serious papal defeat suffered at Desiderius's hands. In the process, he would also redeem a personal defeat, for Christopher had helped to shape the *plenaria iustitiae* concept.

After the papacy advanced the *plenaria iustitiae* claim again, and after both Carloman and Charles had replied positively to Stephen III, King Desiderius intervened in an internal problem in the papal republic. The trouble stemmed from a dispute over the succession to the archepiscopal throne of Ravenna.[21] Archbishop Sergius, who had been brought to submission by Pope Paul I, died in late August 769. Those in Ravenna loyal

---

[15] See above ch. 5, pp. 85–86 and n. 18.

[16] For example, Bertolini, *Roma*, p. 641; Jan T. Hallenbeck, "Paul Afiarta and the Papacy: An Analysis of Politics in Eighth-Century Rome," pp. 45–46; idem, "Pope Stephen III," pp. 294–296; Llewellyn, *Rome in the Dark Ages*, pp. 225–226; Ottorino Bertolini, "La Caduta del primicerio Cristoforo (771) nella versione dei contemporanei, e le correnti anti-longobarde e filolongobarde in Roma alla fine del pontificato di Stefano III (771–772)," pp. 366–367.

[17] Bertolini, *Roma*, p. 639.

[18] Ibid., p. 641.

[19] Ibid.; idem, "La Caduta del primicerio Cristoforo," p. 367.

[20] See Hallenbeck, "Paul Afiarta and the Papacy," p. 45 and n. 39.

[21] For what follows see *VS III*, 25.477. Secondary accounts are Hodgkin, *Italy and Her Invaders*, 7.339–340; Bertolini, *Roma*, pp. 643–544.

to Rome advanced the candidacy of archdeacon Leo, who was perhaps Sergius's natural successor. But a strong party favoring separation of Ravenna from Rome, that is, Ravenna's secession from the papal republic, backed a rival, the *scrinarius* of the Ravennese church, Michael, who, like Christopher in Rome, was a layman. Michael had the support of troops commanded by Maurice, the duke of Rimini, indicating that the secessionist movement reached well beyond Ravenna. Maurice's forces entered Ravenna and effected the election of Michael, who was then installed in the archepiscopal palace. In the meantime, ties were formed between Michael and Desiderius, for at the king's request Archdeacon Leo was taken as a captive to Rimini by Duke Maurice. And when Pope Stephen steadfastly refused to consecrate Michael as archbishop on the grounds that lay occupancy of episcopal office was forbidden, Michael turned to Desiderius for support. After receiving gifts from Michael, the Lombard king placed royal troops at his disposal, thus strengthening him against Rome. In the meantime, apparently with the connivance of Michael, Desiderius attacked the nominally Byzantine regions of Venetia and Istria, including patrimonies belonging to the important patriarch of Grado.[22]

A plausible explanation for Desiderius's intervention in the disputed Ravenna succession and attack upon Venetia and Istria is that both were retaliations for Christopher's renewal of the *plenaria iustitiae* claim. Desiderius's action hurt the papacy in several respects. It protected lay occupancy of the episcopal office, forbidden in Rome only a few months previously—a direct challenge and insult to Christopher, Stephen III, and their Lateran council. It also furthered factional division within the papal state and promoted those elements in Ravenna and the Pentapolis which wanted no part of subordination to Rome and the papacy.[23] As for the Venetian and Istrian operations, they created a Lombard menace, especially to the church of Grado which had long been an anti-Lombard bulwark,[24] and generated confusion on the northern limits of the papal republic. In all, Desiderius's activity degraded and humiliated the great church of Ravenna, which was supposed to be dependent upon the pope within the republic, and challenged Rome's ability to rule the entire Adriatic portion of that republic.

The purpose of the royal interventions is not clear. Was it a resumption of the apparent former royal tactic of applying pressure upon the papacy to secure an end to unfavorable papal activity, in this case abandonment of the *plenaria iustitiae* claim? Or, did it herald a second effort by Desiderius to alter his treatment of the papacy, the first being the 768 bid to install a puppet pope, and this one being an attempt to prepare the way for annexation of the papacy's Adriatic districts?[25] One suspects that it was a

[22] The situation in Venetia and Istria is visible in *Ep. Lang. Col.*, ep. #19, pp. 712–713.
[23] Bertolini, *Roma*, p. 644.
[24] Ibid.
[25] An essentially similar view is Cutler, (*Carolingian Italian Policies*, pp. 89–93) who holds that Desiderius was seeking to disturb the Italian equilibrium by extending Lombard influence in Italy.

tactic rather than a sign of a new departure, but the matter never developed to the point that its intentions were clear. There was great concern in Rome over the situation, and an understanding may have evolved between Christopher and Stephen III that this was the harvest of Christopher's return to the *iustitiae* claim.

## THE MARRIAGE ALLIANCE

While Lombard-papal tension mounted over the situations in Ravenna, Venetia, and Istria, late in 769 or early in 770 Pope Stephen began to hear of impending marriages, one between a daughter of Desiderius and either Charles or Carloman[26] and the other between Gisela, the sister of Charles and Carloman, and Desiderius's son.[27] Desiderius, the pope had heard, had persuaded the Franks to accept these unions. Immediately Stephen acted to oppose both marriages by writing to both Charles and Carloman,[28] who were already aware of and agitated by the Lombard intrusion in the papal state.[29] It would be diabolical, Stephen began, for one of the two to marry Desiderius's daughter. The union would contaminate the illustrious Franks, for the Lombards were a foul people, cursed with leprosy. The kings were warned that Scripture shows that princes who marry foreign wives are driven by them from holy ways. Stephen continued that the kings should both stay in lawful, canonical marriage with their present wives. Here the pope was in error, for Pepin's wife, Hilmitrude, was a concubine, not a canonically sanctioned spouse.[30] In any event, the wives were extolled as virtuous, beautiful, and Frankish, and any remarriage of the kings was pronounced canonically impossible. Nor should the sister, Gisela, become the wife of Desiderius's son. Why, inquired the pope, should she go to the Lombards when Pepin would not permit her to become the wife of Emperor Constantine V?[31] The kings were ordered to keep Gisela in Francia. Stephen then went on to raise political objections to the projected unions. The emphasis was that Charles and Carloman should both remain faithful to the Frankish support of and obedience to the papacy which had been promised by both their father and themselves. Desiderius was an enemy of St. Peter, and it would not do to have Charles, Carloman, or Gisela in any respect allied to him. Instead, the kings should help the papacy against Desiderius by forcing him to restore the republic—a reference to either the renewed *iustitiae* dispute or to the royal intervention in Ravenna and on the northern frontiers of the republic or perhaps both. Again one hears the warning that Charles and Carloman should not believe the assertions that Desiderius had already restored the claims. The letter ended with impressive strength: St. Peter, the pope, the curial bureaucracy, all Rome's clergy, the military

---

[26] CC #45, 561.

[27] Ibid., p. 562.

[28] Ibid., pp. 560–563.

[29] Cutler, *Carolingian Italian Policies*, p. 90.

[30] Peter Munz, *Life in the Age of Charlemagne*, p. 45.

[31] Byzantine envoys in about 764 proposed to Pepin that Gisela marry the emperor's son, but the offer was not accepted. See Miller, "Byzantine-Papal Relations," p. 60.

and judicial leaders, and all the people of the republic joined in urging the kings to retain their present wives, keep Gisela from Desiderius's son, and resist the Lombards for the church. If the pope was not obeyed there would be anathema on the authority of St. Peter, but obedience would be rewarded by heavenly bliss.

For several reasons Christopher was probably the author of this important letter.[32] First, nothing had happened to lessen his great power over the Lateran or the pope, in whose name the letter was sent: Christopher was in a position to dictate the letter if he wished to do so. There is also ample reason to suppose that he indeed wanted to write it, for the news from Francia involved potential advantage for his enemy, Desiderius. If Charles were to marry Desiderius's daughter, the *patricius Romanorum* solidarity of the two kings could easily end and the revived *plenaria iustitiae* claim could be easily nullified, with Charles being lured into becoming a papal enemy as a friend of Desiderius. The same division and nullification might well occur were Carloman to marry the Lombard princess. To Christopher, such gain for his bitter enemy was intolerable, a hateful prospect to be vigorously opposed, as in the long letter which he evidently composed for both kings. But the most convincing point favoring Christopher's authorship is the extensive vituperation of the Lombards found in the letter, surely a product of Christopher's pen as a reflection of his remorseless hatred for Desiderius and his long experience as an anti-Lombard leader.[33] In the letter the Lombards are lepers, treacherous, even pagans; they threaten corruption of the Franks, in comparison to whom they are base and vile. Desiderius is the worst of kings, an agent of the devil, worthless in every way. Surely this was the rhetoric of the *primicerius*, reason to think that he composed or at least dictated Stephen's letter resisting the prospective marriages.

It would soon become apparent that the marriage arrangements so dreaded in Rome involved the union of King Charles with Desiderius's daughter and marriage of Gisela, Charles's sister, with Desiderius's son Adelgis. If we may believe Stephen III's remark about the genesis of the Franco-Lombard marriage question, Desiderius was the initiating party. That is, the Lombard approached the Frank on the matter. What aims did Desiderius have in wanting to join his daughter and Charles, and Gisela and his son? As usual, no source specifically addresses the problem.

It would seem Desiderius's principal aim was to create a division in the Frankish kings' *patricius Romanorum* solidarity with the papacy.[34] As the Lombard monarch understood recent developments, Pavia stood to be

---

[32] Clearly recognized by Bertolini, "La Caduta del primicerio Cristoforo," pp. 355–356. See also Étienne Delaruelle, "Charlemagne, Carloman, Didier et la politique du mariage Franco-Lombard (770–771)," pp. 213–224, p. 218.

[33] Again clearly understood by Bertolini, "La Caduta del primicerio Cristoforo," p. 356.

[34] A generally recognized but undeveloped point. See for example Delaruelle, "Charlemagne, Carloman, Didier," p. 218. Normally the marriages are viewed almost exclusively from the Frankish and papal viewpoints, as for example in Delaruelle, "Charlemagne, Carloman, Didier"; Hodgkin, *Italy and Her Invaders*, 7.310–319; and Cutler, *Carolingian Italian Policies*, pp. 85–100.

forced into compliance on the *plenaria iustitiae* issue by both Charles and Carloman. They had readily supported the 769 council and both accepted the *iustitiae* claim. To deny papal success in the revived *iustitiae* demand and to keep the Franks out of Italy, it appears that Desiderius sought to break up permanently the joint support of the papacy which had been extended by Charles and Carloman and cultivated by Christopher and Stephen III. The method selected was the double device of activating tension between the two kings and attaching one of them more closely to Pavia than to Rome. If such was indeed the case, it certainly was a masterful conception, and Charles was designated the mainspring. By marrying Desiderius's daughter, Charles would be no less than his new kinsman. Inevitably, Charles could no longer perform his full *patricius Romanorum* services, for they had historically required action against his new ally and could now be performed only indirectly or not at all. Further, the tension between Charles and Carloman was probably heightened, for the alliance of Charles and Desiderius would encircle Carloman, causing him to doubt Charles's good intentions and fear him greatly. Nor could Carloman miss the point of complete encirclement: Duke Tassilo of Bavaria was married to another daughter of Desiderius,[35] making him and Charles both allies and brothers-in-law in their joint alliance with Desiderius, and a potential enemy of Carloman just as Desiderius was a potential foe. In these circumstances, there could be little further thought of shared patrician service by the Frankish kings. There would be only one operative patrician now, Carloman, and he would be so preoccupied with the threat of his brother, Tassilo, and Desiderius that he could not act in Italy in any serious way.[36] King Liutprand's old conquests, presently being demanded by the papacy as the *plenaria iustitiae*, would thus remain in royal hands and the possibility of Frankish military action against the Lombards in Italy would be much reduced. As for Gisela, she would confirm the central liaison, that between Charles and the Lombard princess. But Gisela's role as a royal spouse in Pavia while the Lombard princess dwelt in Francia would also underscore the reciprocality of the arrangement—Charles was Desiderius's ally and Desiderius was Charles's ally, a vital point for Carloman's consumption, and for the papacy's as well.[37]

What of Charles's views of the projected alliance? From his standpoint the preponderant consideration was most likely the bearing which the alliance might have upon his relationship with Carloman. The two brothers had to some degree been reconciled, or so it would seem if Stephen III's

[35] Hodgkin, *Italy and Her Invaders*, 7.311.

[36] Perceived by Lintzel, "Karl der Grosse," p. 13.

[37] Kleinclausz (*Charlemagne*, p. 7) argues that the Franco-Lombard marriage was only one component of a broad effort by Desiderius to dominate Italy and the papacy through marriage bonds—with King Charles and Gisela, Tassilo of Bavaria, and Duke Arichis of Benevento, the royal appointee there who was married to another daughter, Adelperga. The view has merit, but appears to miss the essentially defensive character and special dimensions of the alignment with Charles.

congratulations to the kings on reportedly improved relations in early 770 is any indication.[38] But tensions no doubt remained, apparently to a serious extent in that Charles went ahead with the Lombard alliance. In brief, Charles allied with Desiderius apparently to have Lombard aid in the event of an ultimate confrontation with Carloman.[39] The aid, supplementing Charles's Frankish strength, would give him the decisive edge needed for victory over his brother. If nothing else, Carloman might be deterred from attacking Charles by the Lombard alliance.

## BERTRADA'S GRAND SCHEME

In the summer of 770, Bertrada, the widow of Pepin and mother of Charles and Carloman, put the new Franco-Lombard alliance into effect in a brilliant diplomatic tour.[40] Bertrada first consulted with Carloman and then visited Tassilo of Bavaria, probably informing him of the details of the coming arrangements and enlisting his support for the subsequent dealings with Desiderius, his father-in-law. She then went on to Rome for crucial discussions with Pope Stephen: his opposition to the Frankish-Lombard marriages would have to be converted to support.[41] To achieve the conversion, Bertrada is thought to have assured the pope that her son Charles would have Desiderius make some territorial concessions to St. Peter, drop his support of the lay usurper of the archepiscopal throne in Ravenna, and cease his military operations in Venetia and Istria. In effect, Desiderius would by Frankish pressure return to harmonious relationship with the papacy, ending the mounting tension of recent months.

In this respect Bertrada was evidently responding to Stephen III's letter voicing fears that a Franco-Lombard marriage would terminate the papacy's *patricius Romanorum* relationship with the Carolingians. Further, Bertrada may have promised the pope that Gisela, the sister of Charles and Carloman, would not marry Adelgis, Desiderius's son, thereby meeting one of Stephen's demands in the anti-Lombard letter. As for the canonical obstacle, Bertrada is apt to have assured the pope that none existed since Charles's present wife was merely a folk concubine who could be put aside without objection. In fact, a canonical marriage of Charles and Desiderius's daughter would be a gain for the church in that it would involve a repudiation of the pagan concubinage. In these ways, it appears, Bertrada bought Pope Stephen's approval of the Franco-Lombard marriage.[42]

She then went on to Pavia and secured Desiderius's consent to transfer of some territory to the papacy, terminate his support of Michael in Ra-

---

[38] *CC* #44, 559.

[39] Winston, *Charlemagne*, p. 3; Bertolini, *Roma*, p. 648.

[40] The best account, giving the pertinent source references, is Delaruelle, "Charlemagne, Carloman, Didier," pp. 215–217; see also Bertolini, *Roma*, pp. 648–649.

[41] The interpretive material in the remainder of this paragraph and all of the next is based substantially upon Bertolini, *Roma*, pp. 649–650. Some of the argument is my own, however.

[42] It is often assumed that Stephen III's letter opposing the Franco-Lombard marriage was written *after* Stephen discovered Bertrada's machinations, not before, as argued here. See for example Hodgkin, *Italy and Her Invaders*, 7.314–315.

venna, and suspend his military activity on the northern fringes of the papal state. To secure the king's compliance on these crucial points, Bertrada, we think, played a trump gleaned from Stephen: the papacy would drop its claim to the *plenaria iustitiae*, just as it had done in the days of Paul I. Desiderius was also told that only one marriage would occur, that between his daughter and Charles. Finished in Pavia, Bertrada returned to Francia with the Lombard princess and before the end of 770 her marriage to Charles took place.

In late 770 and early 771 further diplomacy looked to the specifics of the complex accommodation orchestrated by Bertrada.[43] She and Charles sent to Rome Charles's chancellor, Itherius, to satisfy the pope on the promised Lombard territorial concessions. After conversations with Stephen III in Rome, Itherius moved on to the duchy of Benevento and possessed for St. Peter a number of unnamed patrimonies which had long been disputed by the papacy and the Lombard crown. This done, Stephen wrote to Charles and Bertrada, thanking them and Itherius, and emphasizing that St. Peter now had full territorial satisfaction from Desiderius.[44] There was not a word about *plenaria iustitiae*. Evidently, as Bertrada presumably had arranged, the *iustitiae* claim had been yielded by Stephen III in exchange for a territorial concession, the patrimonial contribution in Benevento, which had no connection at all with the *plenaria iustitiae*. In the meantime, Charles and Bertrada sent a second delegation to Italy to settle the Ravenna matter to Rome's advantage.[45] Headed by the veteran diplomat Hugobald who had been active in Italy since the early 760s for Pepin, the envoys discussed the situation with Stephen II and then proceeded to Ravenna where they arrested the usurper Michael and sent him to the pope. They also arranged for a proper archepiscopal election, and when the latter produced the accession of Archdeacon Leo, the original favorite, they saw him on to Rome for consecration at the hands of Stephen III. The Ravenna problem was thus resolved. As for Desiderius, he did not assist his former protégé Michael or obstruct the Frankish-papal restoration of the clerical and pro-Roman rule in Ravenna. Nor is there any sign that he persisted in the cognate disturbance in Venetia and Istria. Again, Bertrada's arrangements were being borne out, this time Desiderius, as promised, leaving aside his extensive intervention in the Ravennese politics of the papal state and abandoning the northern depredations. By early 771, then, the conventions achieved by Bertrada in consultation with Charles, Tassilo, Stephen III, and Desiderius were all in place.

These conventions had the most direct bearing upon the Lombard-papal relationship. Whereas in early 770 there had been great strain between Pavia and Rome there was now, a year later, a very clear accommodation.[46]

---

[43] CC #46, 564–565.

[44] Ibid., p. 564.

[45] VS III, 26.477–478; CC #2467. See also Duchesne, VS III, p. 484, n. 55; Lintzel, "Karl der Grosse" pp. 1–10.

[46] The concept of accommodation is owed to Bertolini, *Roma*, p. 650. Otherwise the following judgments are my own.

Where the popé had recently demanded fulfillment of the *plenaria iustitiae*, that claim was absent, evidently sacrificed for some new Beneventan patrimonies. Where Desiderius had recently given strong support to Michael in Ravenna, he now abandoned him and let Frankish and papal authorities restore a legitimate archepiscopal regime which was obedient to Rome and acceptable to the pope. Where Desiderius had seized patrimonies in Venetia and Istria and threatened the northern borders of the republic, he now was quiet. And where Stephen had recently vigorously opposed any Franco-Lombard marriage, he was now at least implicitly endorsing one between Charles and Desiderius's daughter. In brief, the royal-papal divisions were healed. Stephen apparently abandoned the *iustitiae* claims in exchange for the Beneventan patrimonies, while Desiderius ended his Adriatic manipulations in exchange for the pope's discarding of the *iustitiae* renewal. Through the medium of Bertrada, Desiderius and Stephen III had clearly established the groundwork for a resumption of the harmony between Pavia and Rome which had been subject to severe strain since 768.

To Desiderius, the core of the accommodation was the Franco-Lombard marriage. The king originally regarded the marriage of his daughter and Charles as the device for resisting Christopher's *iustitiae* claim. The marriage in fact achieved those ends,[47] but not in the manner which Desiderius had anticipated. The initial understanding was apparently that the alliance with Charles would gain both goals by heightening Charles's tensions with Carloman and binding Charles more tightly to Pavia than to Rome. But Bertrada's diplomacy changed things. Through her efforts, Charles was actually bound more closely than ever to the pope, for it was through Charles's envoys—Itherius and Hugobald—that Desiderius and Stephen III reached the details of their territorial and Ravennese settlements, both of which were highly advantageous to the papacy. That is, Bertrada succeeded in intensifying Charles's *patricius Romanorum* service and commitment, exactly the opposite of what Desiderius may have originally expected from the marriage.[48] But, ironically it was in this intensified commitment to Rome that Desiderius gained his likely objective in the marriage project—denial of papal expansion of the republic at Lombard expense. In accepting the settlements negotiated by Charles's envoys, who were sent to Italy in the *patricius Romanorum* context, Desiderius also accepted amity with Rome, a resolution of all outstanding royal-papal problems which was so much in keeping with papal and Frankish wishes that no hostile Frankish action could be expected. Thus, in the end Desiderius's route to security for the monarchy through the marriage was apparently not his but Bertrada's.

In participating in Bertrada's plan, Desiderius necessarily gave up what-

---

[47] F. L. Ganshof, "Charlemagne," p. 520.

[48] The normal understanding is that the marriage separated King Charles and Rome, with the king taking a non-traditional or unnatural approach toward the Lombards. The theme is well articulated by Lintzel, "Karl der Grosse," pp. 12–17. However, see Cutler, *Carolingian Italian Policies*, p. 60.

ever radical ambitions concerning Rome he may have entertained in the period from 768 onward. That is, in his accommodation with the papacy it seems clear that Desiderius could no longer realistically contemplate such expedients as imposing his personal control over the papacy by installing a pope of his own choice or recovering the lands once possessed by Aistulf but lost to the papacy in 756. Rather, Desiderius was returning to the conservative pre-768 approach to Italian politics and the acceptance of the limitations which had marked his reign up to that date.

It is furthermore evident that Bertrada's settlement also revived the Italian *modus vivendi* of 760 which had endured until the emergence of the royal-papal discord in 768 but which was threatened by it. In the 760–768 equilibrium the Italian environment was stable, with Pavia and Rome dwelling in reasonably harmonious co-existence; such was the case in Bertrada's settlement in 771. In the earlier period and in 771 the papacy possessed its republic. In the 760–768 enviornment, the republic, Rome, and the papacy were all kept free of danger from Pavia, the Lombard king being held in check by Pepin's patrician activity within the papal-Frankish alliance. Conditions were essentially similar in 770–771 as Bertrada and Charles had begun to look after the papacy, persuading Desiderius to compromise and abandon his menacing action. As before, in 771 the Carolingian moderation of the Italian scene was through the medium of diplomacy rather than force. In the 760–768 *modus vivendi* Lombard royal interests were met in Pavia's control over the duchies of Spoleto and Benevento, the right to traverse the papal republic to enforce its rule in the duchies, the consequent possession of a partially restored Lombard Kingdom of Italy, and continued royal possession of the *plenaria iustitiae* claimed by Rome. The same royal interests were still being met in 770–771. In the 760–768 equilibrium the Lombard monarchy observed dependence upon the Frankish crown, and that dependence was visible in 770–771 in Desiderius's compliance with the envoys of Charles and Bertrada. Likewise, the Lombard autonomy in Italy, respected in the 760–768 period, was not terminated in 770–771, for Desiderius continued to enjoy the considerable latitude for royal action and sovereignty over Spoleto and Benevento which he had known earlier. In every respect, then, the Italian *modus vivendi* of 760–768 reappeared in 770–771. The personnel were different, as for example in the emergence of Bertrada, Charles, Carloman, and Stephen III after Pepin's death. There were also new conditions, especially the marriage alliance between Charles and Desiderius, two Frankish kingdoms, and sharp tension between their respective monarchs. But the essential Italian realities prevailing in 760–768 after the basic alterations flowing from the establishment of the papal-Frankish alliance, the foundation of the papal state, and the failure of Aistulf's Kingdom of Italy were all recaptured by Bertrada's efforts in 770–771. As in 765, the point at which the 760 *modus vivendi* was fully in effect, the 771 prospect was for a stable Italian future, especially in the central concern of a peaceful relationship between the Lombard monarchy and the papacy.

### CHRISTOPHER AND CARLOMAN THREATENED

The eclipse of Christopher in Rome[49] is of major importance. The *primicerius* was bitterly hostile to Desiderius because of the 768 attempt to seize the papacy in addition to the venomous maligning of Desiderius in the letter which opposed the Franco-Lombard marriage came from his pen. Christopher was evidently ignored in the accommodation of 770 and early 771 by Stephen III. More precisely, Christopher's anti-Lombard point of view, which had been dominant at the Lateran since the beginning of the pontificate, was apparently being set aside by the pope. Christopher had advanced the *iustitiae* claim presumably to harmonize Charles and Carloman against Desiderius, perhaps even to bring the kings into Italy against him; but Stephen evidently ended the claim and refused to provoke Desiderius further. Christopher had treated Desiderius as a foul enemy who was never to be trusted; but Stephen showed considerable trust, seeing the Lombard as capable of negotiation and compromise. In brief, Stephen II was repudiating the policy of his minister. But this was more than a policy repudiation, for Christopher was so dominant in Rome that in rejecting his policy the pope was rejecting the minister himself. Stephen III apparently took advantage of Bertrada's diplomacy and Desiderius's willingness to accommodate to assert his independence of the overmighty *primicerius*. Christopher gave stiff resistance and had to be removed violently from the scene. But Stephen III had taken the first step toward liberating himself from Christopher's control.[50]

Stephen's motives for accepting Bertrada's initiatives are not difficult to discern. Certainly one vital consideration was the opportunity to escape Christopher's rule. Compliance with the components of Bertrada's scheme required treatment of the Lombard and Frankish kings different from that acceptable to Christopher, and in that difference lay the beginning of Stephen's release. Further, Bertrada's initiatives offered strengthening of the papacy's association with the Frankish monarchy. True, the former joint exercise of the *patricius Romanorum* service by Carloman and Charles was being superseded by the essentially single service of Charles, giving the papal-Frankish association a weakened appearance. But Charles's emergence as unique *patricius*, or at least as single effective *patricius*, was a gain in that his diplomats in 770–771 energetically and effectively performed services of the highest importance for the papacy in settling the divisions between Rome and Francia. That is, by accepting the lead of Bertrada, Stephen III discovered in Charles the source of renewed strength for the papal-Frankish association at large and a rededicated commitment for the

---

[49] Recognition of this point is found in varying degrees in Bertolini, *Roma,* pp. 650–651; idem, "La Caduta del primicerio Cristoforo," pp. 367–368; Delaruelle, "Charlemagne, Carloman, Didier," pp. 218–219; and L. Homo, *Rome médiévale, 476–1420,* p. 50; Lintzel, "Karl der Grosse," p. 14.

[50] This judgment runs counter to the general impression of Stephen III—that he was a weak and vacillating pontiff. For the argument that Stephen was nothing of the kind but a man of experience, ability, and strength, see Hallenbeck, "Pope Stephen III."

patrician obligation in particular—an especially vital discovery in view of the distinct possibility that the Franco-Lombard marriage could have ended in virtual elimination of the Frankish crown as an effective force in Italy. Finally, Stephen III endorsed Bertrada's scheme because it brought the papal republic peace with the Lombard monarchy, an end to the tensions which were reaching serious proportions by 771–772. The friction over the *iustitiae* ceased, as did the trouble in Venetia-Istria and the see of Ravenna, leaving a new calm and positive gain in the security on the northern frontier of the republic and in resolution of the Ravennese intervention. Christopher would not have accepted Bertrada's initiatives, but Stephen III, striking out boldly on his own, knew that the advantages were considerable and so followed where Bertrada led.

Something should be said of Bertrada's motives since her actions had a profound effect upon the Lombard-papal relationship. The standard view is that Bertrada saw the Lombard marriage for Charles as the gateway to a general European pacification within which peace between her sons would be maintained.[51] She strove for an equilibrium satisfactory to the aspirations of all parties whereby no party would feel driven to war. In this reconstruction, Carloman would feel safe from Charles because Charles, in the Lombard alliance, would have access to Italy denied him by Pepin's division. In turn, Charles would not fear attack by Carloman, for Carloman would be checked by the alliance with Desiderius. Nor would the sons suffer division over war in Italy or even be drawn into an Italian war, for pacification would be brought to the Italian world: the friction separating Pavia and Rome would be resolved, and as the two settled into peaceful relationship neither Charles nor Carloman would find an Italian ally to use against the other in Francia and no Italian war would tempt either king to cross the Alps. The papacy would be satisfied by the Lombard concessions in Benevento and Ravenna, while Pavia would be content with papal renunciation of the *iustitiae* claims. Rome would find comfort in Charles's arrangements as a *partricius Romanorum* function, and be assured of continuing peace with the Lombards through the dialogue established during the concession negotiations. Through this planned stabilization and through mutual gratification Bertrada sought harmony in Francia, a means of holding Pepin's kingdom together despite the incompatibility of her sons and the tensions arising from the division of the kingdom.

This view may be defended with considerable success, but there remains a suspicion that it may not be accurate, for it is possible that Bertrada was siding with Charles.[52] That is, Bertrada's complex diplomacy may have aimed at isolating Carloman to Charles's benefit.[53] The supporting evidence seems strong. For example, the marriage which Bertrada arranged for

[51] Kleinclausz, *Charlemagne*, p. 9; Delaruelle, "Charlemagne, Carloman, Didier," p. 217; Hodgkin, *Italy and Her Invaders*, 7.310–314; Mohr, *Studien*, pp. 55–60; Abel-Simson *Jahrbücher*, 1, pp. 61–63.

[52] Lintzel, "Karl der Grosse," p. 10.

[53] Ibid., p. 17.

Charles with Desiderius's daughter favored Charles and weakened Carloman, for it was Charles who would enjoy Lombard aid in the event of war between them. Further, the marriage and the simultaneous accommodation which Bertrada arranged between Desiderius and Stephen III denied Carloman aid or even support from the pope to be used against either Charles or Desiderius, for the Lombard-papal accommodation placed the pope in support of both Desiderius and the Franco-Lombard marriage. Finally, and most important, Bertrada arranged all the components of the 770–771 settlement in conjunction with Charles; she negotiated the marriage for Charles at Pavia and took the Lombard princess back with her to Francia for him to marry; envoys of *Charles* and Bertrada saw to Desiderius's concession of the Beneventan patrimonies; and envoys of *Charles* and Bertrada provided for the end of Desiderius's intervention in the Ravennese situation. Up to the time of these activities Carloman and Charles had acted jointly in Italy; now it was only Charles and Bertrada. A reasonable assumption is that Bertrada's 770–771 settlement was undertaken on behalf of Charles to the detriment and exclusion of Carloman.[54] Only Christopher in Rome was in similar eclipse, making him and Carloman potential allies in the future.

### THE FALL OF CHRISTOPHER AND SERGIUS

Soon after the completion of Bertrada's diplomacy, there occurred in Rome a series of developments which clarified the new conditions considerably.[55] Reportedly wanting to kill Christopher and Sergius, King Desiderius early in 771 secretly bribed the papal *cubicularius* or chamberlain, Paul Afiarta, and had him denounce them to Stephen III. Learning that Paul and his followers were discrediting them, and hearing that Desiderius was coming to Rome with an army to discuss papal territorial rights, Christopher and his son maneuvered to protect themselves. They were able to gather into Rome supporters from Tuscany, Campania, and Perugia, that is, from various quarters of the papal republic. Romans were also armed, while the city gates were closed and some were even walled up. Desiderius thereupon appeared before Rome requesting that Pope Stephen come out to St. Peter's Basilica beyond the walls to confer with him. Stephen complied with such alacrity as to suggest forethought. Meanwhile, having conspired with Paul Afiarta and his adherents, Desiderius tried to arouse mob action against Christopher and Sergius to kill them. Threatened from within and without, Christopher and his son led a rampaging crowd through the Lateran, to which the pope had just returned after his conversation with Desiderius. Joining Christopher and his men in this intrusion was Dodo, a

---

[54] Ibid., pp. 16–17.

[55] The following account is based upon *VS III*, 28.478–33.480, except where otherwise noted. The most important secondary works are Bertolini, "La Caduta del primicerio Cristoforo"; idem, *Roma*, pp. 651–668; Halphen, "La papauté et le complot Lombard de 771," pp. 238–244; Hallenbeck, "Paul Afiarta and the Papacy," pp. 33–54; and Lintzel, "Karl der Grosse," pp. 17–22.

*missus* of King Carloman who was in Rome at this time with a contingent of Frankish troops[56] and was in full cooperation with the *primicerius* and his adherents.[57] Stephen III was appalled by the unruly intrusion, regarding it as an attempt by Christopher and Dodo to assassinate him.[58] But when the intruders actually confronted the pope they meekly submitted to a furious pontifical berating. Christopher and Dodo had failed in their bid to overcome the pope by violence.

But, fearing what the threatened *primicerius* might try next, Stephen soon went to King Desiderius for protection, to "our most excellent son."[59] The pope also wanted to discuss the territorial rights, but Desiderius would consider only what he termed the "deceptions" of Christopher and Sergius. In the meantime, Stephen steadily sent clergy to them ordering them to come out to St. Peter's where the pope was. But they refused, with Dodo and his Franks closing the gates again and boldly denying the pope admittance.[60] Two bishops were thereupon sent to Christopher and Sergius with the message that they should enter a monastery or appear before the pope at St. Peter's. By this time the strength of the *primicerius* and his son was waning, for the Romans now deserted them and even threatened to kill them once their perfidious treatment of the pope became generally known.[61] The frightened pair declared that they were willing to turn themselves over to what was termed "their Roman brethren," presumably meaning surrender to the pope and his people rather than to Desiderius and the Lombards. Seeing that his kinsmen were in deep trouble, Duke Gratiosus, the son-in-law of Christopher and the brother-in-law of Sergius, slipped from Rome and gave himself up at St. Peter's. Left with only Dodo and his Franks, who were evidently seen as an inadequate defense, Christopher and Sergius soon followed suit, only to be arrested by Lombard guards on the steps of St. Peter's. Desiderius promptly turned them over to Stephen III, who enclosed them in the church for safety until he could secretly move them back into Rome at night. The pope thereupon re-entered the city, and before long the helpless father and son were seized, removed from St. Peter's, and blinded, with Desiderius's approval, by Paul Afiarta and his followers. Pope Stephen insisted that the terrible deed was done without his knowledge or consent, and professed great sorrow about it.[62] Christopher was taken to a monastery where he soon died of his wounds, while Sergius lived on blind and imprisoned in a Lateran cell. The regime of the great Christopher had fallen in blood.

We are not told what happened to Carloman's *missus* or to Duke Gratiosus, but they appear to have had no further role in Rome after the

---

[56] CC #48, 566.
[57] Ibid.
[58] Ibid.
[59] Ibid.
[60] Ibid., 567.
[61] Ibid.
[62] Ibid.

brutalizations. As for the territorial issue, we find that Desiderius satisfied the pope "in whole and in full."[63] Stephen soon wrote to Bertrada and Charles[64] dwelling upon the "malicious" deeds of Dodo and his men. Surely, Stephen wrote, Carloman would be most distraught to learn of the sad and diabolical disobedience of his *missus*. The pope should be able to expect obedience to St. Peter and service to the papacy from the Franks. But only St. Peter and the aid of "our most excellent son, King Desiderius," delivered the clergy and all the faithful of the church from mortal peril. The emphasis was clearly upon Dodo's "treason" in conjunction with Christopher and Sergius, and upon Desiderius's cooperation with Stephen III and the church.

The fall of Christopher and Sergius has been variously interpreted, but an accurate analysis depends upon a grasp of the antecedents. The roots of the episode lay in the friction between Desiderius and Christopher in 768, Pope Stephen's apparent initiation of action to escape the *primicerius'* dominance in 770-771, the Lombard-papal accommodation of the same moment, and the likely isolation of Carloman by Bertrada and Charles in the diplomacy surrounding the Franco-Lombard marriage. Each strand seems to have fed directly into the fall of the two ministers.

The beginning point was probably some form of agreement between Desiderius and Stephen in the 770-771 negotiations that they would co-operate to remove Christopher and Sergius from power.[65] Perhaps Bertrada introduced the idea as part of her intricate and subtle plan. There is no specific proof of such an entente, but its existence is nevertheless likely because both the king and the pope stood to gain from it, could easily have agreed to it as one aspect of their 770-771 accommodation, and obviously worked closely together when the fall occurred. Desiderius surely wanted Christopher and his son deposed because of the brutal maltreatment of Waldipert in 768 after he had failed to install the monk Philip as pope, a matter of revenge as it were.[66] Moreover, as long as Christopher and Sergius remained influential in Rome, their intensely anti-Lombard bias might lead to an end of the recently attained accommodation. Stephen III also very likely desired the removal of Christopher and Sergius. He could further his apparent initial steps toward liberation from their tutelage, and, like Desiderius, he could protect the harmonious relationship between Pavia and Rome.[67] The latter gave Rome and its state security from royal menace, and had the effect of binding Charles very closely to his patrician service. If Christopher and Sergius were able to retain their power at the Lateran,

---

[63] Ibid.: ". . . Desiderius rege, et omnes iustitias b. Petri ab eo plenius et in integro susce-pimus."

[64] Ibid., 566–567.

[65] Bertolini, *Roma*, p. 651.

[66] Llewellyn, *Rome in the Dark Ages*, p. 226; Duchesne, *The Beginnings*, p. 60; Amann, *L'époque* p. 47.

[67] Bertolini, *Roma*, p. 651. This view is sharply different from the normal understanding that Stephen, deplorably weak, simply capitulated to pressure from Desiderius to abandon Chris-topher and Sergius. See for example, Halphen, "Complot," p. 242; Hodgkin, *Italy and Her Invaders*, 7.320; and Kleinclausz, *Charlemagne*, p. 10.

they would be apt to threaten the vital entente with Pavia, again owing
to their anti-Lombard sentiments.[68] Both Desiderius and Stephen had so
much to gain from the removal of Christopher and Sergius that they probably cooperated in securing it.

There can be no doubt about the cooperation itself, and that began when
Desiderius bribed Paul Afiarta to malign Christopher and Sergius to the
pope. This was evidently a case of practical politics, for Desiderius needed
a Roman for the shadier aspects of the project while Stephen III required
an element in the curial administration which could discredit and oppose
Christopher and his son. Afiarta, who was clearly an unprincipled and
violent person, was more than willing to engage himself against the two.
His ambition was to advance from *cubicularius* to pope after the death of
Stephen III, and to prepare for that step he had to destroy Christopher and
Sergius, or at least their power, and supersede them as the dominant curialist at the Lateran and in Rome.[69] Afiarta cared nothing at all for the
interests of either Desiderius or Stephen, and served as their hatchet man
simply to smooth his own way to the papacy, taking Desiderius's money
in the bargain. In this way Paul Afiarta joined the royal-papal conspiracy.

Against this background, the subsequent developments are easily grasped.
Desiderius came to Rome so that he would be able to give Christopher and
Sergius his immediate and undivided attention. He brought his army with
him for use in the extreme event that his two enemies could be broken
only by a siege of Rome or some forceful action within the city. The territorial discussion may have been a cover adopted by the king and the
pope, although there may have been a substantive concern in unfinished
details surrounding the recent royal transfer of patrimonies to the papacy.
Since Desiderius and Stephen needed close and personal cooperation in
order to oust Christopher and Sergius, they required both an opportunity
to meet and a reason for doing so. Both could be provided in a discussion
of the territorial rights, whether there was a problem or not. Nobody would
be surprised if pope and king convened to discuss territorial matters, least
of all the Franks, to whom Stephen III would have to report on the removal
of Christopher and Sergius. The latter pair no doubt grasped the situation.
They were experienced politicians, possessed many sources of information,
and knew that in the 770–771 accommodation Stephen III had begun to
undercut them. Their gathering of external and internal Roman allies and
their association with Dodo against the pope was simply their effort to
counteract the conspiracy which they knew was being forged between
Desiderius, Stephen III, and Paul Afiarta. Nor should we be surprised that
Dodo was in Rome, in league with Christopher, and opposed to the pope:
as soon as Carloman discovered that the diplomacy of his mother favored
Charles and clearly isolated him, he naturally sought some effective political
response.[70] It was thus that he sent Frankish arms to Rome in the hope of

---

[68] Bertolini, "La Caduta del primicerio Cristoforo," p. 371.
[69] The principal argument advanced in Hallenbeck, "Paul Afiarta and the Papacy."
[70] Lintzel, "Karl der Grosse," pp. 17–20.

either deposing or killing Stephen III in cooperation with the two threat-ened ministers, or else forcing Stephen to forsake the arrangements recently made by Bertrada.[71] This was scarcely appropriate activity for a *patricius Romanorum*, a son of Pepin, but Carloman was severely threatened, perhaps damaged to the point of ruin by Bertrada. That Christopher, Sergius, and Dodo intended to assassinate the pope seems clear from both the source statement that the murder was planned and the violent, desperate, and frenzied nature of the Lateran intrusion. Further, the pope was evidently thoroughly frightened, for immediately after the intrusion he fled directly to Desiderius.

The final stage of the ministers' fall was at hand. They could not with-stand the loss of Roman support, which was apparently caused by the intolerable sight of the pope's being hounded from Rome and his own palace by two fading politicians and some Frankish troops. It came down to a matter of what to do with Christopher and Sergius. We may be sure that Stephen wanted no more than their departure from active political life through retirement to a cloister. There is little likelihood that he envisioned and sanctioned any sort of harm to their persons. But Desiderius was surely more violently inclined, for he had the blinding and death of Waldipert to avenge as well as the same political ends as the pope to secure. One surmises that Desiderius was prepared to acquiesce in their brutalization but not to engage openly in it, for if his involvement became known it would damage his effort to maintain amicable relations with the Romans. What probably happened is this: once Christopher and Sergius were both within St. Peter's, in effect in papal custody, Stephen and Desiderius met to decide their fate. Judging from Stephen's vehement condemnation of the brutalizations, the understanding was that the two would be placed in a monastery. The pope returned to Rome, satisfied that the matter was settled, but Desiderius secretly carried out his own solution by allowing Paul Afiarta to carry out the blindings and incarcerate the wounded Sergius. Desiderius may well have expressed as much shock, surprise, and dismay as Stephen, but only the latter's was genuine.

There is no sign that Stephen and Desiderius suffered any significant division over the royal betrayal of Christopher and Sergius to the brutality of Paul Afiarta. That was perhaps because Desiderius may have been able to conceal his connection with Paul, leaving it to the latter's doing only, but more likely the pope simply settled for the public condemnation and then moved comfortably into the new reality of an autonomous pontificate, which Desiderius had been instrumental in achieving. It was a time of royal-papal solidarity and mutual success, a moment to be hailed to King Charles and his mother, Bertrada, both of whom had done so much to establish the accommodation between Pavia and Rome from which the cooperation requisite for the defeat of the ministers had sprung. It was thus that the letter reporting the fall of Christopher and Sergius, the intervention

---

[71] Ibid.; Bertolini, *Roma*, p. 652.

of Dodo on their side against the pope, and the extension of Desiderius's support to St. Peter was sent to Charles and Bertrada.[72] But there were other purposes as well—to inform the two of the hostility of Carloman and Dodo, explain it, and use it as a device for applauding Charles for his continuing devotion, further isolating Carloman, and warning him away from additional machinations. The letter also signalled an end to the territorial problem, whatever it was, for Bertrada and Charles were told that Desiderius had complied in all respects, a notice which they would receive gladly.

The episode of the fall of Christopher and Sergius obviously had a major impact upon the Lombard-papal relationship: it strengthened and extended the royal-papal accommodation which Bertrada, Charles, and Stephen III had contrived in 770–771. There may have been some tension over the manner of the disposal of the two curialists by Afiarta, but otherwise there was apparently cooperation at every point as king and pope jointly endeavored to protect the accommodation from its enemies. They evidently shared a single view that Christopher and Sergius had to be removed and together advanced the territorial discussion, held at least two meetings to plan and orchestrate the plot, contrived to have Paul Afiarta serve them both, and generally saw a most complex and challenging project through to a successful conclusion. In the process Desiderius and Stephen III must have grown close in mutual trust and regard. There was no other moment like it, no other point in the entire eighth-century relationship in which king and pope joined so fully as one. The effect was surely to build upon the good relations which had already been established in 770–771, for the collaboration against Christopher and Sergius both advanced and deepened the personal association of Desiderius and Stephen and protected the institutional gains achieved through the recent accommodation. At no time in the eighth century were relations between Pavia and Rome on a more harmonious and integrated footing than they were during and just after the fall of Christopher and his son.

It goes almost without saying that the renewal of the 760–768 *modus vivendi*, which was so much a part of the recent 770–771 accommodation, was also strengthened by that fall. Obviously, nothing happened in the leaders' removal to disrupt the equilibrium just established; rather, it was made more stable by the further harmonization of Pavia and Rome. Moreover, the elimination of Christopher and Sergius removed a potentially disruptive and explosive force from the environment: with them gone there was no significant Italian opposition to the restored stability. Finally, with the exclusion of Christopher and Sergius, and with the failure of Carloman's effort via Dodo to kill, depose, or manipulate Stephen in conjunction with them, Carloman became even less able than before to militate against Bertrada's reorganization and was therefore virtually powerless to disturb the

---

[72] Normally the letter is seen as a dictation of Paul Afiarta and Desiderius, allied in their pro-Lombard sympathies against the pope. See for example Bertolini, "La Caduta del primicerio Cristoforo," p. 354; Halphen, "Complot," p. 242; and Hodgkin, *Italy and Her Invaders*, 7.325.

revived equilibrium. Turbulent though it had been in itself, the episode of the fall of Christopher and Sergius ended by enriching the stable and integrated environment restored in 770–771.

One is inclined from all this to propose the argument that Desiderius was in early 771 acting as Charles's deputy in Italy, that is, he was doing for the pope what the *patricius Romanorum* would do—under Charles's auspices. The fact of Desiderius's protection is obvious: Christopher, Sergius, and Dodo all threatened the life and safety of the pope, and Desiderius aided him against them. As the papal letter to Bertrada and Charles after the event stressed, Stephen owed his success against his foes to Desiderius. The possibility that the king was explicitly serving as the delegate of the patrician is somewhat less clear, but it is not untenable because at the time of his service to the pope Desiderius had special bonds with Charles arising from the Franco-Lombard marriage. Given the familial association between Charles and Desiderius there was sufficient familiarity and opportunity for communication to suppose that Charles indeed might have called upon Desiderius to see to his *patricius Romanorum* responsibilities, at least for the time being. If so, it is further testimony to the growth of the 770–771 *modus vivendi*.

This view concerning the fall of Christopher and Sergius varies from another argument, or rather impression, which is nowhere summarized in well-developed and coherent form, but exists instead in scattered statements and inferences found in a number of works. The basic assumption is that Desiderius struck against Christopher and Sergius to destroy Stephen III's most able supporters and thereby establish royal Lombard control over Rome and the papacy.[73] Aiding Desiderius in this lunge at Rome was the despicable Paul Afiarta, who was the king's Roman agent and whose supporters were a pro-Lombard party in Rome, a Lombard fifth-column devoted to subordinating Stephen III to Pavia.[74] The collaboration of Desiderius and Paul Afiarta was successful, Christopher and Sergius being eliminated despite the valiant efforts of Dodo and his Franks to support the pope and prevent the papacy from falling under royal sway. Once Christopher and his son were gone, Stephen was Desiderius's virtual prisoner, or more exactly, the prisoner of the king's Roman deputy, Afiarta.[75] As for the letter from Stephen to Charles and Bertrada extolling Desiderius and vilifying Christopher, Sergius, and Dodo, it is viewed as a dictation by Desiderius, a false version of the fall imposed on Stephen after the fact and

---

[73] Implicit in all the references cited in notes 74, 75, and 76 below.

[74] Bertolini, "La Caduta del primicerio Cristoforo," p. 354; Homo, *Rome médiévale*, p. 50; Hartmann, *Geschichte Italiens*, pp. 254–256; Hodgkin, *Italy and Her Invaders*, 7.320; Romano, *Dominazioni*, p. 441; Lintzel, "Karl der Grosse," p. 18.

[75] Hartmann, *Geschichte Italiens*, pp. 253–256; Halphen, "Complot," p. 238; Romano, *Dominazioni*, p. 441; Haller, *Das Papsttum*, 1, pp. 446–447; Kleinclausz, *Charlemagne*, p. 10; Jan T. Hallenbeck, "The Election of Pope Hadrian I." The degree to which Afiarta actually dominated Rome is discussed in Hallenbeck, "Paul Afiarta and the Papacy," pp. 47–52.

calculated to place a strictly royal construction upon it for Frankish consumption.[76]

This impression seems untenable in every key respect, first regarding its basic assumption that Desiderius always wanted to capture Rome and dominate the pope. There was only one moment when such an aim may have been held—in 768 when the king had Waldipert attempt to install Philip as the successor of Pope Constantine. Otherwise Desiderius's long record from 757 to 771 reveals no such aim or interest, his general pattern being basic compliance with the key realities of independence and security for Rome and the papal state. Therefore, especially in view of the 770–771 royal-papal accommodation, one must doubt that Desiderius in 771 was interested in governing the pope. Doubting this, one must also doubt that Desiderius attacked Christopher and Sergius in order to gain such an end. And, if it is not supportable that *Desiderius* was trying to dominate Rome in the action against the two curialists, it follows that *Paul Afiarta* was not involved in any such project either, meaning that Afiarta was not likely to have been a Lombard agent in Rome[77] and his supporters no Lombard party.[78] In short, the view that Desiderius and Stephen III were adversaries locked in a struggle for control of Rome and the papacy fails to hold in front of key questions raised from the context of the long-term development of Lombard-papal relations, especially those pertinent to Desiderius's reign. One is better off with the interpretations posited earlier, which, while they are not entirely certain, have the merit of being firmly rooted in that context.

In summary, the events and developments from the division of Pepin's kingdom in September 768 until the fall of Christopher and Sergius in early 771 promised to disrupt the *modus vivendi* of 760–768 but did not in fact do so. The tensions between Charles and Carloman, the marriage of Charles and Desiderius's daughter, Christopher's renewal of the *iustitiae* demand, and Desiderius's interventions in Ravenna, Venetia, and Istria individually and collectively threatened to upset the Italian equilibrium. But there were stronger forces, those working for perpetuation of the harmony: Bertrada's determined diplomacy favoring isolation of Carloman via encouragement of Lombard-papal peace under Frankish auspices, Stephen III's apparent will to be free of domination by Christopher and Sergius, and Desiderius's acceptance of cooperation with Rome, Bertrada, and Charles. By early 771, the equilibrium appeared to be firmly in place.

---

[76] See above, note 72.

[77] Argued in depth in Hallenbeck, "Paul Afiarta and the Papacy."

[78] See Hallenbeck, "The Lombard Party in Eighth-Century Rome."

## VIII. THE BEGINNING OF THE END

Within months of the fall of Christopher and Sergius, both the strengthened Italian *modus vivendi* and the attendant royal-papal harmony were seriously threatened by events in Francia. As early as April 771 Carloman was apparently relinquishing exercise of government in his kingdom, some of it being taken over by Charles.[1] The likelihood is that Carloman was ill and that Charles, knowing of the illness, was preparing to annex his territory in anticipation of his death.[2] As Carloman's brother, Charles had a strong claim of succession. But there were competitors, Carloman's two minor sons, who were probably seen by many as no less legitimate successors than their uncle.[3] Thus, when Carloman did die in early December,[4] Charles moved quickly into his kingdom and secured the support of Carloman's clergy and nobles, intending, we are told, to possess the entire kingdom.[5] The hopes of Charles's nephews were thus preempted by Charles, and their mother, Carloman's widow Gerberga, felt unsafe enough to flee the kingdom with them and a number of Carloman's leading men, including the prominent Duke Autchar.[6] Gerberga and her sons found refuge at the court of King Desiderius,[7] who had recently become estranged from Charles when the latter, at about the same time as Carloman's death, repudiated Desiderius's daughter and married a Swabian woman of noble birth named Hildegard.[8] In short, late 771 saw three major changes: the death of Carloman, Charles's subsequent reunification of the Frankish kingdom, and his termination of the Frankish alliance with King Desiderius.

### TENSION BETWEEN CHARLES AND DESIDERIUS

There are several possible explanations for Charles's rejection of Desiderius's daughter and the alliance with Pavia. It has been argued that the

---

[1] Delaruelle, "Charlemagne, Carloman, Didier," pp. 220–221.

[2] Ibid.

[3] Kleinclausz, *Charlemagne*, p. 12; Donald Bullough, *The Age of Charlemagne*, p. 45.

[4] Einhard reports (3.4) simply that Carloman died of disease.

[5] *ARF*, a. 771, p. 32; *Ann. Ein.*, a. 771, p. 33. Of Carloman's men who came over, Archbishop Wilchar, Fulrad, and Counts Warin and Adalhard are named. Duchesne, (*The Beginnings*, p. 88) characterizes Charles's accession in Carloman's realms as a selection by the magnates, not a seizure.

[6] *ARF*, a. 771, p. 32; *Ann. Ein.*, a. 771 p. 33. Bullough (*Age of Charlemagne*, p. 45) speaks of Charles's "ruthlessness and apparent disregard of the possible rights of his nephews. . . ."

[7] *Vita Hadriani I, LP I*, 9.488.

[8] Einhard, *Vita Karoli Magni*. 18.16. The date of the repudiation is deduced from Einhard's statement that it occurred "at the end of a year"—a year after the December 770 marriage. For the possibility of repudiation before late 771, see Cutler, *Carolingian Italian Policies*, pp. 107–111.

actions stemmed from Pope Stephen's resistance to the marriage, as expressed in the 770 letter which was probably dictated by Christopher.[9] But this view seems incorrect since Stephen III came to accept the marriage as a political necessity. Another suggestion is that Charles was apprehensive about the growing rapprochement between Desiderius and Stephen III,[10] and by repudiating the Lombard princess withdrew his sanction of that accommodation. However, it is impossible to demonstrate convincingly that Charles had anything but satisfaction in the Lombard-papal cooperation—which he, of course, had done much to help establish after Bertrada's great embassy. A third explanation is that Charles ended his alliance with Desiderius because he was deeply disturbed by the Lombard's treatment of Stephen III, Christopher, and Sergius.[11] There may be truth to this approach, but it is likely that Charles believed that there was no royal maltreatment of the pope and that the fall of Christopher and Sergius was jointly managed by Stephen and Desiderius. A further possibility is that Charles's concern was to strengthen his ties with Hildegard's family,[12] giving the repudiation a specifically domestic hue. This view may be too restricted to be authentic, however. We are left with only one convincing interpretation, that the repudiation resulted from the death of Carloman, the accompanying end of tension between Charles and Carloman, and Charles's reunification of the two kingdoms.[13] Charles had allied with Desiderius in order to have Lombard strength should it be needed against Carloman and to have direct access to Italy and its politics, from which he had been excluded by Pepin's division. With Carloman dead, Charles had the direct Italian contact he desired without alignment with Pavia. The latter was simply unnecessary in the new circumstances, an expendable arrangement which had outlived its usefulness.

In late 771 there was thus a restoration of some of the principal conditions which had prevailed before Pepin's death in 768. Charles's denial of the throne to Carloman's heirs amounted to a return to single Frankish rule, and by seizing Carloman's territory Charles reconstituted Pepin's single Frankish kingdom. There was also a return to earlier conditions in Italy, for in excluding Carloman's sons from the throne Charles revived the former reality of a single *patricius Romanorum*. Moreover, Charles's repudiation of Desiderius's daughter returned to the relationship between Francia and Pavia its essential character of Pepin's day.[14] That is, instead of Desiderius's being Charles's father-in-law and favored ally, he was once

---

[9] Hefele, *Histoire des conciles*, 7.2.955; Gasquet, "Le royaume lombard," p. 90.

[10] Hauck, *Kirchengeschichte Deutschlands*, 2.78; Romano, *Dominazioni*, p. 369.

[11] Halphen, *Les Barbares*, p. 237; Kleinclausz, *Charlemagne*, p. 10.

[12] Bullough, *Age of Charlemagne*, p. 12.

[13] A view well advanced in Delaruelle, "Charlemagne, Carloman, Didier," pp. 213–214, 221–224.

[14] Lintzel, "Karl der Grosse," 21–22; Delaruelle, "Charlemagne, Carloman, Didier," pp. 223–224; Calmette, *Charlemagne*, p. 53; Kleinclausz, *Charlemagne*, pp. 12–13. As such, it is seen as a repudiation by Charles of Bertrada, a view which may be difficult to sustain if, as we have argued, Bertrada was advancing a policy on Charles's behalf alone.

more simply a Frankish vassal, subject in his Italian political activity to Frankish royal limitation and sufferance which flowed from Charles's exercise of his *patricius Romanorum* service. For both Francia and Italy, then, there were major recurrences in late 771 of conditions which had not been seen in the three years since Pepin's death.

There was nothing in this development which was inherently dangerous to the Lombard monarchy, for as Desiderius was well aware he had been able earlier to arrive at coexistence with Pepin. He had partially restored the Lombard Kingdom of Italy by repossessing Spoleto and Benevento for the crown, achieved agreement and cooperation with Pope Paul I, and enjoyed surprisingly wide freedom of action in Italy relative to both Frankish and papal restriction. These were all major accomplishments, leading us to suppose that Desiderius found the return to the conditions reminiscent of Pepin's day acceptable.

But other considerations were less positive. First, since it appears that neither Desiderius nor his daughter gave Charles cause to repudiate his Lombard wife, Desiderius was bound to have regarded the rejection as a gross personal offense.[15] That is, Charles's action, highly insulting to his erstwhile father-in-law, introduced tensions into the Lombard-Frankish relationship.[16] That strain could only have been exacerbated by Desiderius's reception of Gerberga and Carloman's sons at the court of Pavia. Charles, having just taken his brother's land and throne, was of course sensitive to the problem of potential resistance there in the name of Carloman's heirs,[17] who could conceivably serve as focal points for both generating and coordinating opposition if they were to remain at large.

The trouble might become severe were Desiderius to assist the sons by actively forwarding their interests in Francia, or if he had his friend Pope Stephen III anoint the boys as Frankish kings and Roman patricians. The latter act would make the boys in some respects Charles's equals and deny Charles the advantage of being the sole Frank having papal unction. Thus, in harboring Carloman's sons King Desiderius threatened Charles's restoration of the united Frankish kingdom.[18] Both Desiderius and Charles had grievances against one another, ample reason for them to understand that the renewal of the conditions obtaining before Pepin's death did not include one of those conditions, harmony between the Frankish and Lombard monarchies. Now, in late 771, the prospect was for Frankish-Lombard hostility, meaning that an important new circumstance had grown out of the late 771 alterations.

In granting refuge to Gerberga and Carloman's sons, Desiderius was seeking revenge for Charles's rejection of his daughter.[19] There was risk in

---

[15] Perceived by Winston, *Charlemagne*, p. 60; Hodgkin, *Italy and her Invaders*, 7.327; Cutler, *Carolingian Italian Policies*, p. 114.

[16] Winston, *Charlemagne*, p. 60, 73. Hartmann, "Italy Under the Lombards," p. 219.

[17] On this subject see Jörg Jarnut. "Quierzy und Rom. Bemerkungen zu den 'promissiones donationis' Pippins und Karls," pp. 289–90.

[18] Duchesne. *The Beginnings*, p. 88.

[19] Hodgkin, *Italy and Her Invaders*. 7.349.

this position for Desiderius, for the presence of the fugitives at his court invited Frankish invasion of Italy. Furthermore, the Franco-Lombard marriage which had effectively kept Charles from any prospect of Italian war was no longer a restraint. Even so, there were reasons why Charles might not come to Italy, leaving Pavia free at least for the moment to continue backing Gerberga and her sons. First, Charles would be unlikely to risk an Italian campaign so soon after the annexation of Carloman's lands for fear of treason there. Further, Charles would be reluctant to invade Italy without a request for such action from the pope.[20] That is, Charles would be apt to attack only in a *partricius Romanorum* capacity, specifically ordered by the pope. Such an order would be unlikely to come from Stephen III because of his accommodation with Pavia and the intimate Lombard-papal cooperation recently experienced in the deposition of Christopher and Sergius. The bonds of mutual support and respect between Stephen and Desiderius were too strong to permit any immediate rupture of the sort required if Stephen were to call upon Charles to assault the Lombard kingdom. Frankish domestic limitations and the lack of papal desire for Frankish aid might be sufficient to keep Charles from undertaking any Italian action, making the risk involved in his support of Carloman's sons relatively low.

It was thus vital to Desiderius that his accommodation with the papacy last. As long as he maintained Carloman's sons at his court and continued through them to threaten Charles's reunification of the *regnum Francorum*, Desiderius required friendship with the pope to keep his policy of supporting the sons from leading to the highly undesirable end of an Italian campaign by Charles against Pavia. The accommodation with Rome was important to Desiderius in the general sense that it was the lynchpin of the Italian *modus vivendi* which, as observed, he had come to accept. But now there was the new ingredient of his devotion to Carloman's sons as the means of gaining revenge against Charles for the dismissal of his daughter. This consideration gave the accommodation the added role of discouraging Frankish intervention in Italy for the purpose of Charles's possessing the sons and ending their menace. The accommodation with the pope would deny the latter reason to apply for Carolingian arms in Italy, and in the absence of such application Charles would be reluctant to attack, partly because the attack would lack justification and partly because it might provoke the outright resistance and condemnation of the pope. Such a reaction Charles could ill afford for domestic considerations and the fear that the consequence would be a papal anointing of the sons as kings and patricians. To Desiderius, the accommodation was vital to his pursuit of revenge against King Charles.

### Desiderius and Pope Hadrian I: End of Royal-Papal Harmony

During the year 772, however, the accommodation with Rome dissolved into a bitter struggle which eventually led to the fall of the native Lombard

---

[20] Perceived by Cutler, *Carolingian Italian Policies*, p. 115.

crown in Charles's assumption of Pavia's throne in April 774. The final stages of the Lombard-papal relationship were at hand beginning with the death of Pope Stephen III on 3 February 772 after an illness of some length.[21] As we have noted, the villainous chamberlain Paul Afiarta hoped to succeed Stephen as pope and had exploited the plot against Christopher and Sergius to erase their opposition to his acceptance. In procuring Christopher's death and Sergius's blinding and imprisonment, Afiarta had no doubt considerably strengthened his hand in Rome, but not to the point of dominance since he was constrained to inflict further indignities upon the Romans.[22] Thus, when Stephen fell mortally ill, Afiarta and his followers exiled and imprisoned an unspecified number of Roman military and clerical officials.[23] Then, as was learned later from an inquest after the event, Afiarta and some Roman and Campanian associates had Sergius strangled in his Lateran cell.[24] In both actions the atrocious Afiarta was attempting to consolidate his power in Rome in preparation for his election as pope or was trying to overcome very strong opposition to him and his candidacy which materialized after the fall of Christopher and Sergius so that he would have at least some chance at election.[25] He probably sought to reduce his opposition, for Afiarta did not in fact become pope, yielding to the deacon Hadrian, who gained the throne in some form of coup after Stephen's death.[26]

The accession was likely a matter of force because Hadrian had a powerful opponent in Afiarta, and within hours after his elevation recalled Afiarta's exiles and released his prisoners.[27] Furthermore, Hadrian seems likely to have been the leader of the evidently numerous, powerful, and active enemies of the chamberlain.[28] Certainly Hadrian was known as an enemy of Paul after the fall of Christopher and Sergius, for he won the papacy in competition with him. And certainly he had a more or less organized party at his disposal since he gained election in a situation in which no man could have become pope without one.

The composition of this group and its reasons for looking to Hadrian are discernible. There were probably a number of members of the curial administration, disaffected by the evil of Afiarta's presence in their midst, who were favorable to Hadrian because of his reputation for moral purity and clerical excellence.[29] The same men were no doubt pleased by the fact

---

[21] *VS III*, 480.

[22] Hallenbeck, "Paul Afiarta and the Papacy," p. 47.

[23] *VH*, 4.486–487. Here it is reported that Hadrian recalled the exiles and released the prisoners—who had suffered their afflictions at Paul's hands during Stephen's illness.

[24] *VH*, 10-11.489–490.

[25] Hallenbeck, "Paul Afiarta and the Papacy," pp. 47–53.

[26] On the election of Hadrian as a coup see Ibid. and ibidem, "The Election of Pope Hadrian I." The latter article proposes that the coup was against Lombard power in Rome and over the papacy generally; but this view is modified in "Paul Afiarta and the Papacy," which sees the coup as being against the independent power of Afiarta.

[27] *VH*, 4.486–487.

[28] Hallenbeck, "Paul Afiarta and the Papacy," p. 50.

[29] *VH*, 2.486.

that Hadrian's uncle, Theodotus, had once been in their ranks as *primi-cerius*.[30] In addition to curial administrators, at least some of the military nobles, angered at Afiarta because he had ousted Duke Gratiosus[31] and assumed military airs himself,[32] must have been among the followers of Hadrian. The latter was by birth a member of the military aristocracy,[33] and Theodotus, who had raised him from boyhood, had once served as *dux*.[34] Finally, outraged by Afiarta's maltreatment of the chiefs of the legal profession, Christopher and Sergius, legalists may have supported Hadrian, drawn to him by his former service to Pope Paul I as a regional notary.[35] In sum, one presumes that in the months between the fall of Christopher and Sergius and Hadrian's election, the enemies of Paul Afiarta were not only numerous, important, and active but also organized to a certain extent and committed to Hadrian as their leader.[36] He and his men were also effective, for they won the throne on Stephen's death, denying it to the unprincipled chamberlain via some form of swift action.[37]

King Desiderius, who naturally watched the Roman developments closely, wasted no time in getting in touch with Hadrian. Soon after the elevation, the king sent three high-ranking envoys to greet Hadrian at his consecration—the duke of Spoleto, another duke, and his own *vestararius* or wardrobe master.[38] We are told that these Lombard dignitaries assured the new pope that Desiderius remained firm in his friendship. But Hadrian gave the envoys a sharp lecture. To be sure, he began, he both wanted peace "even with your King Desiderius" and supported the peace between "Romans, Franks, and Lombards," referring to the 755-756 treaty involving Stephen II, Pepin, and Aistulf.[39] But, Hadrian continued, Desiderius cannot be believed, for Stephen III "told me that he [Desiderius] had lied in all respects concerning the restoration of the rights of the church."[40] Further, Hadrian complained, Stephen had been able to get no satisfaction on the rights when he sent an embassy to the king on the matter. "Such is the honor of your King Desiderius," Hadrian told the envoys, "and the degree to which I may trust him."[41] The Lombard emissaries thereupon swore that

[30] Ibid.
[31] See Hallenbeck, "Paul Afiarta and the Papacy," p. 50.
[32] Paul took the military title of *superista*. VH, 6.487 and p. 515, n. 9.
[33] VH, 1.486.
[34] Ibid., 2.486.
[35] Ibid.
[36] See Hallenbeck, "The Election of Pope Hadrian I," pp. 264-266.
[37] The most recent treatment of Hadrian's election is found in David S. Sefton, "Pope Hadrian I and the Fall of the Kingdom of the Lombards," pp. 206-220. Sefton's view is that Hadrian was elected without opposition and gained the papacy because he was known as a supporter of papal territorial independence.
[38] VH, 5.487.
[39] For Hadrian's speech and what follows, see VH, 5-7.487-488.
[40] Ibid., 5.487,, lines 10-12: "domnus Stephanus papa de fraudulenta eius fide referuit, inquiens quod omnia illi mentitus fuisset que ei in corpus b. Petri iureiurando promisit pro iustitiis sancti Dei ecclesiae faciendis. . . ."
[41] Ibid., lines 22-23: "Ecce qualis est fides Desiderii regis vestri, et qua fiducia illi credere possim."

their king wanted only amity with the papacy and would turn over "*omnes iustitias*," all the rights which he had not transferred to Stephen III. Hadrian responded by sending two papal envoys to Desiderius, one of whom was the recently-defeated Paul Afiarta.[42] But the envoys had not traveled as far as Perugia when it was learned in April 772, two months after Hadrian's accession, that Desiderius had invaded the papal state, seizing the two exarchate towns of Faenza and Comacchio and the duchy of Ferrara,[43] all territories which were within the limits of the papal state recognized by Desiderius according to the treaty of 755–756.[44] After occupying these places, Desiderius went on to place Ravenna under siege and inflict severe ravaging upon the countryside.[45] Archbishop Leo, turning to the capital of the papal state for aid, called upon Pope Hadrian for help lest Ravenna fall. Hadrian responded by ordering his envoys to hurry on to Pavia and press Desiderius for return to St. Peter of all the territories which he had illegally taken, especially those rights of the church which "he had promised but not restored."[46] The king would not comply, and as the envoys stayed on in Pavia for some time Hadrian made them swear that they would remain faithful to the papacy. The papal anxiety may perhaps be attributed to the presence of Gerberga and her sons at the Lombard court. Desiderius, reports Hadrian's biographer, believed that the sons should have had Carloman's kingdom and therefore "attempted to get Hadrian to hurry to him so that the pope might anoint the sons of Carloman as kings."[47] Desiderius's aim, asserted the biographer, was "to cause a division of the kingdom of the Franks, to separate Charles, the king of the Franks and the *patricius Romanorum*, from the pope and to subjugate the city of Rome and all Italy to Lombard rule."[48] The source implies that Desiderius sent an embassy to Hadrian requesting the anointings, and it is clear that the pope turned it down.[49]

Analysis of these major developments suggests that after Hadrian's election Desiderius sought to extend the royal-papal accommodation[50] which had obtained under Stephen III. The Lombard's desire for continued amity is clear: immediately after Hadrian's election, Desiderius gave assurances in the embassy sent to the consecration that Pavia wanted only peace with

---

[42] *VH*, 6.487.
[43] Ibid., 6.488.
[44] Sefton, "Pope Hadrian and the Fall of the Kingdom of the Lombards," p. 212.
[45] *VH*, 7–9.488.
[46] Ibid., 8.488, line 15: "etiam quia iustitias b. Petri iuxta ut repomiserat not reddidit. . . ."
[47] Ibid., 9.488, lines 21–23: "et ob hoc ipsum sanctissimum praesulem ad se properandum seducere conabatur ut ipsos antefati quondam Carulomanni filios reges ungueret. . . ."
[48] Ibid., lines 23–25: "cupiens divisionem in regno Francorum inmittere ipsumque beatissimum pontificem a caritate et dilectione excellentissimi Caruli regis Francorum et patricii Romanorum separare, et Romanam urbem atque cuncta Italia sub sui regni Langobardorum potestate subiugare."
[49] *VH*, 9.488.
[50] Duchesne, *The Beginnings*, p. 88. Compare with the inaccurate view that Desiderius began to attack the papacy immediately after Charles's repudiation of his daughter and Hadrian's election. See for example Pepe, *Il medio evo*, p. 189.

Rome, that is, that he hoped for continuation of the royal-papal accommodation. It is equally clear that Hadrian was not at all similarly motivated or inclined toward the monarchy, despite his protestations to the contrary. The tone of his speech to the envoys was highly belligerent, openly accusing Desiderius of the most faithless dealing with Stephen III and suggesting to the envoys that there was little hope of successful cooperation with the king. This was hardly the way to perpetuate a harmonious relationship.

Also discouraging to the continuation of the Lombard-papal accommodation was Hadrian's position on the rights of the church which the pope asserted Desiderius had promised to Stephen III but not returned. Presumably Hadrian was referring to details of the Beneventan patrimonial transfer with which Desiderius and Stephen were dealing in the context of the fall of Christopher and Sergius, for no question of *plenaria iustitiae*—the conquests of Liutprand—seems to have been involved. The pope's assertion is a surprise since, as observed, Stephen III reported to Charles and Bertrada that Desiderius rendered full satisfaction on the matter. Perhaps the problem was that in the last months of Stephen's reign Desiderius failed to make the actual territorial transfer, or perhaps Hadrian was in some degree misrepresenting what Stephen had told him. In any event, Hadrian made the territorial problem a feature of his confrontation with the Lombard envoys, stressing it as a reason why he could not easily trust Desiderius. Hadrian apparently hoped to work the matter out, for he sent an embassy to Desiderius to discuss the situation. But the pope's emphasis upon the territorial difference and his generally negative framing of the problem could not have made Desiderius confident that Hadrian was as open as Stephen III to a positive royal-papal relationship.

The next matter to be considered is Desiderius's request that Hadrian anoint the sons of Carloman as Frankish kings and, no doubt, as Roman patricians as well. Clearly, Desiderius had begun to further his effort to inflict revenge upon Charles for the repudiation of his daughter. But Hadrian refused to comply, meaning that there was now a second serious rift between Desiderius and Rome. Hadrian had already indicated willingness to end Stephen III's accommodation with Pavia, choosing to emphasize the Lombard's untrustworthiness and the territorial problem; now he refused to cooperate with Desiderius's ambition to elevate Carloman's sons to the Frankish kingship. This refusal was a difficult problem for Desiderius, for implicit within it was papal identification with the cause of Charles. In resisting Desiderius's request for the anointings Hadrian was extending at least some degree of recognition to Charles's seizure of Carloman's throne. But the deeper problem was that in identifying with Charles, Hadrian raised the possibility that in time he might end in full cooperation with Charles against Desiderius. It is true that Hadrian had kept his distance of the Franks, neither notifying Charles of his own pontifical election nor calling upon him for aid against Desiderius.[51] But, unless the accommo-

---

[51] Sefton, "Pope Hadrian and the Fall of the Kingdom of the Lombards," p. 215.

dation with Rome was restored, and unless Hadrian was brought to anoint Carloman's sons, papal-Frankish collaboration to the point of a papally-endorsed Frankish war in Italy was not an unreal prospect.

In the first months of Hadrian's pontificate, Desiderius thus had two major questions before him. How could the accommodation between Pavia and Rome be restored for the sake of both preserving the Italian *modus vivendi* with which Desiderius was content and providing him with the papal neutrality which was necessary for his manipulation of Carloman's sons against Charles? And, how could the pope be brought to anointing the sons, also for the sake of damaging Charles? The answer which Desiderius evidently found was application of force in the papal state, a return to the apparent royal tactic of intimidation to secure papal acceptance of peace and cooperation with the monarchy. Desiderius evidently invaded the republic, seized the various places, and assaulted Ravenna to mount a serious threat to the republic—probably Desiderius's most damaging action in the republic to date—in order to persuade Hadrian to crown Carloman's sons[52] and revive the faltering accommodation. Desiderius also may have wanted to push Hadrian away from his territorial claim, but that concern could not have been as great as the other two. Desiderius's sudden return to force against the papacy was apparently his avenue to both recovery of the Italian *modus vivendi* and attainment of vengeance upon Charles without war by the latter against Pavia in Italy.

It should be recognized, of course, that the strong pressure applied by Desiderius invited what he wanted to avoid, Frankish action in Italy on behalf of St. Peter. If Hadrian felt too threatened, he could inevitably be expected to solicit Charles's active intervention and perhaps gain it. But Desiderius went ahead with his intimidation, suggesting that he believed that no such developments were likely in the future. Despite his disinclination to continue Stephen III's solidarity with Pavia, Hadrian was also in no rush to establish close relations with Charles. His refusal to crown the sons of Carloman may have been an indication of papal cooperation with Charles, but it nevertheless involved no direct approach to the Carolingians. As such, it did not preclude a papal reversal under such duress as Desiderius was applying. In short, the king had at least some reason to hope that Hadrian was not entirely likely to call upon Charles for aid. As for Charles, Desiderius probably gambled that he was still too concerned about conditions in Carloman's former kingdom to be easily moved into Italy without strong papal insistence upon aid—which, as just noted, had not yet materialized. There was apparently enough maneuvering room left for Desiderius to see if his depredations would lead Rome back into accommodation with the monarchy and into performance of the desired coronations.

Hadrian's *Vita* contains the assertion that Desiderius's aims in trying to secure anointing of Carloman's sons were "to cause a division of the king-

---

[52] Hodgkin, *Italy And Her Invaders*, 7.350; Bertolini, *Roma*, p. 670; Halphen, *Charlemagne*, p. 95.

dom of the Franks, to separate Charles, the king of the Franks and the *patricius Romanorum*, from the pope and to subjugate the city of Rome and all Italy to Lombard rule." Unquestionably Desiderius did want "to cause a division of the kingdom of the Franks," for such a division would entail Charles's loss of Carloman's kingdom and give the Lombard ultimate satisfaction for the rejection of his daughter. The claim that Desiderius wanted to separate Charles from Hadrian, that is, to disrupt the king's *patricius Romanorum* tie with Rome, may be true since he hoped to keep Hadrian from requesting Frankish aid in Italy and Charles from campaigning there. But it cannot be sustained that Desiderius sought some basic alteration of the Frankish crown's patrician relationship with Rome. As emphasized, Desiderius was still in acceptance of the 760 *modus vivendi*, which obviously involved a central place for the Frankish patrician. Finally, the assertion that Desiderius aspired to "subjugate the city of Rome and all Italy to Lombard rule" is patently wrong, despite some supportive modern assessments.[53] He had never indicated such an interest in his reign, and his concerns in 772 were to gain revenge upon Charles and to revive the solidarity between Pavia and Rome which had prevailed under Stephen III. Moreover, the hostility to the papacy which Desiderius was showing in the northern part of the papal republic was related to both of these ends, not to the capture of Rome and the conquest of the republic. We must suppose that the papal assertion was a matter of papal rhetoric designed to contribute to an eventual papal case against Desiderius for Frankish consumption should Charles's aid be required in the future.

### Failure of the *Modus Vivendi*

In the summer of 772, after Hadrian refused to anoint the sons of Carloman, relations between Pavia and Rome continued to deteriorate. One of the papal envoys in Pavia, Paul Afiarta, promised Desiderius that he would bring Hadrian to the court by force if necessary.[54] But Afiarta's best days were past. In Rome Hadrian opened an inquest into the murder of Sergius which had taken place during Stephen III's fatal illness, and Afiarta soon had to flee Hadrian's arrest, taking refuge in Rimini in the papal state. There followed a complex series of events which ended in Afiarta's execution by the *consularis* of Ravenna, the city's highest civil authority. The deed was apparently ordered by Archbishop Leo of Ravenna in defiance of papal instructions which commanded Afiarta's return to Rome. As such, the execution was a further instance of resistance to papal authority in the papal republic, but there was also gain for Hadrian in that Afiarta had been a dangerous rival and something of a collaborator with Desiderius. Meanwhile, the Lombard king launched a full-scale offensive in the former Pen-

---

[53] See for example Hodgkin, *Italy And Her Invaders*, 7.355–356.
[54] For this and the long source treatment of the fall of Paul Afiarta, see *VH*, 9–17.489–491. Of the various secondary accounts see Llewellyn, *Rome in the Dark Ages*, pp. 231–233; Bertolini, *Roma*, pp. 673–675; and Duchesne, *The Beginnings*, pp. 89–91.

tapolis.[55] Keeping Ravenna under siege, he attacked and took Sinigaglia, Jesi, Montefeltro, Urbino, and Gubbio,[56] thereby severing Rome's connection with Ravenna, seat of the recently rebellious archbishop, and, in the seizure of Gubbio, threatening an attack against Rome itself through Perugia down the Via Amerina. Desiderius also opened a second front, this one north of Rome from Lombard Tuscany, using forces from the same Tuscan region which had been his sole support when he had struggled with Ratchis for the Lombard crown sixteen years earlier. This invasion, which Desiderius himself directed, first struck the strategic town of Blera near the border with the Lombard kingdom on the Via Clodia about thirty miles from Rome.[57] It was one of the four towns which Liutprand had taken from Gregory III in 739 and returned to Zachary at Terni in 742. The Lombards slaughtered Blera's chief men, inflicted terrible destruction upon the countryside, and moved on to visit similar depredations upon other Roman towns. Otricoli, a town on the Via Flaminia near Narni was taken, perhaps by Spoletan Lombards. With the papal state on the Adriatic lost except for Ravenna, Rimini, and a few other places, Lombard troops poised at Gubbio and around Blera for a potential rush on Rome, and the old Roman duchy having suffered severe ravaging, Pope Hadrian continued to rely upon diplomacy. Envoys from Rome begged the king to cease his malice and restore the places which he had taken. But Desiderius was reportedly adamant, continually perpetrating what were termed cruel and intolerable evils in the Roman district.

But Hadrian would not yield, sending the abbot of Farfa and twenty of his senior monks to plead the papal cause.[58] Again Desiderius was unmoved, but he did send some important envoys to the pope requesting that he confer with him "on equal terms." Hadrian replied:

If your king satisfies me that he is willing to return to me the cities of St. Peter which he has taken from me in my time,[59] whether those of Ravenna, Perugia, or Rome, or even gives evidence of peaceful intention, I will hasten to meet and talk with him. . . . And if he doubts my good will, that I will not negotiate with him once he has returned the cities, he has my permission to reoccupy them. But if he does not restore the cities and their rights he shall not see my face. . . . In the same hour that my *missi* receive word that these cities are restored to me, I will hasten to negotiate with him anywhere he pleases.[60]

Hadrian was apparently beginning to feel the Lombard pressure.

---

[55] The usual view is that Pavia's movement into war was triggered by the fall of Paul Afiarta. See for example Hodgkin, *Italy And Her Invaders* 7.355–356; Llewellyn, *Rome in the Dark Ages*, p. 233; Bertolini, *Roma*, pp. 675–676.
[56] *VH*, 18.491–492.
[57] Ibid., 492 for this and what follows.
[58] Ibid., 19.492.
[59] Hodgkin *Italy and her Invaders*, (7.358) translates "in my time" ("tempore meo") as "in my pontificate."
[60] *VH*, 20.492: "Sic regem vestrum ex mea persona satisfacite, me vobis firmiter quoram Deo omnipotente promittente quia si praedictis civitates b. Petri quas tempore meo abstulit mihi reddiderit, continuo, sive Ticino voluerit, sive Ravenna, sive Perusia, sive hic Roma, vel

But the Lombard responded by raiding throughout Roman territory, investing many towns, and sending the Lombard army to besiege Rome itself.[61] Hadrian closed and strengthened Rome's gates and then, "since he stood in great danger and tribulation,"[62] sent a *missus*, Peter, to King Charles with apostolic letters begging the *patricius Romanorum* to aid the church and the afflicted provinces of Rome and the exarchate and to have Desiderius give up both the cities which he had taken and the *plenaria iustitiae*,[63] that is, the conquests of Liutprand in the exarchate and the Pentapolis. The *Vita Hadriani* observes that Peter went by sea and a Frankish source, the *Annales Regni Francorum*, adds that a sea trip to Marseilles was necessary for Peter because the Lombards forbade Romans to travel the roads.[64] From Marseilles Peter went to Charles's court at Thionville on the Moselle River in the northern part of Carloman's former kingdom. Peter met with Charles and requested that he and the Frankish people remain faithful to God and the cause of St. Peter against the Lombards.[65] Peter also reminded Charles of the royal Frankish *patricius Romanorum* commitment to the papacy: "Pope Stephen of holy memory," Peter recalled, "having endowed you with holy unction, ordained you then king and *patricius Romanorum*."[66]

In analyzing these developments one notices first that in the summer of 772 fighting Desiderius altered the nature of his campaign in the papal republic from a limited effort against Ravenna and the northern exarchate to an apparent effort to conquer the entire state. No part of the republic was spared as royal operations took place in the exarchate, the Pentapolis, Perugia, and the Roman district. Ravenna was besieged and Lombard arms approached Rome itself. In many areas extensive ravaging debilitated the resources of the republic and spread demoralizing terror. Rome was separated from Ravenna and the monarchy evidently came to control the great majority of the republic's highways. To Pope Hadrian, at least, a systematic royal effort to conquer and severely damage the papal republic was in progress, a marked and obvious change from the king's limited war of the spring.

Was Desiderius in fact intending to conquer Rome and the republic? That is, was he actually aiming to secure restoration and augmentation of Aistulf's Lombard Kingdom of Italy by annexing the papal exarchate, Pe-

---

etiam ubiubi illi placabile fuerit, ad eius properabo presentiam, cum eo pariter me coniungendum atque conloquendum quae ad salutem populi Dei utrarumque partium respiciunt. Et si foristan de hoc dubitationem habet, me cum eo minime debere coniungi postquam ipsas civitates reddiderit, si me cum ipso non coniunxero, licentiam habeat eas denuo occupandi. Nam si prius ipsas civitates non reddiderit et iustitias nobis minime fecerit, sciat pro certo meam nequaquam videbit faciem. . . . Et de praesenti, qua hora ipsi mei missi receptis eisdem civitatibus ad me hoc ipsum nuntiantes reversi fuerint, continuo ad eius, ubi voluerit, ut dictum est, properabo praesentiam, cum eo simul loquendum."

[61] *VH*, 21.493.
[62] Ibid., 22.493, line 12: "Et dum in magna angustia ac tribulatione consisteret. . . ."
[63] Ibid., 22.493, line 16.
[64] *ARF*, a. 773, 34. See also *Ann. Ein.*, a. 773, p. 35.
[65] *ARF*, a. 773, p. 34.
[66] *Chron. Moissac.*, p. 295.

rugia, and the Pentapolis to it and by adding Rome and its old duchy? Probably not, despite the strong impression to the contrary, for the king surely had the gravest doubts that Charles the patrician would tolerate conquest of Rome and the republic and the attendant loss of St. Peter's independence. The lesson of Aistulf for Pavia was that sooner or later the Franks would descend upon Italy with irresistible force, compel the crown to disgorge what it had gained, and subject the monarchy to the old restrictions and perhaps new ones as well. What, then, *was* the purpose of the campaign, which had every appearance of a systematic conquest? Still, it is suggested, Desiderius was applying pressure to force Hadrian into compliance with royal interests,[67] specifically, effecting an exchange of all royal conquests and termination of the now-extensive war for restoration of the lost accommodation and the coronation of Carloman's sons. The strong pressures being exerted to achieve these ends were provocative and risky, for they looked very much like attempted conquest and therefore significantly increased the possibility that Charles would invade Italy. But Desiderius knew that in the summer of 772 Charles had new difficulties to add to his earlier limitations: he had embarked on his challenging war with the Saxons on his northeastern frontier,[68] taking up the conquest and Christianization project in Germanic areas which had involved both Charles Martel and Pepin and had been important in drawing the Carolingians and the papacy together prior to the foundation of the papal-Frankish association of 753–754. Charles's Saxon commitment was large, and because of it Desiderius could apply as much pressure as he liked upon the pope in 772. The situation might change in 773, but for the moment he could appear to engage in conquest of the papal republic without fear of Frankish intervention in order to hammer Pope Hadrian into return to the accommodation of Stephen III and performance of the unction of Carloman's heirs.

There is some sign that Hadrian was beginning to waver on both issues. In the long speech which appears in the *Vita Hadriani* the pope suggested to Desiderius that his coronation of Carloman's sons might be possible, for he said that if Desiderius yielded the 772 conquests and returned the other territories he would negotiate with him. Perhaps Hadrian meant that they could negotiate a *peace settlement* after the transfers, but Desiderius, who had coronation of the sons very much on his mind, could have interpreted "negotiations" to mean discussion about the unctions. The papal concession, if it was that, was much more apparent than real, however, for in order for Desiderius to be sure that Hadrian would actually engage in talks which might lead to the coronations he would also have to keep some stick in hand to hold the pope to his word. Hadrian really wanted to avoid the unctions and in essence would have to be forced to make them. The only compulsion which Desiderius could exercise was his conquests of 772: if

---

[67] Hartmann, "Italy Under the Lombards," p. 219.
[68] *ARF*, a. 772, pp. 32–34. See also Hodgkin, *Italy and Her Invaders*, 7.358–360.

Hadrian would crown the sons he would return the conquests to St. Peter and free the republic of war. He could not simply restore the towns to the pope before discussion on the coronations had occurred, for to do so would leave Desiderius with no means of assuring papal compliance. In sum, it is possible that Hadrian wanted surrender of all the places taken from the republic before he would discuss the unctions with the king, while Desiderius wanted the unction to be followed by surrender of the conquests. Neither leader could afford to alter his position, leaving the royal-papal tension unresolved and far greater than it had ever been before in Desiderius's reign.

The stalemate may well explain why Desiderius increased his pressure, seen in the extension of his ravaging near Rome and his dispatch of his army to Rome itself, and the increased pressure in turn appears to explain why Hadrian appealed to Charles for aid. Having gained nothing by force, Desiderius probably believed that only intensified pressure might move Hadrian to a restoration of the accommodation and the performance of the coronation in exchange for return of the 772 conquests and royal withdrawal from the republic. But Hadrian was proving to be a determined and intensely anti-Lombard pontiff who would concede nothing as long as Desiderius held any of the papal state, no matter what new compulsions were brought to bear. Nevertheless, it was painfully and widely clear that Desiderius's rapid advance was beginning to threaten the very existence of the republic; things had reached the point that aid was needed to protect the republic and Rome and to retrieve the many places which had been lost. Thus was Peter sent to Thionville with the request that Charles and the Franks assist St. Peter against Desiderius and the Lombards.[69]

The appeal to the Franks was undertaken reluctantly by Pope Hadrian who was, as the *Vita Hadriani* puts it, "compelled by necessity."[70] The visit of Peter to Thionville was Hadrian's first communication with Charles,[71] and we are reminded that the pope neither notified Charles of his election nor sought his assistance during the earlier stages of Desiderius's intimidations, although the latter were worse than some of the troubles which had caused Paul I and Stephen II to sound the alarm to Francia. Clearly, Hadrian had perferred no serious dealing with Charles. The explanation is that Hadrian was uniquely devoted to the ideal of papal independence in Italy.[72] While previous pontiffs had encouraged Carolingian military and diplomatic activity in Italy, even lectured the kings upon the necessity of such activity, Hadrian hoped to avoid Frankish intervention, seeing it as a difficulty relative to his objective of independence. But the motif of independence had its limits. If Hadrian was careful not to seek Carolingian aid until there was no other choice, he was also quick to let Charles know that he was no enemy. The steady papal resistance to Desiderius on the

---

[69] Sefton, "Pope Hadrian and the Fall of the Kingdom of the Lombards," p. 215.
[70] VH, 22.493, line 12.
[71] Sefton, "Pope Hadrian and the Fall of the Kingdom of the Lombards,' p. 215.
[72] Ibid.

matter of Carloman's sons, which was of crucial importance to Charles, was more than enough to underscore the fundamental solidarity between Rome and Francia.

But Hadrian's objectives included more than papal independence, for this pontiff had dreams of great territorial expansion. Throughout his long reign Hadrian fought doggedly for papal territorial rights, and the record plainly shows that he intended to expand the republic to include Spoleto, Benevento, Venetia, and Istria as well as the papacy's now-traditional bloc composed of the exarchate-Pentapolis, Perugia, and Rome.[73] In the period under discussion, the first year of Hadrian's pontificate, only a nascent papal interest in territorial growth is visible, the claim advanced at Thionville that Desiderius owed the *plenaria iustitiae* to the papacy and the demand that Charles should help possess them. We recall that Pope Paul had abandoned the claim in 760 and that Stephen II did the same in 770-771 after Christopher had revived it early in Stephen's reign. But now Hadrian was renewing the *plenaria iustitiae* cry yet again, asserting to the *patricius Romanorum* that Rome was the rightful possessor of the conquests of Liutprand in the exarchate and the Pentapolis. The pope was making the first of his attempts to expand the papal state.

Hadrian's twin objectives of independence and territorial growth, the latter emerging as an operative principle by summer 772, go far toward explaining why the pope could and did not continue the Lombard-papal accommodation which he had inherited from Stephen III. At the outset of his pontificate, it may be presumed, Hadrian weighed Desiderius in light of the independence and territorial goals and found him a threat on the one hand and a hindrance on the other. In the past, Desiderius had intervened in Roman affairs, freely exercised right of transit across the papal state to maintain his rule in Spoleto, and continually presented the danger of encirclement of the republic with Lombard power. Desiderius had shown restraint, only twice seriously jeopardizing the autonomy of Rome and its republic—the attempted elevation of Philip and the support of Michael in Ravenna. Nevertheless, those episodes showed that Desiderius had the capacity to threaten papal independence, making him always a potential danger to it. He should, Hadrian concluded, be regarded as such and kept as far as possible from close ties with the papacy. As for the territorial ambition, Desiderius possessed the very territories which Hadrian desired for the papal state. He had not yielded the conquests of Liutprand in the exarchate and the Pentapolis, and he had control over Spoleto and Benevento. Desiderius was naturally not inclined to surrender these places, meaning that if they were to be gained Hadrian would have to discover a way to force the king to give them up. Such a consideration of course precluded Hadrian from maintaining the accommodation with Pavia, for

---

[73] For this point of view see Sefton, *The Pontificate of Hadrian I (772-795); Papal Theory and Political Reality in the Reign of Charlemagne*, especially chapters 3-6. Of Hadrian, Sefton (Ibid., p. 76) says: "the territorial question was uppermost in the pope's mind during his entire pontificate."

the accommodation was predicated upon peace between king and pope, which obviously could not endure if Hadrian became engaged in a struggle to expand the papal state at royal expense.

Hadrian's objectives posed a striking paradox. On the one hand he was reluctant to involve Charles in Italy for fear that some form of Frankish restriction would be imposed upon papal independence. But Hadrian also wanted to greatly augment the territory of the papal state and, as the events of 772 were demonstrating, he lacked adequate military strength to protect the security of the existing republic let alone achieve the expansion which he envisioned. For the sake of both papal independence and territorial growth, then, Hadrian had no choice but to invoke the very Frankish military action in Italy which he wanted to avoid. Hadrian, like Desiderius, was forced to gamble. Wanting to achieve independence and major territorial concessions from Desiderius, Hadrian came to view Carolingian invasion of Italy as a necessary evil to gain both, simultaneously hoping that he could check whatever threats to papal independence Charles might pose. Hadrian postponed his appeal until the last moment, until Desiderius's intense campaign made it abundantly clear that neither independence nor the territorial goal could be achieved on the basis of papal strength alone. But in the end he yielded with misgiving, seeing the appeal as a considerable risk but also as an opportunity to rid the republic of its Lombard menace and greatly expand its borders at Pavia's expense.

In the summer of 772, Desiderius was engaged in a campaign which gave the appearance of a systematic conquest of the papal republic which would end in a siege of Rome. But the royal objectives were probably more limited: to compel Hadrian by force to renew Stephen III's accommodation with the monarchy so that the *modus vivendi* of 760 could be restored and Charles kept out of Italy and to crown Carloman's sons as Frankish kings and Roman patricians so that the royal revenge could be gained. Desiderius was reasonably confident that Charles would not descend upon him because of domestic concerns, which would hold him in Francia despite his desire to possess the sons of Carloman resident in Pavia. Pope Hadrian resisted Desiderius's pressures, wanting to protect the independence of the republic by discontinuing Stephen III's accommodation with Pavia and avoiding Frankish military activity in Italy, and hoping to add the *plenaria iustitiae* and the duchies of Spoleto and Benevento to the republic. Along the way the pope protected his ties with the Carolingians by refusing the unction of Carloman's sons as demanded by Desiderius. In the end, the failure of Roman arms alone to achieve either papal independence or territorial aggrandizement, coupled with Desiderius's apparent effort to conquer the republic and Rome, caused Hadrian to appeal to Charles for aid against the Lombards. The pope feared the consequences of such aid for papal independence, but believed that only through it could the desired autonomy and expansion of the republic be attained. It remained to be seen whether Charles would provide the requested assistance.

### DESIDERIUS'S SIEGE OF ROME

In the Fall of 772 and the early months of 773 relations between Desiderius and Hadrian reached crisis stage.[74] The Lombard army gathered around Rome and Desiderius set out with Carloman's widow and her sons so that the pope would be able to anoint them as Frankish kings. When Hadrian in early 773 received royal envoys announcing that the king, Gerberga, and her sons were all on their way to Rome, he refused any contact at all with the Lombards unless Desiderius returned not only all the cities which he had taken in Hadrian's reign but also the *plenaria iustitiae*. For the first time, it appears, Desiderius heard directly from the pope the demand for the surrender of the conquests of Liutprand. By this time Desiderius also knew of the papal embassy to Charles, for he sent envoys to Francia to dispute Hadrian's territorial claims,[75] presumably the *plenaria iustitiae* renewal. In Italy Desiderius went forth to conduct the siege of Rome in person. Hadrian, fearing the worst, gathered into Rome armed men from Tuscany, Campania, the duchy of Perugia, and even the Pentapolis to defend the city. A general levy of the papal state had taken place. Additional repairs were made upon Rome's defenses, while ornaments and precious vessels from the churches of St. Peter and St. Paul beyond the walls were brought in. All the doors of St. Peter's were locked and placed under strong guard, so that if Desiderius came to the church he would be unable to enter it without papal consent. Then Hadrian resorted to an unprecedented maneuver: three bishops were sent to Desiderius with the warning that he would suffer anathema if he or any Lombards entered Roman territory. For reasons of fear and reverence, we are told, Desiderius returned in great haste to Viterbo, a city in Lombard Tuscany near the border with the papal republic. Neither the siege of Rome nor the coronation of Carloman's sons was any longer an imminent possibility.

Only a few brief reflections seem required here. Desiderius was still apparently trying to intimidate Hadrian into returning to the accommodation with Pavia and into the coronation of Carloman's sons. By early 773 Hadrian was both approaching Charles and advancing the *plenaria iustitiae* claim once more. The Lombard pressures thus had two new purposes: to dissuade Hadrian from further dealings with Charles and to compel him to drop the *plenaria iustitiae* demand. Desiderius's reason for having Gerberga and her sons near Rome while it was under siege was probably to have the sons readily available for coronation in the event that the final pressures upon Rome moved Hadrian to change his mind and perform the unctions. But Hadrian remained adamant in his refusal to anoint the sons, refusing to have any contact at all with Desiderius unless the territorial issues were resolved. The special measures which were taken to protect St.

---

[74] For what follows see *VH*, 23–25.493–494.
[75] Ibid., 26.494.

Peter's were apparently related to the projected unctions. If Desiderius were able to enter St. Peter's and Hadrian were to be forced to join him there, the sons of Carloman could be brought in and crowned under duress in Europe's most appropriate setting. Another possibility, although a remote one, is that Desiderius was planning to possess St. Peter's, elect an antipope, and have him anoint the princes in the great basilica.[76] Either way, or as long as the coronations were on Desiderius's mind and he was near Rome with the boys in hand, it was wise for Hadrian to bar St. Peter's to him. Turning to Hadrian's threat of anathema, it is often noted that no pontiff in the eighth century had previously issued such sentence against a Lombard king.[77] Hadrian's intentions were perhaps at least two-fold, to scatter Desiderius's gathering siege force and thereby end the most immediate royal menace, and to demonstrate to Charles the gravity of the situation which he was being summoned to alleviate: Desiderius could be kept from a siege of Rome only by the extremity of threatened anathema. Further, Charles was being signaled in the anathema episode that Desiderius was not only a political foe but an ally of the devil, an opponent of God and His vicar. The imagery was familiar, an echo of the vilification of Desiderius voiced by Christopher in resistance to the Franco-Lombard marriages. As for Desiderius's retreat after the brush with anathema, it may perhaps be attributed to the fact that the king was a Catholic and therefore worried about the threat in personal terms and in relation to the loyalty of his soldiers. The latter were no less Catholic than he and likely would not follow him further if he risked damnation by forging ahead against Rome.[78] But probably most important in influencing Desiderius to give up the siege was Hadrian's general levy from the republic and the likelihood that by this time the king feared that Charles was taking an interest in the Italian situation.[79] In anticipation that Charles might soon invade Italy, Desiderius had to make defense of the Lombard kingdom his paramount concern, causing him to turn away from the Roman campaign and abandon the pressure to gain the coronation of Carloman's sons.[80]

As the Lombards retired from the republic, Desiderius faced a most difficult situation. His apparent intimidation of Pope Hadrian to achieve restoration of the accommodation between Pavia and Rome, papal coronation of Carloman's exiled sons, and, eventually, papal abandonment of the renewed *iustitiae* claim had ended in abject failure. Moreover, the intimidations had finally driven Hadrian to solicit Carolingian aid agianst Desiderius. There was no hope now that the accommodation of Stephen III's reign could be revived or that Desiderius could have his revenge against

[76] Hodgkin, *Italy And Her Invaders*, 7.362.
[77] Duchesne, *The Beginnings*, pp. 67–68.
[78] Deansly, p. 344. Hodgkin (*Italy and Her Invaders*, 7.363) suggests that Hadrian's defensive measures also encouraged the king to retreat.
[79] Sefton, "Pope Hadrian and the Fall of the Kindgom of the Lombards," p. 217. Hadrian is likely to have told Desiderius in the anathema episode that papal envoys were seeking aid in Francia. Idem., *The Pontificate of Hadrian I*, p. 61.
[80] As briefly recognized in Ibid., p. 62.

Charles through papal unction of Carloman's sons. By early 773 Desiderius's attention was on other matters such as new tensions with Rome and the prospect of a Frankish invasion of Italy. For Desiderius, the changes which had flowed from the death of Carloman, the reunification of the Frankish kingdom by Charles, the failure of the Franco-Lombard alliance, and the accession of the ambitious and very anti-Lombard Hadrian I had not only ended the Italian *modus vivendi* and royal-papal accommodation but also brought him to the brink of the great crisis of his reign.

# IX. KAROLUS MAGNUS: REX FRANCORUM ET REX LANGOBARDORUM ATQUE PATRICIUS ROMANORUM

The invasion of Italy by King Charles of the Franks soon materialized. In early 773, envoys from Charles arrived in Rome to investigate the territorial claims of Pope Hadrian and the counterclaims of King Desiderius.[1] The envoys were soon satisfied that Desiderius owed what Hadrian demanded—the *plenaria iustitiae* and the royal conquests of 772 in the republic. Hadrian was able to attach envoys of his own to the Carolingian trio, arming them with apostolic letters to Charles ordering him to come to the aid of the church and restore to St. Peter all the territories which had been "stolen" by Desiderius.[2] The Frankish and papal *missi* first went before Desiderius, begging him to make the restitutions. But the king would restore nothing, so the envoys went on to Francia where they informed King Charles fully of the Lombard's "evil" and the Italian conditions in general.[3] Immediately Charles dispatched another embassy to Desiderius, begging him to restore the cites in question and offering him 14,000 gold solidi if he would comply. But, the money would not soften Desiderius's ferocious heart, sending the envoys home empty-handed.[4] Apparently in the spring of 773—whether before, during, or after the two Frankish embassies to Italy is not clear—Charles, evidently consulting with his chief men and the assembled nation, agreed to undertake the cause of St. Peter.[5] In the summer of 773 he thereupon gathered the Frankish army at Geneva and divided it into two forces, one under his own command which crossed the Alps into Italy by the Mt. Cenis pass and the other led by his uncle, Bernhard, which moved through the Mt. Jupiter or Great St. Bernard pass.[6] The war which Desiderius had long sought to prevent was beginning.

CHARLES'S INVASION OF ITALY: FRANKISH AND LOMBARD PERSPECTIVES

Although Charles finally invaded Italy he was reluctant to do so. In the first place, he did not automatically accept territorial claims, the implication being that he would not attack Desiderius unless he was convinced of the

---

[1] *VH*, 26.494.
[2] Ibid., 26–27.494.
[3] Ibid., 27.494.
[4] Ibid., 28.494.
[5] *ARF*, a. 773, p. 34.
[6] Ibid., a. 773, p. 36. On the dispute over what route Charles and Bernhard took, see A. Coolidge, "Charles the Great's Passage of the Alps in 773," pp. 493–505.

right and necessity of the invasion.[7] A further indication of Charles's reluctance is seen in his steady commitment to the arts of persuasion. After the Frankish envoys were satisfied that Desiderius indeed owed territories to St. Peter—apparently easily done since Desiderius now did hold both the *plenaria iustitiae* and the conquests of 772—they went on to Pavia and asked Desiderius to return the "stolen cities" and rights, that is, hoping for a voluntary and peaceful settlement of the conflict. The envoys had surely been ordered by Charles to take this pacific approach with Desiderius— even if they were convinced in Rome that the king was a villainous thief— a sure sign that Charles preferred diplomacy to war. The same sign is clear later on in Charles's dispatch of the embassy to Desiderius offering him the large sum of money if he would turn over the territories to Hadrian. Had Desiderius accepted the offer and made some gestures toward return of the disputed places, Charles would perhaps not have thought further of invasion.

The realization that an Italian invasion in 773 or 774 would interrupt the attention to the Saxon war may explain Charles's reluctance.[8] Begun in the previous year of 772, the war had been difficult and was not near completion at the end of 772.[9] To leave the Saxon problem unresolved for campaigning in Italy in 773 and perhaps 774 would be to jeopardize the limited accomplishments of 772 and invite Saxon disruptions in the Frankish frontier areas. Further explanations lie in Charles's probable fear that Carloman's kingdom remained potentially too mutinous to risk a long Italian absence,[10] the possibility that Charles worried about new trouble in Aquitaine, and the chance that he saw in Desiderius's considerable military success of 772 · an opponent strong enough either to defeat or stalemate Frankish forces in Italy.[11] Finally, it may be that Charles was really less reluctant than it appeared, for the resort to diplomatic persuasion may have been conscious repetition of Pepin's dealing with Aistulf before the invasion of 775.[12] Charles, in brief, may have been following a pre-war ritual which had been established in the days of the great Pepin and Stephen II. Even if this was the case the problems of the Saxon war surely gave Charles the greatest pause about the wisdom of going to Italy.

But Charles did resort to war, and we must ask why.[13] Certainly a variety of motives was at work, not the least of which was Charles's own sense of obligation to his *patricius Romanorum* duties, his responsibilities to the vicar of St. Peter.[14] One is reminded again that Charles had been raised by

---

[7] Sefton, *The Pontificate of Hadrian I*, p. 64.

[8] Amann, *Histoire de l'Église*, 6.54.

[9] Deansly, *A History of Early Medieval Europe from 476 to 911*, p. 344.

[10] Cutler, *Carolingian Italian Policies*, p. 114.

[11] It has been suggested that the peace overtures were designed to pacify pro-Lombard nobles in Francia. Ibid., p. 119.

[12] Hodgkin, *Italy and Her Invaders*, 7.366.

[13] See Cutler, *Carolingian Italian Policies*, pp. 118–120.

[14] See the assertion of Halphen (*Charlemagne*, p. 96) that Charles acted because he was convinced by his investigation that Hadrian's complaints against Desiderius were valid.

Pepin in awareness of and respect for the patrician office and function. Furthermore, Charles had become the preferred patrician in Bertrada's orchestration and in Stephen III's crisis with Carloman's Dodo. Finally, Charles had emerged as sole patrician upon Carloman's death, and when Hadrian's envoys asked that he remember Pepin's *pactum* with the papacy, execute his responsibilities to St. Peter, and aid him against Desiderius, it was next to impossible to ignore the papal requests. Charles might and did try to have Desiderius accommodate Hadrian without an Italian invasion, but once it was clear that diplomacy was insufficient, there was little choice but to conduct the invasion expected of a *patricius Romanorum*. To do other was to betray his father, his crown, and his sacred obligation to the church. Perhaps not even the demands of the Saxon war were more pressing. There was also a most compelling political reason for attacking Desiderius: retrieval of the sons of Carloman. Desiderius had persistently attempted to secure Hadrian's coronation of the princes, and just as persistently Hadrian had managed to resist. But Charles no doubt feared that Desiderius might eventually prevail unless the sons were captured and removed from political consideration. Some scholars suggest that the aim of seizing them was primary in Charles's decision to invade Italy;[15] that was probably the case, the burden of the *patricius Romanorum* responsibility notwithstanding. Finally, it has been argued that the invasion decision arose from Charles's determination to thwart recent efforts by Duke Tassilo of Bavaria in 772 and 773 to become a king by papal sanction and cut into the Carolingians' monopoly on institutional and spiritual association with the papacy.[16] If so, the Italian campaign had a significant Bavarian dimension to complement the patrician and dynastic concerns.

It is further notable that Desiderius would not comply with the demands of Charles's diplomacy, thereby practically assuring that the Frank would attack him. As has been observed, Desiderius greatly feared a Frankish invasion of Italy, making his rejection of the diplomacy somewhat difficult to understand. Why did he virtually invite war when by turning over all or even some of the *plenaria iustitiae* and the 772 conquests to Hadrian or by promising to effect the transfer he might have prevented the invasion and improved relations with Hadrian considerably? Perhaps Desiderius felt that his armed strength was adequate to defeat Charles, but this view cannot be definitively defended. More convincing is the hypothesis that Desiderius, having plentiful evidence that Hadrian was a thoroughly anti-Lombard pontiff in the pattern of Gregory III and Stephen II, believed that Hadrian would continually press for Frankish war upon Pavia no matter whether he promised to give up the *plenaria iustitiae* and the 772 conquests or not.[17]

---

[15] For example Kleinclausz, *Charlemagne*, p. 18; and Peter Classen, *Karl der Grosse, das Papsttum und Byzanz*, p. 13; ibidem, "Karl der Grosse und die Thronfolge im Frankenreich," pp. 130–131. Cutler (*Carolingian Italian Policies*, p. 116) argues that in 772 Charles had mollified Carloman's nobles by involving them in the Saxon war; having done that, Charles was by 773 in a better position to fight in Italy without worrying greatly about their opposition.

[16] Ibid., pp. 118–119; Abel-Simson, *Jahrbücher*, 1, p. 132.

[17] Approximately appreciated by Hartmann, "Italy Under the Lombards," p. 219.

Sooner or later Charles would have to be dealt with in Italy. There is also the possibility that Desiderius thought that Charles was bent upon deposing him.[18] Why should he comply with the Frankish diplomacy at all when such compliance would only postpone the inevitable war with Charles and the latter's attempt to seize Pavia's throne? That Hadrian and Charles in their territorial demands were asking Desiderius to do violence to himself and to his kingdom which he could not afford was a central consideration. If Desiderius were to yield the conquests of 772 he would deprive himself of a major bargaining point with Rome which he would need later. More important was the consideration that if he were to surrender the *plenaria iustitiae* he would lose territories which were both integral parts of the Lombard kingdom and vital to royal maintenance of the Lombard Kindgom of Italy. These conquests of Liutprand in the exarchate and the Pentapolis had belonged to Pavia without interruption since the mid-720s. Their loss would constitute a serious blow to the kingdom and the king, perhaps so damaging that Lombard noble hostility to Desiderius would follow. Obvious in Hadrian's demand for transfer of the *plenaria iustitiae* was papal interest in expanding the papal republic, and implicit in this interest was a threat to the free access to Spoleto via Lombard transit of the republic which Desiderius had enjoyed since the reign of Paul I. If he were to yield the *plenaria iustitiae* to Rome he would very likely lose control over the Via Aemilia in the surrendered part of the exarchate and the Old Flaminian Way in the surrendered portion of the Pentapolis. Loss of these road segments would seriously damage the vital royal access to Spoleto—and perhaps even deny it completely—raising the possibility that both Spoleto and Benevento would be encouraged to separate themselves again from the monarchy. In the papal-Carolingian request for Lombard transfer of the *plenaria iustitiae* to St. Peter, then, there was significant menace to the Lombard Kingdom of Italy as well as to Desiderius's relations with the Lombard aristocracy. Simply put, Desiderius could not afford to turn the *plenaria iustitiae* over to the papacy and therefore rebuffed Charles's envoys and went ahead with the war which he did not want.

As far as may be known, Desiderius did not offer to return Carloman's sons to Francia, a gesture which might conceivably have kept Charles beyond the Alps. Perhaps Desiderius retained the exiles simply because Charles's envoys apparently did not ask for their release, or perhaps the Lombard continued to hold out hope that he could eventually use them in gaining revenge upon Charles for the rejection of his daughter. But, more plausibly, the retention of the princes, like the refusal to yield the conquests of 772, sprang from a royal desire to have bargaining points for future dealings with Charles and Hadrian. If Desiderius maintained custody of the boys, he could perhaps use them to advantage in subsequent negotiations, which could be crucial in the event that Charles's campaign proved to be only partially successful. By early 773, it is possible that Car-

---

[18] Cutler, *Carolingian Italian Policies*, p. 120; Abel-Simson, *Jahrbücher*, 1, p. 144.

loman's sons, losing their role as instruments of Desiderius's revenge, were taking on new importance as a royal trump card to be placed at the right time—and were thus well worth keeping on hand.

Having resolved to face Charles, Desiderius attempted to put up a strong defense.[19] The entire Lombard army was sent north to defend the Alpine *clusae*, which Desiderius had heavily fortified. As Charles approached the *clusae*, he turned once more to diplomacy, offering 14,000 solidi if he would "restore the cities." Again Desiderius refused, but Charles sent yet another embassy: the Franks would leave Italy if only Desiderius would give Charles three noble Lombard hostages and *promise* to make the restitutions. But not even this lessened the Lombard's resistance. Then, according to the *Vita Hadriani*, God in retribution struck terror into the Lombard troops, causing them to flee in haste from the *clusae*. Modern scholarship suggests that the divine intervention took the form of the sudden appearance of Bernhard and his forces, arriving unexpectedly from their Alpine passage and taking the *clusae* swiftly from the rear.[20] The Franks next descended upon the Lombard plain with little opposition. Desiderius took refuge in Pavia, while his son, Adelgis, rushed Gerberga and Carloman's sons off to the stoutly walled town of Verona. A substantial amount of the Lombard army simply returned home, leaving only Pavia and Verona to be attacked. By the first of October 773, Charles had arrived at Pavia and had begun the siege of the Lombard capital.

### COLLAPSE OF THE LOMBARD KINGDOM OF ITALY

The Lombard crown once more had been unable to defend northern Italy against the Franks. In fact, Desiderius was now in the gravest trouble. His army had been beaten and had apparently slipped away, leaving him strength only in Pavia and Verona. Moreover, the victorious Charles was not inclined to negotiate, for after the two gestures at the *clusae* he stuck firmly to the business of war.[21] The *clusae* embassies were apparently Desiderius's last chance to keep Charles from waging war in Italy, but the Lombard was as intransigent as before, probably for the same reasons. King Charles, who two years earlier had been Desiderius's son-in-law, was now encamped before Pavia's walls with no intention of leaving before the city fell: having settled in, he had his wife Hildegard and his children sent to Italy to join him. Desiderius could have had only the most serious misgivings.

Part of the royal worry was the loss of the duchy of Spoleto.[22] Even while Charles confronted Desiderius at the northen *clusae*, the principal men of Spoleto came to Rome, commended themselves to Pope Hadrian, swore

---

[19] Sources for the campaign are *VH*, 34–35.495; *ARF*, a. 773, p. 36. Secondary treatments are Coolidge; Hodgkin, *Italy and Her Invaders*, 7.366–370.

[20] *Ann. Ein.*, a. 773, pp. 35–37; *ARF*, a. 773, p. 36. For a discussion of the Frankish routes, location of the *clusae*, and other details see Coolidge.

[21] Noted by Sefton, *The Pontificate of Hadrian I*, p. 66.

[22] Based upon *VH*, 32–33.495–496.

fidelity to him, and tonsured their hair in the Roman fashion, a sign of submission. They declared that all Spoletans wanted to perform similar submission, but fear of Desiderius held them back. But, after Desiderius's defeat at the *clusae* and retreat to Pavia, many Spoletans from various cities of the duchy flocked to Rome and begged Hadrian to receive them as subjects. In St. Peter's basilica the Spoletans swore fidelity to St. Peter and his vicars forever and received Roman tonsure while Hadrian appointed a new duke of Spoleto, a certain Hildeprand, who was one of the initiaters of the Spoletan secession and whom the Spoletans themselves had elected duke. What happened to Duke Theodicius is not known. He was still in power as late as September 773, but by early 774 Hildeprand is known to have ruled,[23] so in the interim Theodicius was somehow swept aside. "And so," wrote Hadrian's biographer, "the whole duchy of Spoleto placed itself under the authority and power of the pope."[24] In the meantime, the towns of Fermo, Osimo, and Ancona in the Pentapolis also submitted to Hadrian. One hears nothing about whether the duchy of Benevento defected or remained with Desiderius. As for King Charles, there is no reason to think that he collaborated with Hadrian in achieving the Spoletan defection or even knew that it was being arranged.[25]

Meanwhile, Charles pursued the siege of Pavia. At some point he learned that Gerberga and her sons were not within the beleaguered capital but at Verona with Adelgis.[26] Taking with him a picked force and leaving the bulk of the army to continue the siege, Charles marched swiftly for Verona, captured it, and gathered in the rich prize of Carloman's widow and sons. Adelgis escaped and fled to Constantinople, however.[27] No source describes the fate of Gerberga or her sons, but a frequently-applied eighth-century technique of political exclusion was banishment to a cloister and one has no reason to suppose that these three experienced anything different.[28] After the Verona triumph, Charles captured a number of Lombard cities in the upper Po Valley and then returned to the siege of Pavia.[29]

Major developments were obviously underway. First, and most important from Desiderius's point of view, the Lombard Kingdom of Italy was dissolved. Its northern districts were virtually in Charles's hand, for with the fall of Verona and the conquests in the Po valley only Pavia was left and that was under relentless siege by the already-victorious Frank. Further, in the losses to Charles Desiderius could no longer think of holding onto the duchy of Spoleto via passage of the papal state. Indeed, the duchy itself had renounced its membership in the Lombard kingdom and attached itself

[23] Hodgkin, *Italy and Her Invaders*, 7.372, n. 1.
[24] *VH*, 33.496: "Et ita, Deo annuente, praedictum ducatum Spolitinum generaliter suo certamine isdem praecipuus pontifex sub iure et potesta b. Petri subiugavit."
[25] Sefton, "Pope Hadrian and the Fall of the Kingdom of the Lombards," p. 249.
[26] See *VH*, 34.496.
[27] See *Agnelli Liber Pontificalis*, 160.381; ARF, a. 774, pp. 38–40.
[28] Hodgkin, *Italy and Her Invaders*, 7.370.
[29] *VH*, 34.496.

to the papacy. Because Arichis of Benevento was Desiderius's son-in-law, his duchy stayed loyal to Pavia, but it was necessarily a most tenuous adherence. Clearly, the northern disasters and the Spoletan defection alone were sufficient for all involved to know that the Lombard Kingdom of Italy, first erected by Liutprand, extended, completed, and then lost by Aistulf, and partially restored by Desiderius, was once more non-existent. Charles's war of 773–774 was a disaster of the greatest magnitude for the Lombard monarchy.

The submission of Fermio, Ancona, and Osimo was perhaps a case of an old Pentapoline district seceding from the duchy of Spoleto by attaching itself to the papacy. The places were originally *iustitiae* concessions by Desiderius, but in some way they evidently became possessions of Spoleto after 757,[30] joining the papal state only in the turmoil surrounding Desiderius's northern defeat and subsequent retreat to his capital. For our purposes, the important point is that the three places, which were natural components of the Pentapolis portion of the papal state, were now joined to that state, giving it the same strategic access to the duchy of Spoleto which King Liutprand had once held.

The Spoletan defection to the papacy warrants special comment. The duchy's departure from the royal obedience at first opportunity is clear indication of the degree of Spoletan separatism. At the time, in 773–774, Spoleto had belonged to the Lombard Kingdom of Italy since Desiderius restored it to royal submission in 758, a period of about fifteen years. Even so, something approaching a universal Spoletan repudiation of Pavia's rule occurred, a clear indication that Desiderius and Duke Theodicius had been able to achieve little or no diminution of the traditional Spoletan insistence upon autonomy. A further point has to do with Spoleto's adherence to the papacy. When the duchy had previously rejected Pavia under Pope Stephen II's guidance, it had accepted dependence upon King Pepin of the Franks. But now in 773 the dependence was upon the papacy, a situation arranged evidently without Frankish participation or knowledge. None of this was accidental, for the process of submission was apparently so smooth that one may fairly envision a matter in some way planned by Spoletans such as Hildeprand and his friends and Romans such as Pope Hadrian. It was no different with the exclusion of Charles from the Spoletan-papal association: that too must have been deliberate. In brief, Hadrian's arrangement of papal suzerainty over Spoleto must be understood as an initial success in his policy of expansion of the papal state.[31] Herein the acquisition of suzerainty over Spoleto is clarified: the suzerainty was the first such capacity claimed and enjoyed by the eighth-century papacy, and the tonsuring of the Spoletans in the Roman fashion appears to indicate their inclusion in the membership of the special people of the republic,[32] that is, it implies

---

[30] Duchesne, *VH*, p. 516, n. 26.
[31] Sefton, *The Pontificate of Hadrian I*, p. 68.
[32] Ibid., p. 66.

Spoletan territorial integration into the papal state. It would seem virtually certain that Hadrian's generation of the Frankish invasion aimed partly at the acquisition of Spoleto, a first step toward what Hadrian regarded as general expansion of the republic.

It remains to consider Charles's seizure of Gerberga and her two sons at Verona. Obviously, one of the main aims of the campaign was met with their apprehension, and that Charles took care of the matter with such dispatch is sure evidence that the custody of the princes and their mother was indeed a primary motivation of the campaign itself. At last Charles was free of the menace that the sons, with Desiderius's support, would receive Hadrian's unction and would galvanize resistance in Carloman's old kingdom. The princes were no longer a factor, and Charles could rest secure in the knowledge that the last vestiges of his old trouble with Carloman were settled. That alone made the Italian war worthwhile.

The final observation is that as Charles returned to Pavia from Verona and the Po, the gains for Pope Hadrian were already very great. The Lombard forces in the papal state were surely gone, the towns taken by Desiderius returned by virtue of his withdrawal, and the pitiless ravaging ended. Moreover, the great enemy Desiderius had suffered the gravest defeats and humiliations at Charles's hands: he had fled without a fight from the *clusae*, seen his army disintegrate, lost Verona, and been forced to make Pavia his last defense, one which had twice before proved inadequate. Rome and the papal state were secure from Pavia. But there was more, for in possessing Carloman's sons Charles removed any future possibility that Desiderius could harass Pope Hadrian on the unction issue. That tense and difficult matter was terminated. Hadrian had also gained a new ally in Duke Hildeprand and could view the duchy of Spoleto as an extension of the papal republic. In the Spoletan defection there was also total damage to the Lombard Kingdom of Italy, which the popes more often than not had regarded as a menace. Finally, Hadrian must have been pleased with Charles's performance: the Frank had faithfully and successfully performed his *patricius Romanorum* duty without posing any apparent danger to papal interests. For Pope Hadrian, then, the fall of 773 and early 774 was a time of satisfaction, a sharp contrast to the dark night of despair being suffered by Desiderius in besieged Pavia.

### CHARLES AND HADRIAN IN ROME AND THE DEPOSITION OF DESIDERIUS: A FRANKISH-PAPAL UNDERSTANDING

The *Vita Hadriani* reports that Charles maintained the siege through the winter of 773–774 and then, in late March 774, some six months after its inception, left most of his army at Pavia and set out for Rome, desiring to spend the coming Easter there with Pope Hadrian.[33] Arriving via Lombard Tuscany near Rome on Holy Saturday, Charles was met and greeted by

---

[33] The sole account of the Roman episode is *VH*, 35–43.496–498.

the Roman army , its officers, and a procession of crosses. Moving ahead on foot as a humble pilgrim, Charles came to St. Peter's basilica and ascended the steps on his knees. At the top the *rex Francorum et patricius Romanorum* was greeted by Pope Hadrian and the assembled Roman clergy. Charles and Hadrian then entered St. Peter's and advanced to the saint's *confessio* where they prayed for victory over the Lombards. Franks and Romans then exchanged oaths of fidelity, after which the visitors were permitted to enter Rome.[34] For three days Charles and the Franks toured Rome and attended paschal services; then, on April 6, king and pope joined at St. Peter's for important political discussions, in the course of which, according to the *Vita Hadriani*, Charles promised to fulfill in every detail the promise which King Pepin, Charles himself, his brother Carloman, and all the Frankish nobles had made to St. Peter and Stephen II when the latter was in Francia. Charles's notary, Itherius, who had before handled Italian territorial matters for the Carolingians, drew up a deed of promise "like the former," i.e., the Quierzy promise, which bestowed

the same cities and territories upon St. Peter, promising that they should be given to the pope according to their boundary definitions, which are contained in the donation deed: from Luna with the island of Corsica, from there to Sarzana, there to Monte Bardone, i.e., Verceto, there to Parma, there to Reggio, and there to Mantua and Monselice, together with the whole exarchate of Ravenna, as it was originally, and the provinces of Istria and Venetia, and the entire duchies of Spoleto and Benevento.[35]

Charles and his entourage thereupon signed the document, which was placed in the *confessio* of St. Peter, and swore to uphold what had been granted to the papacy. At some point during the conference, Hadrian for his part promised to Charles that he would apply in the Frankish cause what one scholar calls "the full spiritual resources of the papacy."[36] This arrangement, not referred to in the *Vita Hadriani* but very clear in the papal letters dating from after the 774 conference, specifically entailed prayer for Charles's success against Desiderius and the Saxons[37] by the pope and the Roman clergy and people in special services petitioning St. Peter for aid and rendering him thanks for it.[38] On the surface, Charles recognized and supported Hadrian's territorial interests while Hadrian granted Charles very special spiritual aid.

---

[34] See Josef Deér, "Die Vorrechte des Kaisers in Rom (772–800)," pp. 44–45, on the nature of Charles's reception in Rome. Deér argues that it differed significantly from that accorded the exarch.

[35] *VH*, 42.498: "ubi concessit easdem civitates et territoria b. Petro easque praefato pontifice contradi spopondit per designatum confinium, sicut in eadem donationem continere monstratur, id est: a Lunis cum insula Corsica, deinde in Suriano, deinde in monte Bardone, id est in Verceto, deinde in Parma, deinde in Regio; et exinde in Mantua atque Monte Silicis, simulque et universum exarchatum. Ravennantium, sicut antiquitus erat, atque provincias Venetiarum et Istria; necnon et cunctum ducatum Spolitinum seu Beneventanum."

[36] Cutler, *Carolingian Italian Policies*, p. 133.

[37] *CC* #53, 575. See also Cutler, *Carolingian Italian Policies*, p. 136.

[38] *CC* #50, 570. See also Cutler, *Carolingian Italian Policies*, pp. 135–136.

After the April 6 conference was concluded, Charles returned to Pavia and led strong attacks against the city, which had been weakened in his absence by plague and military pressure. In Rome, Hadrian commenced the enlistment of divine aid through daily assembly of Roman clergy, monks, deacons, nobles and people "imploring most merciful God to grant Charles the utmost prosperity and joy and to increase his victories."[39] After more than a month of such intercession Pavia was finally taken, with King Desiderius, all his chief men, and the whole Lombard kingdom submitting to Charles. Desiderius and his wife were taken away with Charles to Francia.[40] Fortunately, other sources add important details to this *Vita Hadriani* skeleton. Pavia fell in June[41] and the great Frankish source, the *Annales Regni Francorum*,[42] gives the following account of the subsequent events. Charles captured Desiderius, his wife, and daughter, and took possession of the whole royal palace treasury or hoard. Then Lombards from all over Italy came into Pavia and placed themsevles under King Charles. Desiderius's son Adelgis, who had apparently joined his father in Pavia after the fall of Verona, managed to escape and fled to Constantinople. Then King Charles, having subjected Italy and set it in order, returned to Francia in great triumph, leaving behind an occupation force in Pavia. It is not clear where Desiderius and his wife spent their exile.[43] But Adelgis, having fled to Constantinople, was made a patrician by the emperor.[44] When Hadrian wrote his first letter to Charles after the April 6 conference he saluted Charles as *Domino excellentissimo filio, Carolo regi Francorum et Langobardorum atque patricio Romanorum*—king of the Franks and the Lombards and *patricius Romanorum*.[45]

The deposition of Desiderius and the accession of Charles as Lombard king brought the eighth-century relationship between the Lombard monarchy and the papacy to a close, for Desiderius was the last monarch at Pavia who was of Lombard blood and culture. Charles was a Frank, and while he did come to espouse a number of Lombard perspectives, and did eventually recognize the particular needs of the Lombard realm within the Carolingian empire at large by making his son Pepin king of Italy in 781, he never permitted specifically Lombard interests to prevail again in Pavia. Henceforth in the eighth century the Lombard royal relationship with the papacy was inseparable from that conducted by Charles as Frankish king and then as Roman emperor. Clearly, a new phase in the history of the Lombard monarchy commenced as Charles took Pavia's iron crown and Desiderius made his way to a lonely monastic exile.

---

[39] CC #50, 570: ". . . dominum Deum nostrum exorantes, ut et veniam dilictorum vobis et maximam prosperitatis etiam laetitiam et copiosas victorias vobis multipliciter e caelo concedat."

[40] *VH*, 44.499.

[41] *Chron. Moissiac.*, p. 295.

[42] Anno. 774, pp. 38–40.

[43] One source specifies Corbey. *Annales Sangallenses Maiores*, a. 774, p. 75.

[44] *Ann. Ein.*, a. 774, pp. 39–41.

[45] CC #49, 568.

For our purposes the deposition of Desiderius and the accession of Charles at Pavia are events of primary significance. Most important, perhaps, is the genesis of both. It seems most unlikely that Pope Hadrian was responsible, for his interests were independence and acquisition of as much territory for the papal republic as possible, concerns which were fundamentally incompatible with the lodging of the powerful Franks upon the very frontiers of the republic, the theoretical and ideological bonds between St. Peter and the Carolingians notwithstanding. Perhaps Hadrian even resisted the deposition and Frankish installation at Pavia. This leaves Charles as the only possible inspiration, a conclusion which requires particular investigation because it is not enough to say that Charles took the crown simply as a matter of conquest. There were evidently more complex considerations.

At the April conference, it is recalled, Charles insisted on and obtained papal commitment to special prayer and ritual in support of Charles's military efforts against his enemies, first Desiderius and then the Saxons. The interest, it would appear, generated the concept of the deposition of Desiderius and the substitution of Charles as Lombard king in the Frank's mind. If Pope Hadrian was to bring the full spiritual resources of the papacy to bear on behalf of Frankish arms, he would have to be free of Italian political burdens and dangers, and free of harmful distractions.[46] Surely Desiderius was a substantial burden and danger, a very great distraction, which could be eliminated only by deposing him and replacing him with a papal friend, namely Charles himself. With Pavian-Roman harmony thus assured, Hadrian would be in a position to devote his full attention and energy to the spiritual requirements of the Frankish crown. Robert Cutler, this view's convincing advocate, summarizes the argument well: "Charles probably saw deposition of Desiderius as the surest way to prevent further distracting political quarrels from diverting the pope from his spiritual duties."[47]

It is impossible to know with certainty at what juncture Charles decided upon the rearrangements at Pavia for purposes of enlisting St. Peter's aid. Perhaps the decision was reached in Francia when the campaign was finally decided upon, for the invasion had the earmarks of a conquest.[48] Charles seized Verona and the Po places. Moreover, the siege of Pavia was relentless, Charles giving no terms to Desiderius at any point, as well he might have given the obvious strength and tenacity of the Lombard defense. The campaign was thus no mere attempt to force the Lombard king into compliance with Frankish-papal demands or into cooperation with the papacy, as those of Pepin had been. Rather, the concern was one of conquest, of permanent possession of the kingdom, its capital, and its throne. Also favoring the possibility that the deposition of Desiderius was intended from the outset is the fact that Charles was already engaged with the Saxons and could

---

[46] Cutler, *Carolingian Italian Policies,* pp. 147–148.
[47] Ibid., p. 148.
[48] Sefton, *The Pontificate of Hadrian I,* p. 64; Halphen, *Charlemagne,* p. 97.

already have been mindful of the necessity of papal support. But the fore-going evidence is not conclusive. Moreover, Charles was both reluctant to invade Italy and probably concerned with obtaining control of Carloman's sons. One must therefore conjecture further as to the point of decision to depose and replace Desiderius. Very likely it was made at the siege of Pavia before Charles went to Rome in late March 774.[49] Consider the context. Charles, having recently begun the difficult Saxon war, invaded Italy and earned early quick victories, only to see the Lombard defense stiffen at Pavia. There is no sign even as late as March 774 that the city was near capitulation. Moreover, during the siege the Saxons were again raiding the Frankish frontiers.[50] It may be believed that, being convinced by March that Hadrian's provision of spiritual aid was mandatory for final Carolin-gian victory over Desiderius and the Saxons, Charles went to Rome to obtain that aid and from that point on viewed deposition of Desiderius and substitution of himself as Lombard king as the necessary method for pro-viding Hadrian with the capacity to furnish him with St. Peter's spiritual support. This is, of course, adequate grounds for explaining Charles's visit to Rome in the first place: Hadrian had to be brought to promise the spiritual support and understand the deposition of Desiderius and installation of Frankish rule at Pavia in relation to it. There seems to be little reason to believe, as some have, that the royal concern was loss of Spoleto to the papacy,[51] for Charles in 774 seems to have ignored the whole Spoleto matter, even to the extent of accepting Hadrian's claim to rule it by granting the 774 deed which included the duchy as a papal possession. Finally, it is possible that Charles did not decide to depose and succeed Desiderius until the visit itself, but such a view suggests a hasty decision on vital matters. More credible and less problematical is the view of deposition and succes-sion as a carefully premediated design from February or March 774 onward.

Charles and Hadrian must have discussed the deposition and succession plan in the April 6 meeting and Hadrian must have accepted the plan there. It was surely raised in the context of the demand for spiritual support, for the plan and the demand were inextricably intertwined. The demand must have been made at the conference and accepted by the pope, for, as observed earlier, the intercessions began as soon as Charles returned to the siege of Pavia. Bound as it was to the spiritual support concern, the de-position and succession plan was thus also necessarily accepted by the pope in the April 6 meeting. Further, there is no indication at all of any kind of papal surprise over the deposition of Desiderius and the accession of Charles after the fact, suggesting that both developments were at once expected and acceptable in Rome. Finally, given his general concern for papal independence and reluctance over the Frankish presence in Italy, Hadrian would likely have registered strong protest had Charles surprised

---

[49] Abel-Simson, *Jahrbücher*, 1, p. 150.
[50] *ARF*, a. 773, pp. 36–38.
[51] Abel-Simson, *Jahrbücher*, 1, pp. 154–155; Kleinclausz, *Charlemagne*, pp. 23–24.

him with an unexpected deposition and accession. No such outrage was voiced, again indicating a mutually discussed and accepted situation. Without much question, Charles's accession as Lombard king and deposition of Desiderius was agreed to in Rome in early April 774, the king advocating the reorganization and Hadrian grudgingly going along with it.

A further consideration has to do with the territorial grant made by Charles to Hadrian. It will be recalled that the grant was reportedly like that of 754 made by Pepin to Stephen II, specified a northern boundary running northeastward across the peninsula from Luna to Monselice, and placed the exarchate, Venetia, Istria, and the duchies of Spoleto and Benevento in papal hands. There is no surviving copy of the deed itself and the *Vita Hadriani* account of the April 6 meeting is the only description of its contents. For these reasons and others the grant has long been subject to vigorous and interesting but not always useful debate.[52] The discussions have centered upon the enormous amount of territory which Charles apparently awarded to the pope, nearly two-thirds of Italy including all of Tuscany, Venetia, Istria, the exarchate, and the duchies of the Pentapolis, Perugia, Rome, Spoleto, and Benevento. What was the nature of the grant? Did it convey papal jurisdiction over all the territories specified? Or, was the jurisdiction limited to patrimonial land within the general confines of the vast area specified? How does one account for the assertion that the 774 grant was "like the former," that is, like the Quierzy grant of 754, when the 774 grant was apparently far beyond the territorial recognition given in 754, and when it is not at all clear that the recognition was given at Quierzy in the first place? Why did Charles give the grant at all? Was it perhaps a whole or partial forgery, or the creation of interpolation? As important as these and other questions are, our concern with the grant is restricted to its relationship to the deposition of Desiderius and the accession of Charles as *rex Langobardorum*.

If one follows those scholars who believe that Hadrian did in some respect claim the extensive territories listed in the *Vita Hadriani* and that Charles did in some respect specify the places listed in the *Vita* as papal territory,[53] one may rather convincingly link the grant and the subsequent deposition and succession episode in the manner suggested in the following reconstruction.

Wanting to obtain full papal spiritual support in the struggle against Desiderius and the Saxons, Charles arrived in Rome with the demand for

---

[52] Major works in the discussion are: Ernst Sackur, "Die Promissio Pippins vom Jahre 754 und ihre Erneuerung durch Karl den Grosse," pp. 385–424; Wilhelm Martens, *Die römische Frage ünter Pippin und Karl dem Grossen*; Theodor Lindner, *Die sogenannte Schenkungen Pippins, Karls des Grossen und Ottos I. an die Päpste*; Caspar, *Pippin und die römische Kirche*; L. Saltet, "La lecture d'un texte et la critique contemporaine, les prétendues promesses de Quierzy (754) et de Rome (774) dans le 'Liber Pontificalis,' " pp. 176–206 and pp. 61–85; E. Griffe, "Aux origines de l'État pontifical: Charlemagne et Hadrien I<sup>er</sup> (772–795)," pp. 65–89; P. Kehr, "Die sogenannte karolingische Schenkung von 774," pp. 385–411; Sefton, *The Pontificate of Hadrian I*, pp. 71–105.

[53] For example Lindner, *Die sogenannte Schenkungen*, pp. 17–19; Abel-Simson, *Jahrbücher*, 1, 156–158; Sefton, *The Pontificate of Hadrian I*, p. 96.

such support and the proposition that Desiderius be deposed and replaced by Charles as the means to free the pope to fully marshal the divine aid. Hadrian had other things on his mind, however. He feared that the massive Frankish intervention potentially threatened papal independence. Further, as his recent arrangement of Spoletan dependence upon the papacy revealed, Hadrian held territorial growth of the papal republic as a priority. As it turned out, it appears, the royal and papal interests were not irreconcilable: Charles evidently accommodated Hadrian's independence and territorial interests while Hadrian in turn accommodated Charles's spiritual and deposition-accession requirements. One stresses the mutuality of the situation. Approached by the pope and his men, Charles easily complied with their demands for the grant of a new deed which, though reportedly like the Quierzy grant, in fact specified a greatly increased papal territorial jurisdiction. But, it is argued, Charles gave it only in the corollary understanding that Hadrian for his part would commence the solicitation of God's help and acceded to Desiderius's deposition and the institution of Frankish rule at Pavia. Again, Charles willingly accepted the Luna-Monselice line, which was likely in some way a demarcation line between the about-to-be-established Frankish power in the north at Pavia and the expanded territory of the papal republic,[54] and, hence, a guarantee of sorts of the independence of the republic, Rome, and the papacy. But, it is asserted, the assurance of independence was afforded only in the corollary understanding, as before, that Hadrian would furnish the spiritual aid and accept the change of rule at Pavia. In the most basic sense, it appears that Charles in Rome at the April conference traded recognition of a much-increased papal state and acknowledgment of papal independence for papal spiritual aid and permission to free Rome from the distractions of tensions with Pavia. It was, in a sense, the grant or donation of 774 by which Charles secured the end of the native Lombard monarchy.

Unfortunately, there is no specific evidence that the territorial grant and Charles's spiritual concerns and deposition-accession plan were so linked, all the more since Hadrian's spiritual support of Charles is not even mentioned in the *Vita Hadriani* recitation. Nevertheless, the linkage seems tenable in that through it both parties were able to achieve goals which were clearly respective rather than mutual in nature before the conference occurred. Charles wanted St. Peter's assistance and the deposition-accession eventuality to free Hadrian for spiritual service—and obtained both at the conference. Hadrian needed assurance of papal independence in the face of the new circumstance of Frankish power in Italy and Frankish support for substantial growth of the papal republic—and gained both at the conference. The cognizance of one another's interests is obviously sufficient grounds for believing that accommodation of interests was the hallmark of the meeting, wherein the deposition of Desiderius and accession of

---

[54] Sefton, Ibid., p. 93; G. Schnürer, *Die Entstehung des Kirchenstaats*, pp. 45–47; Halphen, *Charlemagne*, pp. 101–102.

Charles as Lombard king and Charles's grant of 774 were entirely har-
monized.

### Frankish Rule at Pavia: New Conditions and Old Perspectives

Implicit in the arrangements of April–June 774 were a number of implications of revolutionary proportions. First was the introduction of Frankish rule at Pavia. In the past there had been occasional Frankish military
intervention and, from about 752 on, fairly steady diplomatic activity.
Henceforth, however, royal Carolingian rule would be exercised in Pavia
on a permanent basis. Further, the Lombard Kingdom of Italy, a persistent
reality since the 720s, was gone, *Charles's* Lombard kingdom being restricted
to north Italian districts because of the 774 grant which placed Spoleto and
Benevento in royal hands and perhaps because of the Luna-Monselice line.
There was also the prospect of a greatly expanded papal republic, territory
embracing nearly two-thirds of Italy and thus far larger than the exarchate-
Pentapolis-Perugia-Rome entity claimed and held by Stephen II, Paul I, and
Stephen III. Present, too, was the Frankish expectation of greatly reduced
papal participation in the energy-draining commitments of Italian politics
to generate and maintain the high degree of spiritual support for victory
over the Lombards and Saxons. Finally, because of the harmony between
Charles and Hadrian, between Francia and Rome, arising from their historical cooperation and the *patricius Romanorum* relationship, there was the
novel prospect of absence of war and serious tension between the Lombard
monarchy and the papacy. In a word, the April–June developments placed
before contemporaries a series of startling innovations which collectively
raised the possibility of the dawn of a new era in Lombard-papal relations
and Italian political life in general.

To some degree the novelty promised in 774 bore fruit. For example
Charles was not long in rooting Frankish rule in Pavia very firmly. At first
content to accept the submissions of the northern Lombard dukes and leave
the governance of the kingdom to them, Charles by 775 was cultivating
favorable relationships with Lombard abbots to check the ducal power,[55]
and, following a rebellion by the duke of Friuli and other prominent Lombards in 776, replaced rebel dukes with Frankish counts.[56] Charles thereafter
generally substituted Frankish for Lombard officers on the latter's deaths.
There was no attempt to merge the Frankish and Lombard peoples, as
Charles's maintenance of the Lombard laws shows,[57] but the designation
and coronation of Charles's son Pepin as Lombard king in 781 suggests
concern for steady and thorough attention to Lombard affairs.[58] The point

---

[55] K. Schmid, "Anselm von Nonantola. Olim dux militum—nunc dux monachorum," pp.
114–116.
[56] Sefton, The *Pontificate of Hadrian I*, p. 124; K. Schmid, "Zur Ablösung der Langobardenherrschaft durch die Franken," pp. 3–4.
[57] Sefton, The *Pontificate of Hadrian I*, p. 125.
[58] Ibid., p. 152; Kleinclausz, *Charlemagne*, pp. 113–114.

seems clear: Frankish rule in Pavia, the most revolutionary of all the 774 novelties, was unquestionably borne out in subsequent years.

It was otherwise with the other innovations, however, most importantly concerning the disappearance of the Lombard kingdom of Italy. Simply put, from an early time after the deposition of Desiderius Charles displayed the keenest interest in exercising the traditional eighth century royal Lombard sovereignty over the dukes of Spoleto and Benevento, that is, in reigning over the Lombard Kingdom of Italy. By late 775 Charles was treating Hildeprand of Spoleto as a royal subordinate, wholly ignoring Hildeprand's 773 submission to Pope Hadrian and his own grant of 774 which specified Spoleto as part of the papal republic.[59] Arichis of Benevento also submitted, but this kinsman of Desiderius was never satisfactorily subdued and became a sharp danger to Charles. Nevertheless, the latter saw the *regnum Langobardorum* not in the restricted northern terms of the pre-eighth-century crown but in the pan-Italian perspective of Liutprand, Aistulf, and Desiderius.[60] As for the promise of a much-expanded papal state, it never materialized, for in coming to share Pavia's traditional eighth-century view of the kingdom's scope, Charles could accept only a small papal republic, essentially that of the exarchate, Pentapolis, Perugia, and Rome entity which had been acknowledged by Desiderius. Charles never recognized the Venetian, Istrian, Spoletan, or Beneventan claims of the 774 deed, despite agreeing to them at the 774 conference. Nor did Hadrian ever possess the places claimed. Thus, Charles would tolerate no significant growth of the republic beyond what might be termed the classical outlines which had been achieved by Stephen II and Paul I. Nor was the expectation of decreased papal political activity in Italy for the sake of massive and persistent prayer support for the Frankish crown visible. Considerable marshaling of spiritual aid did occur, but instead of reduction of political activity one finds Hadrian behaving exactly as Stephen II, Paul I, and Stephen III had in their protection and advancement of papal interests.[61] Papal agents dealt steadily with the Franks and other interested parties regarding land claims, rights, and pressing ecclesiastical matters. Primary papal commitment remained in the political-territorial realm. And, papal resistance to Frankish political growth in Italy was extensive. If anything, Hadrian was even more devoted to the "distractions" of Italian politics than any of his predecessors. Finally, because Charles was determined to possess the eighth-century Lombard Kingdom of Italy rather than the pre-eighth century north Italian kingdom, and because Hadrian persistently attempted to place most of Italy under the republic, there was nearly constant tension between Charles and Hadrian over Italian territorial matters. The claims, counterclaims, negotiations, and ambiguities were not unlike the earlier problems between Desiderius

---

[59] Sefton, *The Pontificate of Hadrian I*, pp. 117–120; Abel-Simson, *Jahrbücher*, 1, p. 242; Hodgkin, *Italy and Her Invaders*, 7.50–51.

[60] Martens, *Die römische Frage*, p. 154.

[61] Cutler, *Carolingian Italian Policies*, pp. 148–149.

and Paul I and Desiderius and Hadrian, the difference being that no open
military conflict occurred. Thus, the promise of a high degree of peace and
cooperation between Pavia and Rome offered in 774 failed to appear. In
the main, then, the revolutionary implications of 774 were overwhelmed
and succeeded by a return to the basic Italian political realities as they had
been prior to the changes of 774, save for the permanent and deep rooting
of Frankish power in Italy.

It was thus that Desiderius's deposition, the fall of the native Lombard
monarchy, and the institution of Frankish power at Pavia failed to alter
the fundamental attitudes held by the Lombard kings toward Italy in general and Rome, the papacy, and the papal republic in particular. Desiderius
was gone—dethroned, banished, and humiliated—but Pavia's king still
looked to Italian unity, supremacy over Spoleto and Benevento, and protection of royal interests and territory from papal encroachments. For Lom-
bardy's discredited and maligned kings, Charles's post-774 behavior as Lombard monarch was at once a vindication and a triumph.

Those who hoped for a restoration of the native Lombard monarchy
naturally looked to Desiderius's son, Adelgis. The latter, it will be recalled,
fled to Constantinople upon the fall of Pavia and was warmly received by
the Emperor Constantine V, who granted him the title of patrician and
promised him military support.[62] Partly to nullify these ties between Adelgis and the empire and thus to reduce the danger of recovery of Pavia by
Adelgis, Charles in 781 arranged for one of his daughters to marry the heir
to the imperial throne.[63] Charles also worried about Duke Arichis of Benevento, who represented the heart of Lombard national strength after 774
more than Adelgis. Ambitious and energetic, this son-in-law of Desiderius
and brother-in-law of Adelgis called himself *princeps*, aligned with Byzantium, and otherwise resisted the subordination to Charles accepted by Hildeprand of Spoleto.[64] Understanding by 787 that Arichis and Adelgis could
pose considerable threat if they joined in Italy with Byzantine help, Charles
confronted the problem directly by forcing Arichis into an oath of submission and making a hostage of his son, Grimoald. But the duke was soon
allied with Byzantium in an arrangement whereby Arichis would help
restore imperial Italy while the Byzantines would recognize Arichis as patrician and allow him to possess the duchy of Naples. His kinsman Adelgis
would help lead the Byzantine army, his goal being restoration of the fallen
monarchy.[65] Arichis died before the imperial force appeared, but it and
Adelgis arrived in Benevento in 787, only to be soundly defeated by Hil-

---

[62] Adelgis evidently retained some strength in the kingdom, for at least some leading nobles
took part in the 776 revolt against Charles which had the restoration of Adelgis as one of its
aims. CC #3, 583.

[63] Sefton, *The Pontificate of Hadrian I,* p. 154.

[64] Ibid., pp. 167–169; H. Belting, "Studien zum beneventanischen Hof im 8. Jahrhundert,"
pp. 144–155.

[65] Sefton, *The Pontificate of Hadrian I,* pp. 171–172, 177.

deprand of Spoleto and Duke Grimoald of Benevento, the son of Arichis and grandson of Desiderius whom Charles changed from hostage to duke when Arichis died.[66] The beaten Adelgis retired anew to Constantinople, never again to affect affairs in Italy. Only in Grimoald as Duke of Benevento did the pride, determination, and ambition of the Lombard kings live on as this grandson of Desiderius, the former Frankish hostage, maintained Benevento's independence of King Charles and carried on the far-reaching policies of his father Arichis. Pavia would have been well-served had Grimoald been its king.

---

[66] Ibid., pp. 178–179, 183–184.

# SUMMARY

The fundamental issue of eighth century Italian political life was the search for political stability following the sixth-century Lombard entry, the subsequent conflict between the Lombards and the empire, and the Italian revolts against Constantinople. It was within the context of the search for stability that the relationship between Pavia and Rome occurred and is most productively studied.

The Italian peace achieved by Justinian's conquest of the Ostrogoths was shattered by the long Lombard-imperial war whereby Italy's unity was replaced by a territorial mosaic of Lombard royal and ducal jurisdictions and those remaining in imperial hands. Clearly, a major issue would be the achievement of an environment wherein the competing Lombard elements could enjoy a stable relationship and the hostile Lombard, papal and imperial elements could co-exist in peace. Progress was made toward Lombard-imperial tolerance by the late seventh century, as is indicated by the royal-Byzantine territorial settlement of 680. But the eighth century brought new disruptions as King Liutprand broke the peace and territorial balance with the empire and the papacy under Gregory II and Gregory III made its long-developing independent Roman and Italian leadership roles active in the Italian revolt of the late 720s. By the 725-740 period there were four competing Italian interests—the Lombard crown, the duchies of Spoleto and Benevento, the papacy, and the empire. All had territorial and jurisdictional concerns foremost in mind, and the situation was so fluid as to permit each to find allies, as Liutprand did when he combined in 728 with Exarch Eutychius or Gregory III did when he joined with Transamund of Spoleto and Romoald of Benevento. The division came to have a potential fifth ingredient when Gregory III approached Charles Martel and the Franks for help against Pavia.

In the end, however, Liutprand was able to move successfully toward Italian order by placing Spoleto and Benevento under royal rule, thereby creating a Lombard Kingdom of Italy, and arriving at a very promising peace settlement with Pope Zachary at Terni in 741. For the first time since the 720s there was Italian peace and political coherence, though the peace did not involve settlement with the empire, as is shown by the attacks upon the exarchate by Liutprand after Terni and by the major offensive of King Aistulf. By 751 that offensive had extinguished Byzantine power and established royal rule everywhere north of Rome. Italian coherence was nearly a reality: the Lombard crown provided Italian unity through its jurisdiction from the Alps to Apulia, except for the duchy of Rome, and peace and harmony characterized Pavia's relations with the papacy, now the only independent Italian political entity apart from the monarchy.

But Pope Stephen II was able to deny this new Italian integration, at least in part for purposes of creating a papal republic and attaining protection for it. Securing Frankish military intervention against Aistulf, Stephen took on the role of a determined enemy of Pavia, made Pepin do the same, and, by 756, after Pepin's second campaign, had replaced Aistulf's Italian organization with another which involved a papal state composed of the former Byzantine central Italian territories, a north Italian Lombard kingdom dependent upon the Frankish crown, and the duchies of Spoleto and Benevento, now liberated from Pavia but newly-dependent upon Francia. Implied in this revised pattern was Frankish military and diplomatic supervision, a general peace between all parties, and Lombard royal subordination to the Franks and Rome. In brief, Stephen II had been able to set aside the Italian community achieved by Liutprand and Aistulf and replace it with another planned in the Lateran and Francia.

Between 756 and 772 the Italian organization imposed by Stephen and Pepin endured despite many complex challenges arising in both Italy and the Frankish kingdom. The fundamental new conditions of the papal republic and peaceful relations between Pavia, Rome, and Francia remained in effect. Nothing gave the empire real hope that it could ever regain its lost Italian place. But there was also one major change within the pattern devised by Pepin and Stephen II—the reemergence of the Lombard Kingdom of Italy through Desiderius's successful reacquisition of royal control over Spoleto and Benevento during the pontificate of Paul I. In effect, Stephen's reorganization was significantly revised to allow for the peaceful presence of a Lombard Kingdom of Italy, a change which was accepted by Pope Stephen III, who seems to have worked consciously to promote Roman harmony with Pavia as the key to Italian stability.

But once more the balance was upset. This time the agent was Hadrian I, who, worrying about papal independence and holding great ambition to expand the papal state, found Desiderius's reinstitution of the Lombard Kingdom of Italy intolerable, refused Stephen III's harmony with Pavia, and ended by taking Spoleto and Benevento from Desiderius by bringing the Franks back to Italy as Lombard foes, this time under the leadership of Charles the Great. Hadrian appears to have gotten more than he expected or wanted, however, for Charles demanded liturgical support of St. Peter against the Lombards and Saxons and made himself Lombard king to facilitate provision of that support. Suddenly in 774 there was in place a new and potentially revolutionary Italian organization. Henceforth, the promise was that Pavia and Rome would enjoy relations free of tension, the pope would not be distracted by ceaseless preoccupation with Italian political problems, and St. Peter's republic would include both its older central Italian districts and the duchies of Spoleto and Benevento. Desiderius's restored Lombard Kingdom of Italy would have no part in the new community, once more denied existence by combined Frankish and papal action. As in the days of Stephen II the papacy had joined with the Carolingians to impose an Italian settlement.

But Hadrian's revision was far less lasting than that of Stephen II and Pepin. By 775 Charles had rejected Spoletan membership in the papal state and had restored the Lombard Kingdom of Italy by bringing the duke of Spoleto back into obedience to Pavia. Hadrian's vision of a greatly augmented papal republic thus failed, returning the republic essentially to the dimensions of the 756–774 period. And, since Charles was as interested in ruling an *Italian* kingdom as Liutprand, Aistulf, or Desiderius, the problems experienced by the latter with the papacy were also known by Charles in his dealings with Hadrian. The upshot was that the Italian *modus vivendi* established during the reign of Desiderius, which included a Lombard Kingdom of Italy, a central Italian papal state, Frankish supervision, lack of imperial power north of Naples, and general Frankish-Lombard-papal peace, reappeared after Desiderius's deposition. It was, it seems, the most durable of the Italian arrangements made during the century.

In the broadest sense, then, the eighth-century relationship between Pavia and Rome was governed by the two parties' reactions to one another's view of the most desirable Italian political organization. Beginning with Liutprand, the crown's vision was of a Lombard Kingdom of Italy ruling all of Italy with the exception of Rome and its territory (first as a duchy, later as the republic of St. Peter) and the Byzantine fragments of Naples, Apulia, and Calabria. Northern Italy, the coastal strip from Ravenna to Rome, and Spoleto and Benevento would all be included. Rome and its territory would be left in peace, and harmony would prevail between king and pope. But the popes frequently refused to accept this vision, explaining why tension between the monarchy and the papacy was frequently present. Gregory III resisted the royal vision bitterly. The wise and temperate Zachary acknowledged Liutprand's rule of Spoleto and Benevento, but obstructed his effort to take Ravenna. Stephen II ended by opposing even royal rule of the duchies and insisting that the kingdom be both confined to the north and subordinate to the Carolingians. Further, he took the central Italian Byzantine territories from Aistulf and bestowed them upon St. Peter. Pope Paul was highly uncomfortable when Desiderius restored Pavia's authority in Spoleto and Benevento, and Hadrian devoted the first two years of his pontificate to opposing Desiderius and finally took the duchies from him. The point seems clear: the Lombard royal perception of the Italian future was often unacceptable to Rome, and as Rome resisted, frequent royal-papal tension was inevitable. The reverse is also true, for the crown could not tolerate the papal view of an Italian organization wherein Pavia was restricted to the north, with either the empire or the papacy holding central Italy and Spoleto and Benevento enjoying independence. Thus did Liutprand struggle against Gregory III's bid to end royal rule in the duchies and resist Zachary's pressures to stop his post-Terni war against the exarchate. Thus also did Aistulf try to protect his conquests and his kingdom against Stephen II and Pepin, especially attempting to contradict their foundation of the papal state. In the same way Desiderius fought Hadrian as the latter resisted the settlement which the king, Paul I, and Stephen III had reached. Again, the point is evident: the papal perception of the Italian future was unacceptable to Pavia, and as Pavia resisted, royal-papal tension was inevitable. What broke the impasse and brought genuine peace was mutual royal and papal support of a jointly-held perception of Italian order, the *modus vivendi* of the period from 760 to 772 developed by Desiderius, Paul, Stephen III, and Pepin, the accommodation which allowed both papal possession of St. Peter's republic composed of the exarchate, Pentapolis and Perugia, *and* the Lombard Kingdom of Italy in the shape of royal control over Spoleto and Benevento. As noted, despite Hadrian's attempt to seize Spoleto for Rome, this *modus vivendi* was maintained by Charles, testimony to its validity as the sole means of achieving a lasting Italian settlement. In this respect, eighth-century relations between the Lombard monarchy and the papacy produced the Italian political equilibrium which had been largely absent since the outset of the century, if not since Alboin's entry from Pannonia.

# BIBLIOGRAPHY

## PRIMARY SOURCES

*Agnelli qui et Andreas Liber Pontificalis Ecclesiae Ravennatis.* ed. O. Holder-Egger. *MGH Scriptores rerum Langobardicarum et Italicarum saeculum VI–IX.* Hanover, 1878.

*Annales Laureshamenses.* ed. G. H. Pertz. *MGH Scriptores,* I. Hanover, 1826.

*Annales Mettenses.* ed. G. H. Pertz. *MGH Scriptores,* I. Hanover, 1826.

*Annales Qui Dicuntur Einhardi.* ed. F. Kurze. *MGH Scriptores Rerum Germanicarum in usum Scholarum.* Hanover, 1895.

*Annales Regni Francorum,* ed. F. Kurze. *MGH Scriptores Rer. Ger. in usum schol.* Hanover, 1895.

*Annales Sangallenses Mairores.* ed. G. H. Pertz. *MGH Scriptores,* I. Hanover, 1826.

*Benedicti Sancti Andrae Monachi Chronicon.* ed. G. H. Pertz. *MGH Scriptores,* III. Hanover, 1839.

*Chronicon Moissiacense.* ed. G. H. Pertz. *MGH Scriptores,* I. Hanover, 1826.

*Chronicon Salernitanum.* ed. G. H. Pertz. *MGH Scriptores,* III. Hanover, 1839.

*Chronicon Venetum.* ed. G. H. Pertz. *MGH Scriptores,* VII. 1925.

*Clausula de Pippini in Francorum Regum Consecratione, Recueil des historiens de Gaul et de la France.* ed. M. Bouquet; new ed. L. Delisle. Paris, 1869.

*Codex Carolinus.* ed. W. Gundlach. *MGH Epistolae Merowingici et Karolini Aevi,* III. Berlin, 1892.

*Codicis Carolini Epistolae.* ed. P. Jaffe *Bibliotheca rerum Germanicarum,* IV. Berlin, 1867.

*Codice Diplomatico Longobardo,* IV. ed. C. Troya. Rome, 1885.

*Concilium Romanum a. 769.* ed. A. Werminghoff. *MGH Concilia,* II. Hanover, 1906.

*Einhardi Vita Karoli Magni.* ed. G. Waitz and O. Holder-Egger. *MGH SS Rer. Ger. in usum Schol.* Hanover, 1880.

*Epistolae Langobardicae Collectae.* ed. W. Gundlach. *MGH Epp. III, Mer. et Kar. Aevi,* I. 1892.

*Fredegarii Chronicon. The Fourth Book of the Chronicle of Fredegar With Its Continuations.* ed. and trans. J. M. Wallace-Hadrill. London and New York, 1960.

*History of the Lombards,* Paul the Deacon. tr. William Dudley Foulke. Reprint, Philadelphia, 1974.

*Leges Langobardorum.* ed. F. Bluhme. *MGH Leges,* IV. Hanover, 1869.

*The Lombard Laws.* tr. Katherine Fischer Drew. Philadelphia, 1973.

*Pauli Historia Continuatio Casinensis.* ed. G. Waitz. *MGH Scriptores Rer. Lang. et Ital. Saec. VI–IX.* Hanover, 1878.

*Pauli Historia Continuatio Lombarda.* ed. G. Waitz. *MGH Scriptores Rer. Lang. et Ital. Saec. VI–IX.* Hanover, 1878.

*Pauli Historia Continuatio Tertia.* ed. G. Waitz. *SS Rer. Lang. et Ital. Saec. VI–IX.* Hanover, 1878.

*Pauli Historia Langobardorum,* ed. L. Bethman and G. Waitz. *MGH SS Rer. Lang. et Ital. Saec. VI–IX.* Hanover, 1878.

*Pauli Historia Langobardorum Continuatio Romana.* ed. G. Waitz. *MGH SS Rer. Lang. et Ital. Saec. VI–IX.* Hanover, 1878.

*Vita Gregorii II.* ed. L. M. O. Duchesne. *Liber Pontificalis,* I. 2nd ed. Paris, 1955.

*Vita Gregorii III.* ed. Duchesne. *LP, I.*

*Vita Zachariae.* ed. Duchesne. *LP, I.*

*Vita Stephani II.* ed. Duchesne. *LP, I.*

*Vita Stephani III.* ed. Duchesne. *LP, I.*

*Vita Pauli I.* ed. Duchesne. *LP, I.*

*Vita Hadriani I.* ed. Duchesne. *LP, I.*

## SECONDARY SOURCES

ABEL, S. and B. SIMSON. *Jahrbücher des frankischen Reiches unter Karl dem Grossen.* Vol. 1. Leipzig, 1888.

ALEXANDER, PAUL J. *The Patriarch Nicephorus of Constantinople. Ecclesiastical Policy and Image Worship in the Byzantine Empire.* Oxford, 1958.

AMANN, ÉMILE. *L'époque carolingienne.* Paris, 1937. Vol. 6 of *Histoire de l'église.* ed. A. Fliche and V. Martin.

ANASTOS, M. V. "Iconoclasm and Imperial Rule, 717–842," *CMH* (2nd ed. Cambridge, 1966), 4.

——. "The Transfer of Illyricum, Calabria, and Sicily to the Jurisdiction of the Patriarchate of Constantinople in 732–33." *Studi Bizantini e Neoellenici* 9 (1957): 14–31.

——. "Leo III's Edict Against Images in the Year 726–727 and Italo-Byzantine Relations Between 726 and 730," *Byzantinische Forschungen* 3 (1968): 5–41.

BACHRACH, BERNARD S., *Merovingian Military Organization, 481–751.* Minneapolis, 1972.

——. Review in *CHR* 59, 3 (October, 1973): p. 534.

BAUMONT, MAURICE "Le pontificat de Paul Iᵉʳ, 757–767," *Mélanges d'Archeologie et d'Histoire,* 1930: 7–24.

BAYET C. "Remarques sur la caractère et les conséquences du voyage d'Étienne II en France," *RH* 20 (1882): 89–94.

BELTING H. "Studien zum beneventanischen Hof im 8. Jahrhundert," *Dumbarton Oaks Papers* 16. 1962.

BERTOLINI, OTTORINO *Roma di fronte a Bisanzio e ai Longobardi.* Bologna, 1941.

——. "I rapporti di Zaccaria con Constantino V e con Artavasdo," *Archivio di Societa romana di storia patria* (3rd ser., 9) 1955.

——. "Sergio arcivescovo di Ravenna (744–769) e i papi del suo tempo," *Studi Romagnoli,* I (1950): 43–88.

——. "I papi e le relazioni politiche di Roma con i ducati longobardi di Spoleto e di Benevento," *RSCI* 9 (1955): 1–57.

——. "Le relazioni politiche di Roma con i ducati di Spoleto e di Benevento nel periodo del dominio longobardo," *Scritti Scelti di Storia Medioevale* 2, ed. Bertolini. Livorno, 1968.

——. "La Caduta del primicerio Cristoforo (771) nelle versione dei contemporanei, e le correnti anti-longobarde a filolongobarde in Roma alla fine del pontificato di Stefano III (771–772)," *RSCI* 1 (1947): pp. 227–261 and 349–378.

——. "Il primo 'periuria' di Astolfo verso la Chiesa di Roma, 752–753," *Studi e Testi* (125) *Miscellanea Giovanni Mercati* (5), 1946.

——. "Il problema della origini del potere temporale dei papi nei sui presupposti teoretici iniziali; il concetto di 'restituto' nelle prime cessioni territoriali (756–7) alla Chiesa di Roma," *Miscellena Pio Paschini, Lateranum* 14 (1948): 103–171.

——. "Le prime manifestazione concrete del potere temporale dei papi nell' esarcato di Ravenna, 756–7," *Atti dell' Istituto Veneto di Scienze Lettere ed Arti. Classe di Scienze Morali e Lettere* 106, pt. 2, (1948): 280–300.

BOUSSARD, JACQUES. *The Civilization of Charlemagne.* New York and Toronto, 1968.

BRÉHIER, LOUIS. *La querelle des images.* Paris, 1904.

—— and René Aigrain, *Grégoire le grand, les états barbares et la conquête arabe (590–757).* Paris, 1938. Vol. 5 of *Histoire de l'église.* ed. A. Fliche and V. Martin.

BRÜHL, CARLRICHARD. "Chronologie und Urkunden der Herzöge von Spoleto im 8. Jahrhundert," *QFIAB,* 51 (1971): 1–92.

BULLOUGH, DONALD A. "The Writing-Office of the Dukes of Spoleto in the Eighth Century," *The Study of Medieval Records: Essays in Honour of Kathleen Major.* ed. D. A. Bullough and R. L. Storey. Oxford and New York, 1971. pp. 1–22.

——. *The Age of Charlemagne.* New York. 1966.

——. "Germanic Italy: The Ostrogothic and Lombard Kingdoms," *The Dawn of European Civilization.* ed. David Talbot Rice. London, 1965.

CALMETTE, JOSEPH. *Charlemagne, sa vie et son oeuvre.* Paris, 1945.

CASPAR, ERICH. *Das Papsttum unter Byzantinischer Heerschaft.* 1933. Vol 2 of *Geschichte des Papsttums.* Tübingen, 1933.

——. *Das Papsttum unter Fränkischer Heerschaft.* Darmstadt, 1956.

——. *Pippin und die römische Kirche. Kritische Untersuchungen zum frankisch-papstlichen Bunde in VIII Jahrhundert.* Berlin, 1914.

CESSI, ROBERTO. "La crisi dell' esarcate ravennate agli inizi dell' iconoclastia," *Atti del Reale Istituto Veneto di Scienze, Lettere ed Arti,* 93 (1933–34): 1671–1685.

CLASSEN, PETER. *Karl der Grosse, das Papsttum und Byzanz. Die Begrundung des karolingischen Kaisertums.* Dusseldorf, 1968.

——. "Karl der Grosse und die Thronfolge im Frankenreich," *Festschrift für H. Heimpel* 3 (1972): 109–134.

COOLIDGE, A. "Charles the Great's Passage of the Alps in 773," *Ohio Archaeological and Historical Quarterly* 21 (1906): 493–505.

CRIVELLUCCI, A. "Stefano patrizio e duca di Roma (727–754)," *Studi Storici* 10 (1901).

CUTLER, ROBERT. *Carolingian Italian Policies, 739–780.* Unpublished doctoral dissertation, 1970, Michigan State University.

DALY, WILLIAM M. "St. Peter: An Architect of the Carolingian Empire," *SMC*, 4, part 1 (1973): 55–69.

DANNENBAUER, H. "Das römische Reich und der Westen vom Tode Justinian bis zum Tode Karls des Grossen," *Grundlagen der mittelalterlichen Welt*, 1958.

DEANSLEY, MARGARET. *A History of Early Medieval Europe from 476 to 911.* London, 1960.

DÉER, JOSEF. "Die Vorrechte des Kaisers in Rom (772–800)," *Schweizer Beiträge zur allegemeinen Geschichte* 15 (1957): 5–63.

——. "Zum Patricius Romanorum Titel Karl des Grossen," *AHP* 3 (1965): 32–86.

DELARUELLE, ÉTIENNE, "Charlemagne, Carloman, Didier et la politique du mariage franco-Lombard (770–771)," *RH* 170 (Sept.–Oct. 1932): 213–224.

DIEHL, CHARLES. *Études sur l'administration byzantine dans l'exarchat de Ravenne, 568–751.* Paris, 1888; reprint, 1972.

DOWNS, NORTON. "The Role of the Papacy in the Coronation of Charlemagne," *SMC* 3 (1970): 7–22.

DREW, KATHERINE FISCHER, "The Carolingian Military Frontier in Italy," *Traditio* 20, (1964): 437–447.

DUCHESNE, L. M. O. *The Beginnings of the Temporal Sovereignty of the Popes, A. D. 754–1073.* trans. A. H. Mathew. London, 1908, reprint, 1972.

FANNING, STEPHEN C. "Lombard Arianism Reconsidered," *Speculum* 56 (April, 1981): 241–258.

FRITZE, WOLFGANG E. *Pabst und Frankenkönig: Studien zu den päpstlich-fränkischen Rechtsbeziehungen von 754 bis 824.* Sigmaringen (Germany), 1973.

GANSHOF, F. L. "Charlemagne," *Speculum* 24 (1948): 520–527.

——. "Note sur les origines byzantines du titre 'patricius Romanorum,'" *"Annales de l'Institut de Philologie et d'Histoire Orientales et Slaves de l'Université de Bruxelles* 10 (1950): 261–282.

GASQUET, A. "Le royaume lombard; ses relations avec l'empire grec et avec les Francs," *RH* 33 (1887): 58–92.

GRIFFE, E. "Aux origines de l'État pontifical: Charlemagne et Hadrien Ier (772–795)," *Bulletin de la litterature Ecclésiastique* 53 (1954): 65–89.

GRUMEL, V. "L'annexation de l'Illyricum Oriental, de la Sicile et de la Calabre au Patriarchat de Constantinople," *Recherches de la Science religieuse* 40 (1952).

GUILLOU, A. *Régionalisme et indépendence dans l'Empire Byzantin au VIIe Siècle. L'exemple de l'exarchat et de la Pentapole d'Italie.* Rome, 1969.

HALLENBECK, JAN T. "The Election of Pope Hadrian I," *Church History* 37, no. 3 (Sept. 1968): 261–270.

——. "Pope Stephen III: Why Was He Elected?" *AHP* 12 (1974): 287–299.

——. "Paul Afiarta and the Papacy: An Analysis of Politics in Eighth-Century Rome," *AHP* 12 (1974): 33–54.

——. "The Lombard Party in Eighth-Century Rome: A Case of Mistaken Identity," *Studi Medievali* 3rd ser., 15, pt. 2, (1974): 951–966.

——. "Rome Under Attack: An Estimation of King Aistulf's Motives for the Lombard Siege of 756," *Mediaeval Studies* (1978): 190–220.

HALLER, JOHANNES. "Die Karolinger und das Papsttum," *HZ* 108 (1912): 38–76.

——. *Das Papsttum, Idee und Wirklichkeit* Stuttgart, 1950. 5 vols. Vol. 1, 2nd ed.

HALPHEN, LOUIS. "La papauté et le complot Lombard de 771," *RH* 182 (1938): 238–244.

——. *Études sur l'administration de Rome au moyen âge (751–1252).* Paris, 1907.

——. *Charlemagne et l'empire carolingien.* Paris, 1947, reprint, 1968.

HARTMANN, LUDO MORITZ. *Geschichte Italiens im Mittelalter.* Gotha, 1903. Vol. 2, pts. 1 and 2.

——. "Italy Under the Lombards," *CMH*, New York, 1957. Vol. 2, pt. 2., pp. 194–212.

HAUCK, A. *Kirchengeschichte Deutschlands.* Leipzig, 1889. Vol. 2. 1st ed.

HEFELE, CHARLES and H. LECLERCQ. *Histoire des conciles.* Paris, 1910.

HELDMANN, KARL. "Kommendation und Königschutz im Vertrage von Ponthion," *Mitteilungen des Instituts fur österreichische Geschichtsforschung* 38 (1921): 541–570.

HODGKIN, THOMAS *Italy And Her Invaders*, Vol. 5: *The Lombard Invasion, 553–600.* Oxford, 1895; Vol 6: *The Lombard Kingdom, 600–744.* Oxford, 1895; Vol. 7: *The Frankish Invasions, 744–774.* Oxford, 1899.

HOLTZMANN, ROBERT. *Die Italienpolitik der Merowinger und des König Pippins.* 2nd ed. Darmstadt, 1962.

HOMO, LÉON P. *Rome médiévale, 476–1420.* Paris, 1934.

HUBERT, H. "Étude sur la formation des états de l'église. Les papes Grégoire II, Grégoire III,

Zacharie et Étienne II et leurs relations avec les empereurs iconoclastes (726–757)," *RH* 79 (1899): 1–40.

JARNUT, JÖRG. "Quierzy und Rom. Bemerkungen zu den 'promissiones donationis' Pippins und Karls," *HZ* 220, 1975.

KEHR, P. "Die sogenannte karolingische Schenkung von 774," *HZ* 80 (1893): 385–441.

KLEINCLAUSZ, ARTHUR. *Charlemagne*. Paris, 1934.

LEVILLAIN, LÉON. "L'avènement de la dynastie carolingienne et les origines de l'état pontifical (749–757)," *Bibliothèque de l'école des chartes* (1933): 225–295.

——. "De l'autenticité de la *clausula de unctione Pippini*," *Bibliothèque de l'école des chartes* 88 (1927): 20–42.

LEVISON, W. *England and the Continent in the Eighth Century*. Oxford, 1946.

LEWIS, ARCHIBALD R. *The Development of Southern French and Catalan Society, 718–1050*. Austin, Texas, 1965.

LINDNER, THEODOR. *Die sogenannte Schenkungen Pippins, Karls des Grossen und Ottos I. an die Päpste*. Stuttgart, 1896.

LINTZEL, MARTIN. "Karl der Grosse und Karlmann," *HZ* 140 (1929): 1–22.

——. "Der *Codex Carolinus* und die Motive von Pippins Italienpolitik," *HZ* 161 (1940): 33–41.

LLEWELLYN, PETER. *Rome in the Dark Ages*. New York, 1971.

MACAIGNE, RENÉ. *L'Église Merovingienne et l'État pontifical*. Paris, 1929.

MARTENS, WILHELM. *Die römische Frage ünter Pippin und Karl dem Grossen*. Stuttgart, 1881.

MILLER, DAVID HARRY. "Papal-Lombard Relations During the Pontificate of Pope Paul I: The Attainment of an Equilibrium of Power in Italy, 756–767," *CHR* 55, no. 3, (October, 1969): 358–376.

——. "The Motivation of Pepin's Italian Policy, 754–768," *SMC* 4, pt. 1 (1973): 44–54.

——. "Byzantine-Papal Relations During the Pontificate of Paul I: Confirmation and Completion of the Roman Revolution of the Eighth Century," *Byzantinische Zeitschrift* 68, (1975): 47–62.

——. "The Roman Revolution of the Eighth Century: A Study of the Ideological Background of the Papal Separation from Byzantium and Alliance With the Franks," *Mediaeval Studies* 36 (1974): 79–133.

MOHR, WALTER. *Die karolingische Reichsidee*. Münster, 1962.

MUNZ, PETER. *Life in the Age of Charlemagne*. New York, 1971.

MUSSET, LUCIEN. *The Germanic Invasions. The Making of Europe, A. D. 400–600*. tr. Edward and Columba James. University Park, Pa., 1975.

OELSNER, L. *Jahrbücher des fränkischen Reichs unter König Pippin*. Leipzig, 1871.

PABST, H. "Geschichte des langobardischen Herzogtums," *Forschungen zur deutschen Geschichte* 2 (1867): 405–518.

PARTNER, PETER. *The Lands of St. Peter. The Papal State in the Middle Ages and the Early Renaissance*. Berkeley, 1972.

PEPE, GABRIELE. *Il medio evo barbarico d'Italia*. 4th ed. Torino, 1959.

RASSOW, PETER. "Pippin und Stephan II," *Zeitschrift für Kirchengeschichte* 36 (1916): 494–502.

ROBERTI, M. "Liutprando re longobardo," *Rendiconti dell'Istituto lombardo di scienze e lettere, classe di lettere e scienzi morali* 85, (1952): 91–102.

RODENBERG, KARL. *Pippin, Karlmann und Papst Stephan II*. Berlin, 1923.

ROMANO, G. *Le Dominazioni Barbariche in Italia, 395–888*. Milan, 1909.

SACKUR, ERNST. "Die Promissio Pippins vom Jahre 754 und ihre Erneuerung durch Karl den Grosse," *Mitteilungen des Instituts fur österreichische Geschichtsforschung* 16, (1895): 385–424.

SALTET, L. "La lecture d'un texte et la critique contemporaine; les prétendus promesses de Quierzy (754) et de Rome (774) dans le 'Liber Pontificalis'," *Bulletin de la litterature Ecclésiastique*, (1940): 176–206 and (1941): 61–85.

SCHIEFFER, THEODOR. "Angelsachsen und Franken, I: Bonifatius und Chrodegang," *Akademie der Wissenschaften und der Literatur Geistes und Socialwissenschaftlichen Klasse* 20 (1950).

——. *Winifrid-Bonifatius und die christliche Grundlegung Europas*. Frieburg, 1954.

SCHMID, K. "Zur Ablösung der Langobardenherrschaft durch die Franken," *QFIAB* 47 (1972): 1–36.

——. "Anselm von Nonantola. Olim dux militum—nunc dux monachorum," *QFIAB* 52 (1967): 1–122.

SCHRAMM, PERCY ERNST. "Das Versprechen Pippins und Karls des Grossen für die römische Kirche," *Zeitschrift der Savigny-Stiftung für Rechtsgeschichte*, 58, Kanonistische Abteilung 58 (1938): 180–217.

SCHNÜRER, G. *Die Entstehung des Kirchenstaats.* Cologne, 1894.

SEFTON, DAVID S. *The Pontificate of Hadrian I (772-795): Papal Theory and Political Reality in the Reign of Charlemagne.* Unpublished doctoral dissertation. Michigan State University, 1975.

———. "Pope Hadrian I and the Fall of the Kingdom of the Lombards," *CHR* 65, No. 2 (April, 1979): 206–220.

SEPPELT, F. X. *Das Papsttum in Frühmittelalter.* Vol. 2 of *Geschichte des Papsttums.* Leipzig, 1934.

ULLMANN, WALTER. *The Growth of Papal Government in the Middle Ages. A Study in the Ideological Relation of Clerical to Lay Power.* 2nd ed., London, 1962.

WINSTON, RICHARD. *Charlemagne. From the Hammer to the Cross.* Indianapolis, 1954.

# INDEX

Accommodation of 770–771, Lombard-Papal: 123–128, 130, 131, 133ff., 137, 140, 144, 145, 149, 151ff.

Adelgis, son of Desiderius: 119, 120, 122, 161–162, 166, 173–174

Afiarta, Paul, *cubicularius*: 128, 129, 131ff., 141, 142, 143, 146

Agilulf, Lombard king: 8–9, 14, 17

Agiprand, duke of Spoleto: 39–40, 41

Aistulf, King: conquest of exarchate of Ravenna, 52–53; and zenith of Lombard Kingdom of Italy, 53–54; and relations with Pope Zachary, 54–55; early attitude of toward papal republic, 55–57; and peace of June 752 with Stephen II, 56–59; and changing attitude toward Rome, 66–68; and relations with King Pepin, 72–73, 78–79; and siege of Rome, 81–83; dependence of upon Pepin, 84; 52, 87, 88, 101, 103, 105, 109, 125, 148, 149, 158, 175ff.

Alboin, duke of Spoleto: 88, 89, 91, 94

Alboin, Lombard king: 5–6

Ambrose, *primicerius*: 45–46, 56

Aquitaine, duchy of: 104, 104 *n*, 105, 113, 158

Arianism: 13–15

Arichis, duke of Benevento: 163, 172, 173

Arichis, duke of Spoleto: 91, 121 *n*

Aripert I, Lombard king: 10, 14–15

Aripert II, Lombard king: 11–12, 21

Audoin, Lombard king: 5

Authari, Lombard king: 7, 14

Auximum: 23, 28, 91, 162, 163; *see also* Osimo

Benevento, duchy of: foundation of, 6; 10–11, 27–29, 39–40, 53, 80–90 *passim*, 88–90, 91–92, 98–99, 107, 123, 151, 160, 162, 165, 172, 173–174, 175, 176

Bertrada, mother of Charles and Carloman: and diplomacy of 770–771, 122–128; 113 *n*, 130, 132ff., 138, 144, 159

Boniface, St.: 64, 74, 77

Carloman, brother of Charles: and Franco-Lombard marriage, 118–122; and Lombard-papal accommodation of 770–771, 122–128; and fall of Christopher, 129–130, 131–132, 133–134, 135, 137; 72, 76, 113ff.; sons of, 137, 139–140, 143, 144–145, 146, 149–150, 151ff., 159, 160–161, 162, 164, 168; *see also* Gerberga

Carloman, brother of Pepin: 45, 51, 72, 77–78, 165

Cesena: 46–48, 52–53, 70

Charles, King: and Franco-Lombard marriage, 119–122; and Lombard-papal accommodation of 770–771, 122–128; becomes sole Frankish king, 137; and repudiation of Desiderius's daughter, 137–138; and appeal from Pope Hadrian I, 148ff., 150–151, 152; and invasion of Italy, 157–161; and siege of Pavia, 161–162, 168; and 774 Rome visit and conference, 164–165, 167–171; and deposition of Desiderius, 166, 167–169; as Lombard king, 171–174; 176ff.; 70, 72, 76, 113ff., 130ff., 133ff., 139–140, 144ff., 153ff., 163ff.

Childebert, Frankish king: 7

Christopher, *primicerius*: and usurpation of Constantine II, 106–112; and Franco-Lombard marriage, 120–121; decline of 126–127, 128; fall of, 128–135; 86, 117–118, 138, 140ff., 151, 154

Constantine II, papal usurper: 106–108, 109–110, 111, 115ff., 135

Constantine V, Byzantine emperor: 59, 60, 95, 119, 173

Desiderius, King: accession of, 85–86; territorial concessions of to Pope Stephen II, 85–88; and the *plenaria iustitiae*, 90–94, 97–99, 116–117, 118, 120, 127, 142ff., 148, 151, 153, 154, 157–158, 159–160; and the empire, 91, 94–95, 97; recovery of Spoleto and Benevento, 91–92; success of by 758, 96; and relations with King Pepin and Pope Paul I, 97–106; and 768 intervention in Rome, 108–112; and intervention in Ravenna, 117–119, 123; and Franco-Lombard marriage, 119–121; and Lombard-papal accommodation of 770–771, 122–128; and fall of Christopher, 128–135; and failure of the Franco-Lombard marriage, 137–140, and early tension with Pope Hadrian I, 142–146; and 772 attack upon papal republic, 146–150; and siege of Rome, 153–155; and Charles's invasion of Italy, 157–161; and Charles's siege of Pavia, 161–162, 164, 166, 168; deposition of, 166, 167–169; 151, 152, 163, 164, 170, 172ff., 176ff.

*Divisio* of 768, Pepin's: 113–115, map 114, 138

Dodo, *missus*: 129, 130, 131, 133, 134, 159

Emilia, the: 16, 16*n*, 45

Empire, Byzantine: sixth century Italian territories, 7–8, map 9; papal membership in,

www.ingramcontent.com/pod-product-compliance
Lightning Source LLC
Chambersburg PA
CBHW080925100426
42812CB00007B/2371